PENGUIN CANADA

JA, NO, MAN

RICHARD POPLAK was born in Johannesburg, South Africa, in 1973 and immigrated to Canada with his family in 1989. A co-founder of the successful Canadian music label 2wars & A Revolution Records, Richard is also a trained filmmaker and has directed numerous music videos, earning five nominations at the 2005 MuchMusic Video Awards. Richard has written for various publications in Canada and South Africa, including *Toronto Life, Canadian Living,* and the CBC Online.

JA, NO, MAN

Growing Up White in Apartheid-Era South Africa

Richard Poplak

PENGUIN
CANADA

PENGUIN CANADA

Published by the Penguin Group

Penguin Group (Canada), 90 Eglinton Avenue East, Suite 700, Toronto, Ontario, Canada M4P 2Y3 (a division of Pearson Canada Inc.)

Penguin Group (USA) Inc., 375 Hudson Street, New York, New York 10014, U.S.A.
Penguin Books Ltd, 80 Strand, London WC2R 0RL, England
Penguin Ireland, 25 St Stephen's Green, Dublin 2, Ireland (a division of Penguin Books Ltd)
Penguin Group (Australia), 250 Camberwell Road, Camberwell, Victoria 3124, Australia (a division of Pearson Australia Group Pty Ltd)
Penguin Books India Pvt Ltd, 11 Community Centre, Panchsheel Park, New Delhi – 110 017, India
Penguin Group (NZ), cnr Airborne and Rosedale Roads, Albany, Auckland 1310, New Zealand (a division of Pearson New Zealand Ltd)
Penguin Books (South Africa) (Pty) Ltd, 24 Sturdee Avenue, Rosebank, Johannesburg 2196, South Africa

Penguin Books Ltd, Registered Offices: 80 Strand, London WC2R 0RL, England

First published 2007

1 2 3 4 5 6 7 8 9 10 (WEB)

Manufactured in Canada

ISBN-13: 978-014305044-5
ISBN-10: 0-14-305044-3

Library and Archives Canada Cataloguing in Publication data available upon request.

Visit the Penguin Group (Canada) website at **www.penguin.ca**

Special and corporate bulk purchase rates available; please see **www.penguin.ca/corporatesales** or call 1-800-810-3104, ext. 477 or 474

For My Parents

Contents

Author's Note

Ja, No, Man is what I describe as an act of memory—the story of my youth told from my perspective, based on my experiences and my recollections. But it is also a work of journalism; research has played an important role in this reconstruction of my early years. I asked a number of people—especially those who appear in the narrative—to vet the text, and they kindly agreed to do so.

This book owes many of its particulars to a four-month research trip I undertook in early 2006; if I describe a tree as a jacaranda, that's because I returned to the site, cross-referenced the tree with my illustrated pocket botany book, and ascertained it to be a jacaranda. I have nowhere included details if I could not confirm them.

After much deliberation, and some back and forth with my legal counsel, I decided that I would not include the real names of some of the players who appear in this narrative. As a general rule, most (but not all) of my educators' names have been changed, the name of my primary school has been altered, and many of my friends' names have been substituted. I should note here that there are no composite characters, no fictional locations, and no made-up situations within the pages of this book.

Throughout the book, I use the Apartheid-era names for places, footnoting their current designations. As far as racial terminology is concerned, the prefix "African" is, in a South African context, meaningless. To remain true to the time period,

I employ the terminology from the era: Black Africans are blacks, the mixed-race population are coloureds, Southeast Asians are Indians, and Caucasians are whites. Similarly, I have tried to depict the Johannesburg patois of the time as accurately as possible. The vernacular was uncommonly heavy with slang—for this, I ask you to turn to the glossary at the back of the book.

Finally, you'll observe that I capitalize the word *Apartheid.* I'm of the firm belief that the term must be associated with a single place and era: South Africa 1948 to 1994. Misappropriating it as a pejorative for other regimes does an enormous disservice to those who suffered under it and threatens to cloud their history. Apartheid is Apartheid.

Welkom by Suid Afrika
An Introduction

My extra-curricular art teacher came to class prepared. She carried in her handbag a meticulously burnished silver nine-millimetre semi-automatic handgun with an integrated laser site and a spare clip for emergencies. She first showed it to me when I was eleven or so, and the gun was just about the most beautiful thing I had ever seen. It shone like a weapon of the gods, something Zeus would use if he ran short of lightning bolts. My art teacher swore she would use it if necessary. "If they" (and, this being Apartheid-era South Africa, it was clear who *they* were) "come near my car, I will never, ever hesitate to shoot," she once told me. "*Boom!* You can say goodbye to them."

My art teacher, a meaty woman with heavy bovine features, tutored me during my formative years and was a rigorous and inflexible taskmaster. Her mantra was unbending: "Look. Look again. Now paint what you see." I remember the Johannesburg winter sun pouring into the Parktown Primary assembly hall as, along with my classmates, I worked on faithfully rendering a chicken or a mongoose or whatever taxidermied creature she'd exhumed from her well-stocked mausoleum. I looked, I looked again, and I painted what I saw.

So, several years and many thousands of miles later, the mannequin came as something of a surprise. It was assigned to me as a sculptural project at the Claude Watson School for the Arts in January of 1990, on day one of my Canadian scholastic career, a few weeks after my family and I immigrated to Toronto from Johannesburg. The mannequin was long of limb and difficult to work with; every time I shifted her position, we'd engage in a pose so explicitly pornographic—her legs around my neck, one of my hands on a large smooth breast and another on her crotch—that my face flamed with a florid blush. The whole thing was so terribly undignified. "What must I do with her?" I asked my new art teacher in a thick, nearly incomprehensible Johannesburg drawl. Unlike my old art teacher, he did not appear to be packing. "Use your imagination," he said. That would be something of a problem. For the duration of my sixteen years, I'd been told exactly what to do. I did not *have* an imagination.

I had seen *Fame* at the Balfour Park movie theatres back in Johannesburg; on being told of Claude Watson's similarities to the fictional New York City High School for the Performing Arts, I was excited at the prospect of having sophisticated friends who smoked Gitanes and wore leotards as a matter of course. After all, I was rather sophisticated myself. In South Africa, I had pored over every scrap of cultural flotsam and jetsam that drifted over from North America. I read extensively (everything from the Hardy Boys to the entire Stephen King canon), watched any film that I could (by that I mean *any* film—I was so obsessive, I could tell you who gaffed *Honey, I Shrunk the Kids*), was a pop music fundamentalist ("Infidels must *die*," I'd think, cursing those who did not share my passion for Duran Duran's *Notorious*), and filtered all this through my subscriptions to *MAD* magazine and *Fangoria*. An inveterate scrapbook maker, I'd cut out pictures from *Teen Beat* magazine or the newspaper, draw charts, document Tiffany's and Depeche Mode's discographies—anything that caught my interest was glued into a series of large, multicoloured scrapbooks. I cut and pasted what amounts to a definitive anthropological record of 1980s North American popular culture.

But there's a problem with learning about North America through *Magnum, P.I.* and Debbie Gibson: Popular culture is, at best, a variation on the truth. Watching something on television or in a movie theatre and assuming that's how it plays out in real life is a recipe for thermo-nuclear culture shock. So it was with Claude Watson and me.

When my new art teacher walked me through the busy atelier, I was dumbfounded. This was 1990. Black was in, and the class looked like it had just returned from a seance. I must have cut quite the contrast in my tight acid-washed jeans, colourful Smarties up-chuck sweater, and South African–purchased winter jacket, redolent of a Tito-era Yugoslav ski resort. Those black-clad ciphers etched and scoured and scribbled away diligently on their mannequins, incorporating a working knowledge of Dadaism, Der Blaue Reiter, street art, and, one presumes, a thorough understanding of the principles of the avant-garde. As far as I was concerned, Avant-Garde was a cigarette brand, and paint was meant for canvas or, failing that, a sheet of decent-grade paper. With shock, I noted one mannequin's tit read: *Free Mandela.* If my old art teacher had stumbled in here, she would most certainly have needed her emergency clip.

Each day revealed surprising differences between my old life and my new one. The moment that defined this disconnect, that finally brought my hurtling disorientation smack against the brick wall of actuality, occurred in math class. I had yet to process the fact that, for the first time in my life, I was surrounded by people of multifarious ethnicities. I was too obsessed with the mannequin to give this much thought. So, when a black girl raised her hand to answer a geometry question that I could never have answered, and did so succinctly, confidently, without the merest hint of deference, I knew I had taken a running dive down the rabbit hole. I had never been in a room with a black girl my age before, let alone as a fellow student. I had thought I'd be okay with this. But the truth was, it felt extraordinarily strange. When I sat and hid in the library during lunch hour, swaddled in my Tito jacket for safety, I noticed dozens of black and brown and yellow people walking through the halls, chatting and laughing as though this happened every day. Like this was normal.

I was used to a very different kind of normal.

The thing about South Africa during the 1970s and 1980s is this: If you were to take a cursory look at the snapshots that sit in boxes in my parents' basement, you would have great difficulty differentiating my childhood from any other middle-class Western childhood from the same period. That's me, the little boy with golden curls, grabbing the family cat by the fur on its stomach. There I am in a cowboy suit, double fisting cap guns. There I am again, grinning with glee, seated on my first ten-speed. Look at my sister, three years old, her forehead wrinkled in concentration, struggling to dress a dolly while I stare over her shoulder. That's my neighbourhood pal and me fighting over a chunk of Spider-Man birthday cake. Entirely, utterly normal.

Taken in snapshots, even Johannesburg, my hometown, might appear normal. The country itself was an admixture of the First World, the Third World, and the Victorian colonial era. Johannesburg, however, was (and still is) the most industrialized city in Africa. Its excellent infrastructure, modern amenities, and glorious weather made it a fine place to live. Except for a dour feeling of isolation, the unmistakable spice of Africa, and some of the crappiest examples of 1960s aesthetics outside *Barbarella,* Johannesburg could have been anywhere.

Yet, at the same time, there were one or two … let's call them "idiosyncrasies." You'd have to look at the very corners of those family snapshots to find any hint of these. There, right at the back of the Spider-Man cake party, in the pink cloth uniform, is our maid, Bushy, the black woman who reared me for the entire sixteen years of my life in South Africa. In the front pocket of her pink apron she carries her passbook, a document that she must produce any time a white police officer asks her to do so. Without that passbook, ratified by my parents, Bushy will go to jail. Bushy has no freedom of movement, she cannot buy property in our neighbourhood (or anywhere in any white area), and she cannot vote. Bushy has no rights—none whatsoever. She is, by any standards, an indentured servant. She lives in a small room at the back of our house, thousands of miles from her family, who are forbidden from living with her in the city.

How to reconcile the reality of Bushy with the Spider-Man cake and the cowboy suits, or, more specifically, with the reality of a white middle-class family in a modern industrialized city? The answer lies in the mechanics of the system we lived under. Pop the hood and look at the engine that drove the country, and it all becomes terribly clear.

Apartheid was, after all, legislated. It was tabled, debated, refined, written in legalese by parliamentarians, and then transcribed into the law books. This process was central to South Africa's particular brand of institutional prejudice. It pulled race from the emotional realm and placed it in the rational. Denying a black person a bus ride was not the result of an impulsive burst of hatred. It was, very simply, the law. Every instance of racism, no matter how seemingly insignificant, that defined social behaviour in South Africa was in part a product of a grey-suited lawyer's quill. Apartheid was law, which meant racism was law, which removed it from the arena of personal responsibility and quickly and definitively made it normal. Laws are the guiding principals of any society; they define mores and ethics and codes of social behaviour. With the laws we had on the books, South African society could have developed in only one way. And that way was fundamentally racist. The fact that my Canadian classmates didn't call the riot police when that black girl raised her hand in class—the very fact that they didn't blink—suggested that behaviour in Canada could exist separately from racism. In South Africa, nothing existed separately from racism. Everything we did was based on it. It was room tone. It was normal.

In this way, racism became a standard, defining feature of everyday life. Like the bureaucratic Vogons who destroy Earth because of a paperwork snafu in *The Hitchhiker's Guide to the Galaxy,* the ruling party in South Africa whittled evil down to banality. Little laws, little bylaws, tiny subsections of sub-subsections—the glorious minutiae of a country ruled on a poisoned system. The true genius of a system like Apartheid is that it renders the horrific commonplace. And under a regime like this, it takes an enormous act of the imagination to envision anything other than the status quo.

I saw precious little imagination during my childhood, or none of the kind that counts, anyway.[1] This absence—this void—had far-reaching consequences. Revolutionaries are like artists. They have the ability to imagine another possible present—as if it were a symphony or a large-canvas painting (or,

1. Here I'm using the word *imagination* in the social and political sense.

I suppose, a mannequin)—and they then try to implement that vision. Empathy takes even more imagination than revolutionizing does. I was so far removed from those whom we subjugated, the wedge between us so significant, that empathizing with their predicament became a gargantuan leap of the mind. Evidently, too few of us were up to that. I had no relationships with blacks outside the master–servant dichotomy. I had no opportunity to forge any. What's more—I didn't want to. And if I had wanted to, I have no idea what we would have said to one another.

This book, then, is not about revolutionaries. You will find no heroes in these pages. Except for a very few, Apartheid had us all beat. What makes my experience remarkable and my perspective unique is that I lived in South Africa *only* under the Apartheid regime. From my birth in 1973 to several months before Nelson Mandela's release from prison in February 1990 (the symbolic, if not the de facto, end of the Apartheid era), I was a South African. My South Africa, the universe I inhabited as a boy, died three months after I left it.

And things *have* changed. Comparing the country now with the country then is like looking at those pictures of the pasty fat guy next to his muscled likeness in adverts for protein supplements. "Before" South Africa is slow, heavy-lidded, greyish pale, tight-lipped, and grim. "After" is vibrant, dangerously nimble, ever-shifting, and bright—bright with the colours of Africa inexorably moving south to claim this once negative space. South Africa's second-to-last white leader, P.W. Botha, personified the miasmic fog that kept the country in darkness during the Apartheid years.[2] I remember him decaying before our eyes, aging and sickening as he tried to steer the

---

2. P.W. ruled from 1978 to 1987, so he was top dog for most of my South African life.

country into a strange glasnost between Real Apartheid (the pure tincture of Apartheid's founder, the late Hendrik Verwoerd) and a compromised version that our international critics could stomach. Verwoerd and Botha. These gentlemen formed the ideological parentheses in which Apartheid resided. From one year to the next, Botha thinned, the skin around his face sagged, his cheeks became more sallow, and his eyes receded into his skull in preparation for that final, eternal snooze. His pigmentation lost its colour, and I noticed that age and infirmity turned him a hue that he could not stop his country from also becoming—grey.[3]

So, what was it like growing up in all this? This book is my answer to that question, but it itself invites another: "What does *Ja, No, Man* mean?"

Now *that's* a good question.

That I have no good answer, and what's more, that there *is* no good answer, is part of the point. *Ja, no, man!* is the ultimate South Africanism. It means, literally, "Yes, no, man," but that doesn't quite cut it as an explanation. The phrase itself is contradiction epitomized: It is meaningless, yet we South Africans used it all the time.

What you are about to read is a valiant attempt to get to the bottom of the *Ja, no, man!* conundrum. It is an honest recount-

---

3. *Grey* was something of a buzzword in 1980s South Africa. It referred not so much to a colour as to the never-before-heard-of mixing of races in certain geographical areas by loosening the notorious Group Areas Act—principally, in the downtown Johannesburg suburb of Hillbrow. Essentially, it was a great way to provide affordable housing for insane, indigent, drug-addled, and poverty-stricken whites while creating the veneer of slow progress. As far as smoke and mirrors go, it fooled precisely no one.

ing of my early years in a country that was both a very nice place to grow up in and a horrible place to live. South Africa was a wellspring of close families and warm friendships, of sharp hatreds and sheer loathing. It was a place of enormous natural beauty and of deplorable human degradation. It was a country of stark contradictions.

L.P. Hartley said it best: "The past is a foreign country; they do things differently there." Oh, my, yes they do. I will be your humble guide, issuing you a passport and set of maps for this strange region. I will take you from 1973, the year of my birth, all the way through to my leaving for Canada in December 1989. *Ja, No, Man* is my final childhood scrapbook—a patchwork of memories pasted into a collage of what it was like to grow up white in Apartheid-era South Africa.

During my first week at Claude Watson School for the Arts, South Africa seemed a very distant place. I simply could not figure out what to do with my mannequin, and the flesh-coloured, nippleless, featureless facsimile haunted my nightmares. My reticence itself, I learned, counted as a Statement in Claude Watson's conceptual art universe. "Interesting," said my art teacher, stroking his chin, "ve-ery interesting." My time there ended when I saw one of my black-clad classmates sawing a hole in his mannequin's stomach and placing a small television set within. Then he inserted speakers in her breasts. Art that played TV? C'mon.

After a minor breakdown, I transferred to a school closer to my family's new home, with an art program less po-mo and more Old Master. In a matter of weeks, I was used to those chattering kids in the hallways, and I had taken to chewing four pieces of Bubblicious at once in class (a capital offence in a

South African school). I replaced the acid-washed jeans with a pair of used 501s, and I stopped gawking at the black and Asian students. What had been so exotic, so terrifying, a few months earlier was steadily becoming normal.

But by then, I think, I was deeply suspicious of normal.

Beginnings

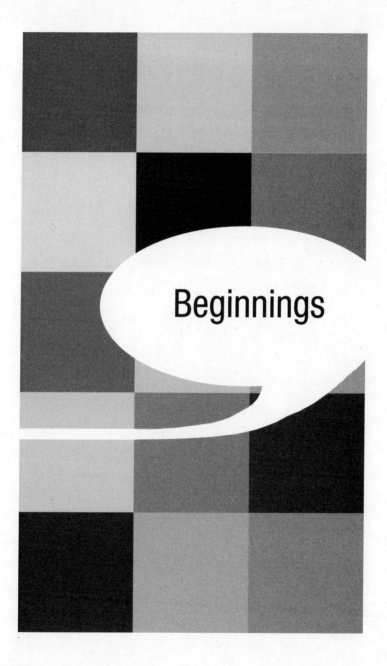

In which we Journey back through Time
to the very Beginning; Grow up under the
Shadow of The Coathanger; Antagonize an
Axe-Murderer; Unravel the Doctor's Canard;
and get Drooled on by a Boerboel.

The Belle of Doorenbos

North Toronto's Whispering Towers is where old South Africans go to die. From a distance, the three high-rise buildings resemble massive sun-bleached bones plonked into the earth by an ancient tribe, like totems. As the semi-alert visitor enters the newly renovated, faux wood, low-lit lobby (which references—unintentionally, I hope—a high-end casket in a tasteful funeral home), he or she cannot help noticing the signs and signifiers of old age—the whiff of camphors, creams, and other topical agents employed to ease broken bodies through their final days; the walkers, sitting canted in the hallways like jets on the deck of an aircraft carrier; the Filipina long-term care workers moving briskly in and out of the elevators, carrying bags full of pharmaceuticals, baby food, and diapers—a perverse inversion of a midwifery ward.

I have no idea why the Whispering Towers are so called. Perhaps it's the wind that constantly whistles though the complex, dancing between the three high-rises, snaking under cracks in doors, and worming down elevator shafts with a low, lugubrious moan. Or maybe it's the unmistakable papyrusy rustle of old age and infirmity that shuffles through those hallways. Cars parked at the roundabout in front of the northernmost Whispering Tower discharge a statistically high proportion of wrinkled, previous-generation white, Jewish South Africans.

As their brittle limbs are uncurled from the car and the icy wind hits them, a baffled expression crosses their faces.

"How did I end up *here*?" they seem to be wondering.

They dodder toward the lobby, steered by a helper or a great-great-grandchild, and look around with puzzlement, as if searching for something familiar—some hint of Johannesburg or Pietermaritzburg or Bloemfontein. It requires a splendid imagination—or failing that, full-blown dementia—to evoke the merest of allusions to the old country on a November day at Whispering Towers.

On this particular day, I'm looking for more than allusions. I'm at Whispering Towers to gather hard facts. There's no other way to start my own story—to make sense of my South African existence—if I don't make a stop here first. Up on the overheated ninth floor, buried alive under a dense synaptic quagmire of lassitude and asthenia, lies the short history of my people. Time, however, is critical—more details are lost to the fog of failing memory with every passing hour. A reporter chasing a scoop, I have hurried uptown, packing a tape recorder and notebook, ready to document a history I could make no sense of as a boy. It has not been easy securing this interview, and I'm warned that I may be biting off more than I can chew. But I'm a professional, and I'll take my chances. After all, without this history, my own story has no context. I take a deep breath, enter the lobby, and key in the buzz code.

"*Why* are you here?" asks Shenella Judelman after I'm let into the apartment. I've tried explaining the book to her, but it's pointless. "*Ag,* who wants to read that nonsense?" she wants to know. As we sit across from each other in her living room, sipping tea, my visit quickly degenerates into the toughest journalistic assignment of my career. Shenella is not being cooperative. This hurts, because Shenella is my grandmother.

Have you ever interviewed a nonagenarian? I have to yell questions so loud that my teeth start rattling loose. The heat in the apartment is jacked up so high that I'm no longer drinking—I'm *hydrating*—and I have a desperate, insistent headache, like something you'd develop in a small village in India during monsoon season. Shenella, whose official appellation is Gaga,[4] is swaddled in blankets on a loveseat. She is bent yet still sturdy. I was astonished to learn that, in her prime, Gaga was only of average height—I always thought of her as basketball-player tall. Although she is ninety-one, remnants of her imperious bearing are still in evidence. Gaga has never been ill; her constitution refuses to fail her. As has been her custom every Saturday morning since the Truman administration, she has her hair styled into a rigid blond coif, then gassed with aerosol lacquer throughout the week to maintain its fixity until the next appointment. She is taken care of by two Filipina caregivers. Today, Grace is on duty.

Often, Gaga will shut down our conversation to break into song (a trait that's become something of a hallmark). "Um, goodbye, er, Piccadilly," she warbles, while I put my head in my hands and wait, like a Floridian during hurricane season, for this to blow over. "Farewell, um, da di dah. It's a long, long way to Tipperary. But my—I think it's—heart's? *Ja,* heart's. My heart's. Right. There."

---

4. Etymology: My uncle Alan apparently mangled the word *grandmother* in a really cute way; it stuck to Gaga's mother and was duly passed down a generation. I shall hereafter refer to my grandmother by that designation.

As her ability to (almost) recall a seventy-year-old pop ditty suggests, Gaga's long-term memory is intact. The problem is her short-term memory. These issues converge when her short-term memory fails to recall what part of her long-term memory she has just related to me. We cover the same ground three times, four times, more. The interview slides quickly into the verbal equivalent of a Benny Hill skit.

Finally, and most painfully, there is The Question. Until recently, Gaga asked me but one Question, one she would forget that she had asked and so ask again. And then one more time. "But are you making any money?" Now, there would be nothing wrong with that query if, of course, I was. But Gaga's Questions have a way of honing in on weaknesses rather than strengths. Even with her faculties failing her and her will ebbing by the day, Gaga still has it in her to find the chink.

I could have lied. I could have said, "Doing quite well, actually. Tech is down a little, but didn't buy with high expectations. And commodities? Hoo-hah!" But that would be useless. The Old Question was not so much a question as a statement of fact. Gaga was actually saying: "You are not making enough money. Get a real job." How she intuited all this, living up there in her torrid estuary, I cannot say. Partly because it was followed by the dispensation of a twenty-dollar bill, I miss The Old Question.

Mostly I miss it because Gaga's New Question is: "Are you very heartbroken?" My recently failed relationship takes the foremost position in her cerebral cortex whenever we see each other. Today, The New Question is on endless repeat, and there's nothing I can do to throw her off the scent. "Are you very heartbroken?"

Grace, the caregiver, gives me the sort of look you'd give the corpse of a drowned kitten.

"I'm asking the questions here," I say.

"Why did you break it off?" asks Gaga, not so much ignoring me as invalidating my right to speak. There is no satisfactory answer to The Question (given that it's not actually a question)—and besides, we've been over it, oh, once or twice before. So I try something different.

"She was stealing money from me. And pregnant, with another man's child. Twins."

A flash of the old Gaga emerges: "What bloody rubbish! It was something you did. Of that I'm sure." I sip my tea and moan slowly. I'm on my ninth tape, and I've got bupkes.

"Are you very heartbroken?" (Translation: That was your last chance at conjugal happiness; you will be lonely for the rest of your life.)

This iteration of The Question does not come with a stipend.

There comes a point in every big assignment when you need a … well, call it what you will: a break, a miracle, an epiphany, a catalyst, religious inspiration, a serendipitous appearance by a celebrity guest star—some damn thing. As I'm about to give up, as I switch off the tape recorder and down the rest of my tea, I hear an insistent, won't-take-no-for-an-answer hammering on the door.

Grace leaps up to answer the knocking. In storms Ethel Shwartz, Gaga's Whispering Towers neighbour. In her early seventies, she's a teenager by Whispering Towers' standards. She is rail-thin, wears a pantsuit accessorized with a pearl necklace, her cropped, unabundant hair adding to a sort of frenzied schoolmarmish appearance. "I'm with the tenants' committee," Mrs. Shwartz screams. (One must get used to significantly elevated levels of noise here—the inhabitants of Whispering Towers are either long past hearing aids or new at English, which means Lots. Of. Loud. Enunciation.) "Last year we..."

A bemused Grace points to Gaga, buried in the loveseat.

"Oh, hello, lovey," booms Ethel in her crisp South African accent. Gaga chokes mid-Tipperary, bewildered, as if Ethel were conjured up by the snap of Grace's fingers. Instinct kicks in.

"Do you want tea?" asks Gaga.

"No, doll," says Ethel. "I want your *money.*" Ethel winks at me conspiratorially and then gets back to business. "I'm with the tenants' committee, and we're doing our annual fundraising drive. Remember last year when they tried to raise the rent 6 percent, but we managed to hold them to 3.7?" It is fair to say, unequivocally, that Gaga does not remember. Ethel sits at the dining-room table, organizing her clipboard and her bankroll. She crosses out a name on a handwritten sheet.

"Ten dollars, doll," yells Ethel.

"Ten? So much?" I can't tell if Gaga is joking.

"*Ja,* well. They're *tupping* with the lobby again, and they're busy with the parking lot, also. You watch—they'll try to raise the rent again, doll. That's why we're here, hey. Stop them from taking advantage."

Gaga is fumbling in her wallet for a ten-dollar bill, gives up, gets Grace to do it. "*Ja,* when I was in South Africa I used to work for the Women's Zionist League every second Thursday. We used to collect money..."

"Sweetie, I have to run." Ethel grabs the cash and adds it to the roll clipped to her clipboard. Her pants are hitched up to her chin, and I get the overwhelming impression that she will never die. "I've got the grandkids coming up from Atlanta tonight. It's the American Thanksgiving, you see. And when their cousins are here, it means the Toronto grandkids must also stay with Granny. It's like a zoo, hey." Ethel winks at me again, as if I know just how it is with the grandkids and the cousins. "*Ja,* I must get back and start the cooking. But I must come for tea soon, hey."

If I was looking for a trigger, some restorative to stimulate the memory and allow South Africa in, Ethel Shwartz is it. I was surrounded by scores of women like her: busy, clucking, indomitable matriarchs. Twelve feet tall. Rulers of planet Earth and all that roam its surface. Indeed, before her slow and steady decline, Gaga was one such creature. She is now, sadly, incapable of anything approaching her old bluster. If Ethel is the Platonic ideal, Gaga is but the shadow on the cave wall. But once it was a very different story. Ethel got away easy.

Gaga's instinctual offer of tea was far from a straightforward gesture of hospitality. It was an act of outright aggression. What could be more painful to Ethel, who was so clearly in a rush, than an impromptu, unscheduled tea? A colonoscopy, maybe? Ten years ago, in South Africa, when she had all her faculties, Gaga would have insisted—there was no way Ethel would *not* be chugging a nice (pronounced "na-aahs") cup of Five Roses, thirsty or not. (I'm not sure Grace does tea parties, so I don't know how this would have turned out at Whispering Towers.) Yes, tea would be made, and slowly. Cookies would be served. The girl[5] would bring the tray to the tea table—the china rattling daintily against the silver, wisps of steam rising lazily from the cups. And hostilities would commence.

---

5. I hate to be the one to tell you this, but domestic servants were referred to as "the girl," as in, "What is the girl making for dinner?" or, "Has the girl set the table?" This appellation was, of course, in no way related to age. The South African Hall of Shame is cavernous and filled to brimming with such terms. My mother has forbidden Gaga from calling Grace "the girl."

The social mores of South African women are dizzyingly complex—mostly because war resembles peace in every way but intent. Depending on the circumstance, a biscuit is a confectionary, an olive branch, or a hand grenade. Gauging these nuances is specialty work, and dangerous besides. I knew, however, where Gaga stood on the Ethel Shwartz equation—those biscuits were bunker-busters. So, it was with real sorrow that I watched Gaga get mauled by her sprightly adversary in the overheated confines of a North Toronto apartment. I should have instead borne witness to an epic battle between Godzilla and Mothra—two well-matched foes tearing at each other to the death with talons of civility, ripping away at infinite carapaces of gentility, city blocks razed in the wake of their politesse. I saw only hints of the old Gaga. She was a lioness once, and queen of the pride in her day.

Ethel, God bless her, has brought energy into the room. In many ways, she is Gaga's spirit and Gaga knows it. What's more, she clearly got the old girl's back up. ("Dropping in like that! Can you bloody imagine?") There's fire in her eyes now, she's sitting up straight—she's ready. It will no longer be such a feat wresting from Gaga's tangled synapses the gist of her younger days growing up at the bottom of Africa.

I click the tape recorder back on, and Gaga and I two-step, tango, and soft-shoe our way through the muddle of her brain, past snippets of Shakespeare, verses of "Old Man River," the roadblocks of long-dead Hollywood matinee idols. ("Who was that in that movie? I can't think until we work it out! He was such a dish.") And when we arrive at the undamaged part of her mnemonic hard drive, it's all there.

The Old Country.

When I was young and slept over at her sprawling one-storey, ranch-style house on Green Street, Gaga would parcel out fragments of her early life, tiny glimpses that made her girlhood seem impossibly exotic. "I never wore shoes—not once—not until I was twelve years old," she'd tell me, her glasses perched magically on her forehead, her lipstick, usually refreshed every fifteen minutes or so, left to fade because of the late hour. Gaga was never less than immaculately turned out—her housedresses were most women's opera wear—so the fact that her feet were, at any point in her life, left bare, struck me as completely fantastical. I thought she *slept* in high heels. "Why didn't you wear shoes?" I'd ask. "Because nobody wore shoes. Barefoot, so the skin under my feet was thick and hard. Now, go to sleep." She'd tuck me in under four layers of blankets, drape another over my feet, give me a peck on my forehead, and switch off the light.

I slept over often, from when I was about three until well into my teens, and there was never the slightest alteration in the proceedings. Stepping into Gaga's domain was to enter a world of rigour; to step outside the prescribed regimen was to risk being churned up by the polished, sharpened cogs of the machine.

Green Street, so named because it runs alongside an enormous sprawling golf course, actually *smelled* green. If you strolled over Gaga's precisely manicured lawn toward the course, you could hear groundwater rushing below your feet, while cool wafts of impossibly rich air brought goosebumps to your arms. Lying in bed, weighed down by forty pounds of blankets (life at 14 Green Street subscribed to Gaga's internal core temperature, which was that of a large iguana), I'd listen to the soporific *shushing* of a line of long-limbed blue gums that stood sentinel at the fringe of the golf course. The house's picture windows looked north over Gaga's garden, where beds of flora were terrified into strict regimental order, and then onto an endless stretch of fairway. Turtledoves cooed from the high branches of the blue gums, and hadedas flew over the house like squadrons of great, grey fighter jets, cawing noisily on their way to tear up the greens that gave Green Street its name. I never once saw hadedas on Gaga's lawn. Somehow, they just knew.

My grandfather, whom we called Oupa, shuffled through this minefield with an irrepressible good nature, which is not to say he didn't come close to losing a limb every now and again. "How many times have I told you, man! Fold the newspaper into quarters and place it on the upper right of the reading table!" Gaga would yell at him. Oupa was stocky and, even in his seventies, rock-solid, attached to the earth like a limpet. In his youth he had apprenticed as a butcher, and his massive hands—with the tip of a thumb missing—suggested the odd costly lapse in concentration. He had a big head with a dash of grey hair on either side of a speckled pate, humorous eyes, and the family trait of enormous, hairy ears. He was not nearly as henpecked as Gaga would have liked. The Yiddish term is *dufkah*—mulishly stubborn—and Oupa was *dufkah* to a fault. He also sported an awful, divorce-worthy sense of humour. He never tired of this one, usually dusted off at restaurants:

Oupa: Vot beer do you haff?

Waiter: Sir, we have Castle Lager, Amstel, Carling Black Label, and Hansa.

Oupa: Hansa? Vot's de question?

Every Friday night, for the duration of my childhood, my mother, father, sister, and I were guests at Gaga and Oupa's for the Sabbath dinner. After Oupa intoned the prayer over the wine and bread in his thick Hebrew, Gaga rang the dinner bell, a signal for her liveried manservant to bring the first course. "Come now, Billy," she'd say. "We can't be here all night." There were three set, rotating menus, and they did not vary in sixteen years. Gaga did not cook the food herself. "I've trained five girls to cook perfectly," she'd say with pride. "Taste that macaroni pudding and tell me if you've ever eaten better." She possessed an encyclopedia of recipes passed down to her through generations, the culinary history of my people inscribed meticulously in blue ink on recipe cards. She stood over her staff in the kitchen until they got it just right. The correct way to mince fish. The only way to baste a chicken. The finest stewed *tsimis* in the world. Consequently, black Africans in Johannesburg were cooking like mamas from the shtetl.

Indeed, Friday dinner conversations were restricted, mostly, to discussions on the quality of the food. My mother, whose personality bore no resemblance to her mother's, would stare into a spot far off in space (I assumed that was the spot where God lived—my mother looked there often) whenever Gaga interrogated us on the cuisine. "My, this is excellent! Really, this is too good for words," Gaga would prompt, staring over at her daughter. "Yessss, Gaga," Mom would drawl in strained tolerance. It was difficult for me to believe that Mom and Gaga were related. Even my mother's wearing pants was enough to garner Gaga's disapproval. ("I wore a pair once," Gaga told me, "and never again. *Never.*") Mom did not get her hair done every week, and would never, as Gaga did, watch our plates like a platoon sergeant observing new recruits at a firing range, though she did share Gaga's more dangerous traits—among them, a penchant for disciplined children with solid academic records. She ran a strict household, my mother, cloaking us in a particularly South African version of motherly warmth—one that carried the whiff of the switch about it.

"More?" Gaga would ask my father, Dr. Poplak. My father was referred to by his professional title, because that's how things worked at his dental surgery. It was a short mental hop from "Pass Dr. Poplak the number three drill, Nurse," to "Pass Dr. Poplak the roast potatoes, Richard." Gaga liked Dr. Poplak, because Dr. Poplak ate. That's all it took to make it into Gaga's good books: chew, swallow, repeat. On those occasions when there were other guests, Gaga was less overt in her ministrations but no less severe in her assessment of those who didn't ask for seconds. As for those who didn't finish their first plate, they were spoken of for years, like wayward apostates, their mortal sins invoked time and time again. "If you're anorexic," Gaga would say, "why come here for dinner? Starve yourself at home, rather."

"Exactly. Stay home and starve," said Dr. Poplak.

"There you go," said Gaga.

"*Ag,* the anorexics…" I'd chip in.

"Shut up," chorused my parents. Children weren't present for the conversation. (Come to think of it, I have no idea *why* we were present.)

My sister, Carolyn, and I were in rapture on Friday nights and at no risk of Gaga's prolonged reprobation. The reason for this was simple: sugar. It was the only night of the week we were allowed to drink pop or eat dessert. (Dr. Poplak disapproved of sugar, and not only because it rotted teeth.) We would spend a good fifteen minutes deliberating over the drinks tray. I am a little over two years older than Carolyn, and she'd eye me intently from under a wild mane of dark curls, waiting for me to make a decision. The difference in my sister's and my looks—she's dark skinned and exotic looking while I was born blond-locked and fair (I turned swarthier over the years)—fooled even the two of us into assuming that we *were* different. This was not the case: We were exactly the same. We faced off this way for our entire childhood—two gunslingers waiting for the other to make a move.

If I was lucky, I won the argument of who got to sleep over at 14 Green Street. ("One child at a time," Gaga would say. "I'm finished with bringing up children.") My first memories include Gaga tucking me into bed while the cries of turtle-doves and cicadas wafted in from the lawn and the golf course beyond. Despite the comfort and routine, an undercurrent of menace ran through that spare room—unsettling mysteries that I couldn't quite unravel, manifest in a Toulouse-Lautrec print that hung on the wall. (Gaga had to remove or cover the offending image—it's as if each of the misshapen dwarf's miserable thirty-six years permeated the room, poisoning my dream life.) A series of old cardboard suitcases lay stacked beneath the bed—suitcases full of photographs of Oupa and Gaga's youth, sepia snapshots of a world bearing no resemblance to my own. Gaga would whisper little pieces of gossip or facts that astonished me ("I couldn't speak a word of English until I was much older than you"), and as I drifted off to sleep, I'd dream of long-forgotten places that were so outlandish even gagas went shoeless and spoke in tongues.

"*Ag,*" Gaga says to me in the Whispering Towers, her eyes milky and faraway, "that place was a godforsaken hellhole."

Sometimes, if you want to know a person, you need to know exactly where they come from. But Doorenbos (the hellhole in question) explains a lot more than just Gaga. It goes a long way to explaining the modern history of South Africa.

"Tell me about it," I say to Gaga.

"No one wants to hear about Doorenbos," says Gaga.

"I do," says Grace, helpfully. After twenty minutes of coaxing, we are on our way.

You'd be hard pressed to find Doorenbos on even a detailed map of the Western Cape. It lies across the Dooren River, a pimple on the ass cheeks of the Cederberg Mountains, about 125 miles northeast of Cape Town. There never has been, and there never will be, much of anything there. The mountains around the Dooren look like they've had their peaks severed; eons of grit and sand and wind have worn them down to harsh nubbins, like the knuckles of a leper. At noon nothing stirs, not the slightest breeze, no birdsong—even the cry of a human voice is swallowed by the endless Cederberg. For those who came here centuries ago, this place must have had a singular Biblical corollary: With the foreboding silence, astonishing heat, and utter isolation, Doorenbos could be purgatory.

Any nation forged in the Cederberg Mountains and beyond—in the vicious land of the Eastern and Western Cape, which is as hard as any country on Earth—is bound to be a tad ornery. This is where an infant South Africa was midwifed, in the seventeenth century, by a white settler population who came to be known as Boers. Afrikaners. These early settlers had what would today be described as chronic authority issues: They fled the land around Cape Town to be free of the pernicious grasp of their colonial masters (the Dutch East India Company was the first to claim the territory, in 1652, and later, the British, who nabbed it from the Dutch in the 1890s), and they moved east in covered ox carts—through settlements just like Doorenbos—a gruelling, blood 'n' guts–drenched excursion through southern Africa, mythologized as the Great Trek.

To come to any understanding of a people, you must first understand their geography. For the Afrikaners, who saw themselves as spiritual descendents of the Israelites—favoured by heaven, persecuted here on earth—every battle won against this arid soil was a confirmation of God's love. Every sound, every echo, was the clatter of an encroaching British hoof clop. Every native they encountered was an enemy, a competitor for territory and scant resources, and a godless fool. This is the land where Boer families were whittled down to nothing, where newborns were buried in shallow graves, where entire clans disappeared. Those who moved through here, or settled, became as wild and arid as the land. They stripped the Bible down to bare bones and crunched those bones to dust in minds that had nothing to do but turn over and over on the concepts of God's mercy and benevolence, and the fact that those dispositions were nowhere in evidence in this life, and perhaps not even in the life to come. The stark Calvinism, the stoicism, the paranoia, the misery, and the hatred—all tendencies I attributed to the Afrikaners who ran the country when I was a boy—found their genesis in Doorenbos and places just like it.

Plonked in the middle of Doorenbos (which is to say, the middle of nowhere) is Katz General Dealers, established 1914, the year before Gaga was born. The store is little more than a trading post for Boers eking out an existence on farms nearby, and for convoys of trek Boers moving north or east. The murky corners are cluttered with bales of feed, maize, sugar, and flour piled high, while shelves are lined neatly with coffee and battered tins. Occasionally, butter and milk can be found in the icebox. Katz General Dealers belongs to my great-grandfather—Gaga's father—one Charles Katz, hereafter known as Oom Koenie. Like everyone who stumbles into Doorenbos and stays for more than ten minutes, he's wondering how in hell he got here. He came, like thirty-five thousand other Jewish Lithuanians, to southern Africa for better (any?) prospects.

Gaga takes her first tentative steps in the vast expanse of veld that surrounds the store, the shimmering, abbreviated Cederberg fading to purple in the distance. She putters around in the rough dust, her little feet thick with calluses, dodging snakes and scorpions while stomping on anything else that wiggles. Gaga's mother—a stout, ginger woman named Bertha—runs the home attached to the store according to the laws of this new land. The old mores—the laws of the Old World shtetls, of the European Judaism of her youth—have as much utility here as fairy tales. Bertha uses a huge tome, a doctor's compendium of ailments (a remnant of a reason-based world that no longer exists for her), to steer her kids through the medical minefields of early childhood. She also has at her disposal all the shtetl home remedies, stored in a battered suitcase that tinkles merrily with multicoloured bottles of snake oil, along with additions from local lore—many of them the product of an unsavoury predilection for dreckopothacary. Crap is the Leatherman multi-tool of Doorenbos—you use it for everything.

("Would you believe it if I told you that our floors were made of s-h-i-t?" Gaga asks.

"If you tell me, I believe it."

"Okay. Our floors were made of s-h-i-t. Shit," Gaga adds, just in case I missed it.)[6]

Two sun-blackened women work for the family (a quiet one named Elsjie and a noisier one Gaga remembers as Behhhh-

6. Gaga, about five thousand miles and twenty years removed from propriety, revels in details like these.

kie!), gathering the steaming shit from the oxen and using it, variously, as construction material, medication, and a means of gently urging uninvited spirits to stay away. The local population,[7] such as it is, are mixed-race people, referred to, unaffectionately and in a way that hints at the social ethos of the area, as *bastes* (bastards or, more properly, Griqua, which refers to the geographical area they settled in—Griqualand). Elsjie and Behhhh-kie!, *bastes* both, work the manure into the floor of the house, packing it so hard that it holds a dull gleam when scrubbed. With their fingertips, the women mix a green paste and paint concentric patterns onto the floors—patterns, with circles spiralling in and in on themselves, that in the gloom of the rudimentary house look like something a scatologically inclined Martha Stewart would be proud of.

Once a year, the church comes to town—an annual highlight (and I use this term loosely) called *nagmaal*. ("*Ja,* that was good fun," Gaga says, with the level of enthusiasm normally reserved for undergoing small surgical procedures.) *Nagmaal* is a version of the Anglican Communion, the point of which is to offer far-flung Dutch Reformed Church members the opportunity to take the sacrament, christen their babies, do a little trade, socialize, and thank God for all the people they'd killed since establishing themselves in the region. The Boer mentality is one of a people under siege, constantly under threat, and *nagmaal* was the physical embodiment of this. Little Gaga watches the Boers outspan their covered wagons

7. The Cape during the early twentieth century was predominantly coloured (mixed race), with whites making up about 20 percent of the population, mostly in and around Cape Town. Jews were a small part of the white population, but they travelled, selling goods, so they got around.

and assemble them in a *laager*—a tight horseshoe formation and a signature Afrikaner military manoeuvre. They'd pitch tents, light fires, and drape thick canvas from wagon to wagon, all to indulge in this pious, God-fearing proto-tailgate party.

Nagmaal, like most military/religious festivities, was an awe-inspiring event, especially in entertainment-starved Doorenbos. The murmur of whispered prayer rises up from the *laager* in steady waves, and Gaga slowly walks around the wagons, peeking through the thick wooden wheel spokes, trying to see what is happening within. The Boers look down at the little Jew running under their feet and pray for the child's soul. These Hebrew wanderers—cursed by God to forever stumble around the Earth without a home—are so unlike the Afrikaners, who have found theirs here at the end of the earth.

Jesus loves me! This I know,
For the Bible tells me so.
Little ones to him belong;
They are weak but he is strong

Yes, Jesus loves me!
Yes, Jesus loves me!
Yes, Jesus loves me!
The Bible tells me so.

At Whispering Towers, Gaga is halfway through this jingle for the J-man before I can quiet her down.

"Please, Gaga, no more!" She sounds like Tom Waits with laryngitis. Screw the tea—I'm pouring myself a whisky.

"*Ja,* they only wanted us to sing about Jesus," she says. "And so that's what we did."

After I do some damage to the Ballantine's, I learn that "they" are the string of teachers who took care of Gaga's education after the Katzes crossed the Dooren River, leaving Doorenbos behind, and began their roving through the Western Cape, trying to coerce both money and a life for themselves from the dust. In rustic brick schoolhouses, often just a room added onto a house (the walls always adorned with a choice Biblical passage and, as a concession to the secular aspects of the curriculum, an alphabet), Gaga was reminded, as often as possible, that the Jews—the *Jode*—were responsible for the death of the very fellow she was obliged to celebrate so regularly in song, and that she should feel bad whenever she got the chance. The *Jode* were very much the Other, lumped in with the genuinely loathed papists (there is no branch of Protestantism quite as inflexible as Calvinism) and treated accordingly. Gaga puts it nicely: "They weren't exactly our biggest fans." Thankfully, because the Afrikaners saw themselves as victims of British avarice and cruelty, they felt some measure of sympathy for the persecuted Jews, a people who had been in the Cape for almost a century and who were (as peddlers, especially) cornerstones of the rural economy.

Cattle speculation—or cow peddling—took Oom Koenie and his brood to Worcester, a spot finally worthy of the descriptor "town." The main street's deep sluices burbled with runoff from the Swartberg Mountains after the rains, and comely double-storey Victorian buildings granted Worcester an imperial, stately appearance that belied its vicious provincialism. The imposing church square formed the centre of town, and the volk here were churchgoers to a fault.

The greatest hint to Gaga's character lies somewhere in the furious, unrelenting heat of this shuttered, straight-backed town. Here, Gaga was forcibly turned into a lady—the calluses scraped from her feet, her elocution polished, her posture corrected, her manner made just so. The person responsible for this—a nightmarish cross between Professor Henry Higgins, Freddy Krueger, and Cruella de Vil—was a woman named *Mevrou* Dees.

"She was bloody *terrifying*," Gaga tells me, close on eighty years later.

Day one at the menacing Worcester girls' schoolhouse immediately staunched any residual excitement Gaga may have had over the purchase of her first pair of shoes. Any decent South African school principal, like any horror-movie villain, requires a trademark. With Dees, it was the keys. A big bunch of them. They would thump against her ample thighs as she walked around the school, an otherworldly jangle that echoed against the brick of the schoolhouse, the sound settling slowly like ash from a newly exploded volcano. As the jangle increased in volume, signalling the impending arrival of the jangler herself, the knocking of knees, chewing of lower lips, and loosening of bladders increased in intensity. I have known women just like *Mevrou* Dees—Afrikaner educators so severe, so outright terrifying, that you never dare to find out if the bark is worse than the bite.

Mevrou Dees used a wooden ruler to assist in the hammering home of the finer points of readin', 'ritin', and 'rithmatic. Gaga's knuckles, she tells me, "still hurt" from the pain caused by her lack of mathematical aptitude (a hereditary defect she passed on to my sister and me). This explains why Gaga was so harsh on us for our math grades when we were in school. "What are you going to be able to do with these math marks? Be a garden boy?" Gaga would ask. This was followed by recommendations to my mother: "He watches too much bloody TV. Get him to stop!" and "Take him to extra lessons. Immediately!"

Gaga, except for one or two minor differences (no keys), was *Mevrou* Dees incarnate. She scrutinized our handwriting—"*No!* Too messy! Your *e* must have a nice, elegant slope. What's the matter with you?"—listened attentively to our English compositions—"*No!* Read clearly. I can't understand one word you're saying!"—and corrected our Afrikaans pronunciation—"*No!* No, no, no. *Ag, nee,* I give up."

Corporal punishment was never Gaga's thing—my theory is that she ran the risk of mussing her hair if she were to move her arms vigorously. But Gaga conjured the ghostly jangle of *Mevrou* Dees's keys every time she corrected my posture or yelled at me for mumbling. Like in a kung fu movie, the protege became the master.

Bertha Katz was nervous. "She thought we were snobs, my mother," Gaga says, sniffing haughtily. "She was exactly right." That her children behaved like landed gentry made Bertha skittish, considering that they were neither landed nor gentry. My grandmother had acquired tastes. Bertha was concerned that these tastes did not include an appetite for fraternizing with co-religionists. And that wouldn't do. In the mid-1930s, they packed for Cape Town.

Here, the boughs of my family tree met the trunk, and the roots become tangled. In what sounds like the plot notes for a Shakespearean farce, Gaga's sister—now living in Johannesburg—met two brothers. She picked one, deeming the other perfect for her sister. He was a Lithuanian named Mannie Judelman, and he had left Lithuania with no money, no English, and even less education. He was a butcher, strong as an ox, with *shtetl kop*—

street smarts. There were, however, complications. First of all, these two brothers had accents as thick as clotted milk. They were uneducated and couldn't mix a martini—if they even knew what a martini was. Jew or no, they were *uitlanders*—foreigners. Gaga, ever the verbal alchemist, could turn romantic sonnets into accountancy textbooks—"*Ag,* the men weren't exactly lining up. So I chose Mannie."

I can't help wondering what Mannie made of this creature, this woman who came from another world, whose aspirations rose far higher than simply bearing children who made it through infancy and maybe having a bit of meat on holy days, God willing. I wonder if Mannie felt a slow rush of pressure when he thought about the fact that putting food on the table would not be enough; that unlike in his shtetl, mere subsistence would amount to abject failure. And how did Gaga know—what Judelman trait did she use as the jumping-off point for her essential leap of faith—that this stocky man from Nowhere, Eastern Europe, would be able to pull the rabbit of wealth from his battered felt bowler?

If you sought wealth in Johannesburg in the 1930s, an excellent way to find it was to look down. The mud beneath your feet oozed rich mineral tinctures—the ground flowed blood red, or green, or fuchsia after the rains, running over with the promise of buried wealth. After all, in 1886, a fellow named George Harrison (don't be silly) literally tripped over one of the largest gold deposits ever discovered. The ensuing rush built the city, quickly making it Africa's largest only ten years after the discovery.

The wealth Mannie saw oozing beneath his shoes was not gold. It was, in fact, clay. Dig it up, fashion it into rectangles, bake it on high—and what you've got are bricks.

"More," Gaga says. "One more." Grace lays another blanket over Gaga's knees, looking mildly astonished, despite her experience with the elderly, at the old girl's boundless capacity for feeling the cold. "Pass him the thing," Gaga tells Grace, who hands me a wedding photo, dated—in scrawled cursive—1938. The woman in the wedding dress is unmistakably Gaga, the man beside her no less definitively Oupa. On a January afternoon, inside Cape Town's Gardens Shul, Mannie and Shenella formalized their union.

Bricks. Millions of them. Billions, even. The quarry at Germiston Brickworks, at first barely a pothole, deepened steadily. I remember it from the 1980s as a massive gouge in the ground, a crater with an ecosystem of its own. A soupy lake formed on the bottom of the quarry—shadowy amphibians darted between the weeds sunk into the depths of the muddy water. Bushes grew into the sides of the bowl; feral cats and dogs, battle-scarred and emaciated, lived out a small-scale Discovery Channel documentary in the caves and crannies pockmarking the cliff walls. I played out many an imagined adventure in this big brown bowl, and I loved the smell of diesel and engine grease that sputtered up from the bulldozers. Oupa conversed with the blacks in the quarry in *Fanagalo*—a Zulu-Afrikaans-English pidgin developed on the mines—and led me around by hand, promising me that yes, one day I would become a forklift driver.

The war years were boom years for South Africa. A country where natural resources litter the ground like discarded Christmas baubles possesses everything necessary to enrich its citizens beyond decency. World War II booted South Africa into the realm of heavy industrialization—creating legions of Daddy Warbucks—and by the war's end, the country's white citizens (those who remained to fuel the war effort) were feeling no pain.

The country's leaders, however, felt plenty of agony. The Afrikaner Nationalists had effectively consolidated their power over the Anglo-friendly United Party and prepared for the 1948 elections by proposing a final and comprehensive segregation of the white and black populations. Looking back, it seems astonishing that institutionalized Apartheid followed so quickly on the heels of Nazism, but the country had never exactly been a hotspot for racial harmony. However, when D.F. Malan and his National Party finally came to the helm and brought the levers of power into the hands of Afrikaner Nationalists, the road to Grand Apartheid was effectively paved, with nary a pothole in sight.

The eve of the 1948 election was ass-clenchingly tense for most English-speaking white South Africans (to say nothing of black South Africans of all linguistic backgrounds). "We all sat around the wireless and listened," says Gaga. "We were too nervous for words." Who would win—the United Party moderates or the National Party extremists? Oupa and Gaga and thousands of other Jewish families wondered what would become of them if ex-Nazi sympathizers were to run the show. But the Nationalists, although far from pro-Jewish, had bigger fish to fry.

Nineteen forty-eight was the beginning of forty long, dark years—a Biblical number indeed. What those Jewish families listening to their wireless sets could not know is that the South African Jewish population would benefit from Apartheid as much as any other segment of the white population. Did the anti-Apartheid movement count a disproportionate number of Jews among its ranks? If you're going by per capita numbers—yes. But doing head counts and census reports seems somewhat counterproductive when considering the question of which race and creed was marginally less supportive of racism and creedism. In the main, the majority of Jews were the same as the majority of the white population. They accepted, they benefited, and their doubts, if they had any, remained private.

Those wireless reports telling Gaga and Oupa that there was a new sheriff in town were the making of my world, the very first crackling transmissions of the universe I was to inhabit. Everything that was born in places such as Doorenbos finally came of age in 1948. The dress rehearsals were over, the stage was set, and the bitter farce was about to begin.

Where I come into the picture, where my memory kicks in, is where the farce starts its ugly denouement. My beginning was the beginning of the end. My first memories under those bedsheets on Green Street coincide all too neatly with one of Apartheid's final Wagnerian movements—the Soweto riots of 1976. The riots grew out of student demonstrations against the mandatory study of Afrikaans in township schools—and when the authorities decided to start shooting, well, the shooting never really stopped. That iconic photograph of the teenaged Hector Pieterson—the first person to die that day—in the arms of an anguished student demonstrator, his grief-stricken sister running alongside them, was not exactly good PR for the Powers-That-Were. The jig was up.

The uprising was a wake-up call for much of the white community. It heralded the first great exodus of white South Africans for a calmer, saner life elsewhere. Mannie's two sons, my uncles, left with their families for Canada shortly after the smouldering Soweto streets turned into hell. Thousands of whites left with them. This was the year Apartheid died, and turned into something else entirely. Whatever possible justification there could have been for the system—no matter how ridiculous that justification—evaporated, and it became a vessel of pure, unreasoning hatred.

Nineteen seventy-six. That was the year I started sleeping over at Green Street, dreaming on top of suitcases packed with history, while the future raged but a few miles away. The wind blew through the leaves of those gigantic blue gums in slow waves, and on stormy nights, the trees would whoosh to the point where a mildly irritated Gaga would have to come in and put me at ease. "Shh, it's just the rain. Be a big boy, hey," she would say.

To soothe me, Gaga would tell me stories of the old days, and I'd drift off to sleep hopelessly confused, imagining a world where people walked around barefoot, chatting in Afrikaans, with their hair perfectly permed, and their clothes immaculately tailored.

Making sense of this confusion took some time. After all, to truly understand someone, you must know where they come from, and to understand a people, you must know their history.

"If you didn't wear any shoes, Gaga, couldn't the *goggas* bite you?"

"Well, *ja*. We had to be very careful of the snakes. And the scorpions. Do you know what a scorpion is? It's like a big spider but with a deadly sting on its tail."

If the point of bedtime stories is to make children scream, Gaga was a master.

Soon, Whispering Towers will no longer be where old South Africans go to die. Filipino families are moving in, as are the Lebanese and many others, with their own histories and their own ancestral memories. You just have to step into Whispering

Towers to understand that being human is an ephemeral state. It lasts forever, and no time at all. From Doorenbos to Worcester to Cape Town to Johannesburg to Toronto. Nine decades and counting. Both an eternity and the blink of an eye. Gaga is one of the last of a generation that was a blip on the chronological chart of her people—native-born rural South African Jews of the early twentieth century. When she goes, it will be all but over. And that, after all, is why I am here today.

She's humming something unrecognizable when her eyes suddenly become clear. I'm holding a half-full glass of whisky that, because of the sauna-level heat in her apartment, is rapidly sending me into somnolence. My eyelids are made of granite, and I'm not falling asleep so much as losing consciousness.

"Richard!"

"Yes! Jesus! What's up?"

"You'll drop that bloody glass and mess the carpet. And sit up straight, man!"

There's something left in the old girl yet. She's not quite ready for the scrap heap of historical footnotes. I reposition my torso and take another sip of whisky.

The wind moans as it whips against the Whispering Towers. I think it's whispered enough for one day.

Or maybe not.

"Richard?"

"Yup?"

"Are you very heartbroken?"

The Coathanger

Before anything else, there was Bushy.

My first memories are of the hunting excursions we shared when I was two years old or so. Our quarry was the lizard population of our neighbourhood, and a particularly good spot to find them was where the large splitpole fence surrounding our house came to a point in the shadow of a great evergreen. As the shade of the tree moved to engulf us, our prey would sluggishly make its way toward the warmth of the sunshine. Using a twenty-cent coin or some other blunt instrument, Bushy would strike, severing the tail of the lizard in one lightning-quick movement. I watched from my stroller as the hacked-off extremity jerked around as decoy, while the freshly shorn lizard scuttled to safety among the cracks where splitpole met aging brick.

I loved those lazy afternoons; Bushy and I trawling our neighbourhood for prey, ready to fall on an unsuspecting lizard like crazed mujahedeen on a lone infidel. We would watch the tail dance around until, slowly, the nerve endings stopped twitching and all was still. That tail was proof—to Bushy anyway—that the lizard was a devious creature, and a cause of untold headaches for mankind.

The lizards, you see, had it coming.

I didn't know this until much, much later in life, but Zulu mythology tells us that we have lizards to thank for Death, which goes a long way to explain local enmity toward reptiles in general and lizards in particular.[8] Actually, Death is not entirely the lizards' fault: They're co-conspirators with chameleons. Unkulunkulu, the Zulus' original ancestor, told the chameleon to find the tribe and tell the people: "Man will not die." The chameleon went the scenic route, stopping to gaze vainly at his multi-hued reflection in the puddles that accumulated after the rains. Shortly after sending the chameleon on his mission, Unkulunkulu ordered the lizard to find the tribe and tell the people: "Man *will* die." The lizard was spitefully expedient, his permanent gash of a grin wider than ever. He hustled and, as you may have guessed, arrived long before the chameleon. Thus, the lizard pronounced: "Man *will* die," and that's why you find yourself in ill-fitting black clothing, listening to Céline Dion songs, and eating shitty cocktail sandwiches at the funerals of people you love.

Like I said: The lizards had it coming.

In one afternoon, Bushy and I could leave five or six tails dancing their spastic dance around the neighbourhood, a slither of lizard gore trailing my stroller like a gruesome wake. Then, it was home, for powdered milk and Marie biscuits.

In a childhood completely sheltered from the continent I grew up in, living in a country that was an idiot-approximation of Christo-European civility (which existed nowhere in Europe, or anywhere else for that matter), I found, deep within the subtext of many of Bushy's actions, an imprint of Africa—almost entirely obscured but present nonetheless. As little white

8. Although Bushy was not a Zulu, African oral traditions are pretty fluid, which means they are passed along from tribe to tribe and either incorporated or discarded. Bushy had certainly adopted this one into her canon.

South Africans, we had only our nannies to link us to the land our stroller wheels trundled across.

I remember Bushy first and foremost among the figures in my early life mostly because of those daily perambulator excursions (random acts of violence and destruction tend to make a lasting impression on small boys). From zygote to chest hair (mine, that is), Bushy was a fixture. I'm told she opened the door when I first arrived home from the hospital, freshly born and swathed in my receiving blanket. Subsequently, she scooped baby mush into my mouth, changed my nappies, wiped and powdered my ass, washed me, dressed me, walked me, yelled at me, and hit me very hard with a vast array of household objects.

Our relationship degenerated into a series of internecine skirmishes and then fell completely apart when I hit the rocky teenage years. But in the early days, before our war, we were conspirators in the serial mutilation of anything unlucky enough to wiggle its way into our neighbourhood. The square mile Bushy and I traversed on our sprees was called Fellside, an in-between burb nestled amid other Johannesburg postal codes that had greater personality, some more desirable than others. For instance, if I was among those to whom these things mattered, I could say, "You know, Fellside? Right next to Houghton?" Let's put it this way: The Shah of Iran had a residence in Houghton. On the other hand, if I was trying to sound tough, I'd say, "*Ja, boet,* Fellside. Y'know, next to Orange Grove?" This was where the Italians and the Portuguese lived, and it was as splendid a place as any for a spontaneous fist fight while someone named Massimo screamed what sounded like a chicken alfredo recipe at you.

Forbes Street was a gap-toothed avenue dominated by several ancient oaks, alternating with a few jacarandas that blossomed a furious purple in October, bestowing on the sidewalks a thick carpet that quickly turned to mush underfoot.[9] Like the burbs surrounding it, Forbes Street had an economic diversity you were unlikely to find elsewhere in the city, at least in such a concentrated space. The elbow of Forbes and Castle streets was home to the Albertis, an amorphous bunch of ethnic Italians who waxed and waned depending on how many family members were born or had died that week. Along with a stocky widow garbed in black and endlessly peeling potatoes, there was always a rusted Alfa Romeo decaying out front of the house, on which the Alberti boys worked when they weren't smoking Peter Stuyvesants on their *stoep*.

At the opposite end of the middle-class spectrum were the owners of Field Force Security, with their cages of rare birds[10] and invitingly scalable wall, which, I feared, if actually scaled to retrieve a lost ball or Frisbee, would result in a bullet fired from a high-powered rifle, removing a section of one's skull. Military Jeeps decaled with the Field Force insignia were usually parked outside on the street, while a bowel-loosening mannequin, garbed in a Delta Force–style uniform, stood sentinel at the front door, with what I'd like to think was a *replica* submachine gun cradled in its frozen arms.

---

9. The jacaranda is a Johannesburg delight, a tree that flowers so vividly in the early summer that the entire city looks like the joyous lead float at a gay pride parade.

10. Several of these birds were unidentifiable, but one was unmistakably a large falcon. Son of Field Force would exercise the tethered bird by having it attack one of those freaky arm-length leather gloves.

I knew Fellside intimately, from all angles and through every season. I knew every crack in the pavement, every pitted section of asphalt; I knew how the summer heat thumped up from the tar to meet the warmth of the sun in a glorious, soporific convection. I knew the people who lived there, the minutiae of their daily routines, and I knew the precise minute Dr. Poplak's car travelled down the street toward home and therefore, in later years, when to screw the cap back on his J&B.

Every afternoon of my infancy and early childhood, regardless of the season—whether it be the dry, sharp winter or the perfect summer, broken only by its punctual four o'clock afternoon rainstorms—Bushy and I traipsed around the neighbourhood during pram-pushing rush hour. Bushy sometimes stopped to talk to other nannies in Sotho (I loved their musical Sotho salutation: *Duhm-eh-lang!*) or to gab with the gathering of blacks sitting kitty-corner to the Albertis' rotting automotive projects, drinking milk stout from cartons.

It's not the walks themselves I remember so much as the feel of the walks: a state of complete well-being combined with an absorption in a universe that was entirely, elementally new. Bushy reminded me of these perambulations many years later. "Boy," she'd say when the war between us raged at full flame, "I used to push you around all the day. You were a nice boy then!" She'd look at me, with my oversize adolescent paws and whiteheads pregnant with the pus of hormonal vigour, and say in what appeared to be genuine disgust, "And look at you *now*!"

While I was no Renaissance sculpture, to look at Bushy was to see the body of a cripple. Standing a good few inches shy of five feet, and then only in her high-soled corrective shoes, Bushy was hobbled by one leg that was a good measure shorter than the other. To compensate for this, she must have made the decision when she was much younger to fold the left ankle of her longer leg in such a way that it was flush with the ground, and to use that ankle as a substitute for her foot. Consequently, she walked like a marionette whose mangled strings were operated by a drunken puppeteer, her shelf-like bottom swinging from side to side with a determined, metronomic rhythm. Despite this handicap, when pressed, Bushy moved with the speed of a feline from some nightmare jungle. Her hands and arms, composed of tiny, birdlike bones, nevertheless possessed enormous strength. She discarded her handicap like a useless accessory that had passed from fashion, and what one part of her body lacked, another made up for with vicious efficiency. Friends who came by the house for the first time (friends who soon learned to fear her) would refer to her handicap, and I'd say, "Huh?" Even now, it's a stretch to think of Bushy as disabled.

Bushy wore exclusively the standard Johannesburg domestic servant outfit: a cotton one-piece dress in a faded light blue or pink, a frilled apron tied around the waist. Then there was Bushy's voice. It had the timbre of a cold steel blade. When she was angry, her left eyebrow rising like the sun over a battlefield, she made my name sound like a dire warning: "Ree-*shat! Uswaba, wena!* Richard! Beware you!" When I heard those words, I knew blood was likely to be spilled that day. Mine. In quantity. She called me "boy" all the years I knew her; even when I was a strapping sixteen-year-old lad, she made me feel like I was a little boy every time she said it. "Don't call me 'boy,' Bushy!" I'd bark at her, pointing a finger in warning (of what, I have no idea). She'd cackle. "I will stop when you ah a *man.*"

The relationship that had started during our walks slid steadily toward a decade's worth of reciprocal torment. Bushy had a dastardly mind. I use, by way of example, the manner in which she woke me in the mornings. She would quietly tip-ankle into my room and whip open the curtains, pouring sunshine into my now half-open eyes. If this failed to fully rouse me, she would worm her hard fingers under the covers at the foot of my bed, find my toes, and yank, cracking them like gunshots. You'd think you'd get used to this, but you don't. "You ah not a man," she'd say as I shrieked in protest. To this day, I am still unable to sleep in.

Those Guantánamo Bay–style wake-up calls instilled in me an advanced appreciation of wanton acts of cruelty. Bushy's diabolical mind was (inadvertently, I assume) transferred to mine. Even my outward appearance became subject to a classic Dickensian characterization flourish—I was born with angelic blond locks and a cherubic countenance, but I morphed into a dark-haired, dark-eyed monster. Bushy enjoyed being mean not because she was intrinsically evil but because being mean is intrinsically enjoyable. I was the same way, and I attribute all the atrocities I visited on my long-suffering sister to Bushy's influence. Oh, the cycle of violence.

You'd think that Carolyn's presence in the house would have spread the hurt. Nope. Her arrival, when I was two and a quarter, was traumatic. She was a tubby Buddha-baby, topped off with a thick thatch of black curls, whose big cheeks and doughy forehead made her look constantly glum. Adults had a word for her: "Cyoooot!" I had to be kept away from her. Although Carolyn necessarily split my parents' attention, Bushy, who was as responsible for Carolyn as she was for me, never really took an interest in her. Carolyn was—obviously—a girl and therefore of far less social importance from Bushy's perspective. I, however, was a man, or at least the carrot of manhood was dangled by Bushy, mine to consume just over the next hill of affliction. "Don't you want to be strong and beeg like me, boy?" Bushy would ask. "Or do you always want to be small?" I'd shove a couple more spoonfuls of Pablum into my maw, my cheeks burning with shame. I'd show her. If she expected a man, a man she would get.

Our two-storey house was not enormous by South African standards; nor was it small. It was a palimpsest, renovated several times during the sixteen years I lived there. Touches of the original structure remained—pressed-tin ceilings, lead-framed windows, an old brick chimney with an anthracite heater. My mother's tastes leaned toward the antique—specifically of the handsome Cape Dutch variety—rather than the 1970s shag-carpet kitsch that adorned so many Johannesburg homes. Dr. Poplak treated her antiques with suspicion, as if the house were populated by a band of thieves conspiring to separate him from his savings. "Jesus Christ—you *bought* that?" he'd ask my mother whenever a new piece moved in. My father's aesthetic sensibilities were severely reductionist: less was much, *much* more. This constant push-pull assured that the house did not look like a living museum, nor did it look like a clearinghouse after a Boxing Day sale.

Forty-one Forbes Street, Fellside, was Bushy's domain. She vacuumed, made the beds, washed the clothes, dusted, cleaned the toilets, beat the rugs (and the kids), polished the shoes, changed the kitty litter, swept the stoep, and fed the dog. She did this all, nominally, to my mother's specifications. The South African maid/madam dialectic is a complex and fascinating social phenomenon. Typically, maids lived with the family and were as much a part of the household as anyone else who lived there (which is distinct from that old South African liberal prevarication, "*Ja,* the maid is just like one of the family"). In a country where labour cost nothing, even lower-middle-class families had live-in servants, and a maid-nanny-cook-disciplinarian would run you approximately 150 rand a month, plus food.[11] In the gruesome context of Apartheid-era economics, this pittance had to feed entire families living in far-flung regions of southern Africa. The quality of a domestic servant's life was subject to the nature of her employers, and that often coincided with the employers' view of black people. Not every woman who worked as a domestic was a saint, of course, and many were downright wretched human beings. (Gaga's maid until the mid-1980s, a dyspeptic old crone named Rebecca, comes to mind.) These women, however, did not have the opportunity to channel those terrible personalities into meaningful careers in law or politics. They had two choices: 150 rand a month as a domestic, or nothing.

Most often, the madam/maid dialectic was dominated by a series of subtle yet intricate power games, silently played out over decades. (Once you've trained a girl, doll, you don't let her go!) Bushy was pretty good at these games. For one thing, she always addressed my mother with her eyes cast downward, almost a parody of obeisance. "Yes m'm," she would say, keeping her sentences short and clipped. Not that my mother demanded unwavering obedience to an inviolable code. Far from it. Somewhere along the line, as a survival technique in her lifelong

---

11. This was in the 1970s, when the rand was stronger than the U.S. dollar. The country *felt* rich in those days, the heavy coins indicative of how much of our natural resources we were pulling out of the ground. But 150 rand was not a lot of money.

vocation as a domestic servant, Bushy had acquired this affectation. Her mastery of these passive-aggressive tug-of-wars is exemplified by the one key area where she bested my mother entirely—and managed to strike from her job description the one thing you'd imagine as central to any housekeeper's duties.

Bushy did not cook for us.

This was because Bushy was either unwilling or unable to render dishes edible. She would happily cook and consume samp and beans,[12] a leaden hunk of boiled meat, or the variety of porridges available to the South African epicure, but her special gift was the ability to remove all the appetizing qualities of even these simple foodstuffs, so that everything she prepared slid down the gullet and nestled sullenly in the stomach, all set to digest slowly and agonizingly over the following week. Her cooking could slam the brakes on a Bangladeshi cholera epidemic.

Everything Bushy made had the pallor of a corpse dredged from a stagnant pond. She would remove pasta à la Bushy from the pot in a steaming gelatinous clump, all flavour and pigmentation gone. And when she wasn't removing taste, she was adding salt. To shake things up, she often dumped in a pound of margarine or added a half bottle of tomato sauce to whatever she was making. Recipes? Not so much. Bushy's level of literacy was hard to pin down: Sometimes she could read, sometimes she couldn't. My mother tried only half-heartedly to coach her. There just didn't seem to be any point. A brick of pasta doused with noisome, salted tomato gloop was not something that appealed, and that's what Bushy afflicted upon us whenever my mother asked her to make dinner.

12. A maize and white-bean dish that could actually taste pretty good if not made by Bushy.

In this way, over the years, my mother and Bushy staked out their relative positions, and peace between them prevailed. They were never close in the way some ostentatiously enlightened South Africans were with their servants. ("Come watch the TV with us, Ruthie; it's your favourite: *Riptide*.") But there was very little discord.

This was in great contrast to the Richards—the family who lived across the road from us. I spent about half my childhood at my best friend Leigh's house (his mother, Ester, was one of the many matriarchs who had a firm hand in raising me). Like me, Leigh had been diagnosed artistic early in life, though he tipped far closer toward genuine talent than I did. We spent our days drawing on chalkboards in the scullery, playing with action figures, inventing imaginary personas (in the pool we were a crime-fighting duo called The Speedo Twins), and bickering. I have no idea how, with his dozy mien and glasses strapped to his head, Leigh made it through childhood alive. His guardian angel was double shifting it—especially when he wandered slowly into moving traffic or absentmindedly pet a rabid watchdog. "Nice kitty," Leigh would say.

I mention Leigh not only because he was a fixture in my early life but also because of his maid, Tryfina. *She* could cook. Her bolognese sauce still holds pride of place in my memory. At the Richards', I would also find cookies, pop, chips, and other goodies that children eat. At dinner, an icy glass of milk was slapped down in front us; there was no milk at 41 Forbes Street (my parents believed in the powdered stuff—another one of Dr. Poplak's complicated nutritional theories that I won't get into here). Tryfina was matronly, a good couple of hundred pounds overweight—and sweet beyond all reason.

But from my perspective, despite the poor cuisine and the lack of decent beverages, Bushy's universe was plenty more interesting than Tryfina's. Bushy was fleet, Bushy was dangerous, and Bushy was mean. For little boys, sweet has its limits.

In retrospect, considering the front garden, the back garden, and the neighbourhood outside our splitpole fence, I didn't need to have the run of 41 Forbes Street between 3:15 and 5:00 P.M., Monday to Friday. But did the French *need* Alsace-Lorraine? Do the British *need* the Falklands? Strategic importance notwithstanding, territory almost always equates to power. In my case, it also equated to fun. Going to war with Bushy was thrilling because it was dangerous—like bungee jumping, except without the bungee cord. Although she inflicted real pain upon my person—something adults were more than free (and expected) to do in South Africa at the time, it never occurred to me to retaliate in kind. The rules of engagement were such that this was not an option. I had to be far more devious.

When I stayed home from school sick, I came to understand the structure of Bushy's day. On her breaks between tasks, Bushy talked on the phone. My room opened onto the end of the hallway, which is where the phone sat. The house would smell of wood varnish and window cleaner, the air still abuzz with the whine of the vacuum cleaner. Her words, spoken in Sotho, a language full of dead halts and harsh turns, sounded like a ninja fight—swords and throwing stars clanging off one another, burnished steel consonants meeting iron vowels in a shower of sparks. I have no idea if Bushy was actually engaged in a prolonged argument with the other domestics in our neighbourhood for the *entire* duration of my childhood, but I have an inkling that her contemporaries were as scared of her as we were.

Her stature qualified her for a Napoleon complex, and what is more lethal than a human who has successfully ignored the fact that she is both tiny and disabled? The only appropriate attitude to Bushy was wariness, and it appeared that her acquaintances felt the same.

I learned from these periods of childhood indisposition that Bushy organized her day into sections. Vacuuming in the morning, dusting around lunchtime, laundry in the afternoon. Bushy's rigidity was eminently exploitable. A typical exchange:

"Get out from he-ya, boy! I'm vacuuming."

"Nah, man. I'm fine here. Maybe you can vacuum in the..."

"Boy! *Uswaba, wena! Hamba!* Go!"

We'd face off for about half a minute or so, and then the chase was on. Bushy was out from behind the vacuum cleaner with astonishing speed. She had a way of spring-hopping, like a wounded buck—leaping from her good leg to her bad and using the centrifugal force to propel herself forward. The *clob-shph-thnk* sound this made was always closer behind me than I would have thought possible, given that I was usually running at a full sprint. *Clob-shph-thnk, clob-shph-thnk, clob-shph-thnk, clob-shph-thnk*—and then the sensation of gravity disappearing and pain appearing as her tiny fingers grabbed my shirt collar, or worse, my ear, yanking me off my feet.

"Boy! I have wehk to do! Go away from he-ya!"

Advantage: Bushy.

Bushy's sanctum sanctorum, I learned (it was a hard, hard lesson), was the laundry room. This was in the scullery behind the kitchen, and with the door onto the backyard open, it was awash, almost bleached, with sunlight throughout the day and operating-room clean. It smelled powerfully of red floor polish and laundry soap—smells I still associate entirely with Bushy. If

Bushy was inflexible about managing the rest of the house, she was a fundamentalist when it came to the laundry. I suppose she was kept fairly busy with my father's safari suits making a thrice-weekly appearance,[13] and there were the bedclothes, school uniforms, sports kits, and civilian clothing. The laundry room was Bushy's nerve centre.

South Africa, for some reason, bred an incredible ingenuity for corporal punishment. I've been beaten with a great variety of objects in my time, and I remember the major figures in my young life as though they were characters from a *Street Fighter* video game, each with their patented moves and their weapon of choice. Bushy's *objet de guerre* was ingenious, both because of its utilitarian aspects (she had unfettered, unlimited access to *matériel*) and because of the severe pain it caused. I imagine her finding what became her trademark as if in a superhero myth, like when Superman outruns the locomotive or the Green Lantern finds the all-powerful alien light source: A beam of sunlight descends from the heavens, illuminating a lone object that sits beside her laundry basket. Bushy picks it up, feels its weight, and a choral surge emanates from God's eight-million-speaker surround-sound system. She whips the object through the air, hears its angry, bird-of-prey whistle, and she knows—she *knows*—she has found her identity:

The Coathanger.

With her simple household weapon, Bushy wrought terror, because a wire coat hanger actually hurts like Christ when

13. Dr. Poplak, as you know, was a dentist. And so, like all dentists in South Africa (and most male professionals in the country, for that matter), he wore safari suits to work. What were they hunting? Incisors?

applied with the appropriate force and technique, and Bushy had that down to a fine art. Her little wrists, stoked with seemingly supernatural force, flicked the weapon in a whizzing arc, generating a velocity that was as impressive as it was painful. She had an intuitive way of guiding her shot through small gaps in clothing so that it struck bare skin with a sharp *thwack.* Sprightly as I was, Bushy always managed to get one good shot in—her reach impressive and her aim true.

To paraphrase Frau Clinton: In my youth, the village beat the child. If my parents were ever to have found out about this egregious child abuse, they would simply have assumed that we must have done something to warrant the beating. Invariably they were right. There were exceptions, mind you, but for the most part, news of a spanking from Bushy, or anyone else, would more than likely lead to a grounding or further spanking. So Bushy spanked with impunity. Besides, I didn't want to tell my mother about the coat hanger—in case she adopted it into her own already well-stocked arsenal.

But, like any superhero, Bushy had her weaknesses: a series of rigorously established phobias that could be exploited when necessary. I loved reading Superman comics primarily for the innovative ways in which Lex Luthor exploited the Man of Steel's weakness—firing kryptonite arrowheads into Superman's back, or attempting to blow him up with a kryptonite-tipped warhead, or serving him a ham-and-kryptonite sandwich. I also learned about The Joker, Dr. Doom, The Green Goblin, characters whom I considered soulmates. If we had a maxim, my supervillain colleagues and I, it was this: "There is *always* a chink."

I found the chinks.

"Come with me," I'd yell to Leigh if he was embroiled in one of Bushy's coat-hanger pursuits. (I liked having him along—he was generally slower and would usually take the brunt of the first few lashings.) I'd head straight for a deep closet.

"Um?" Leigh would say, pushing his glasses up from the tip on his nose. "We'll be trapped."

The *clob-shph-thnk* was approaching—we were running out of time.

I'd just grin my supervillain grin and dive in.

This is like hiding from a samurai in a sword factory, I know. But there was no way Bushy would follow, despite the fact that I was deep within a chamber lined with her weapon of choice. Bushy was terrified of the dark. She would stand by the closet for a minute or two, trying to outwait us, but she had a job and we didn't, meaning time was on our side. "Reeshat, boy! *Hiy ko-nah!* I will get you, my boy!" I'd sink back into the closet a good two feet, enveloped by dusty jackets and musty jerseys, and try to steady my breathing. Maybe I'd whistle a tune. "Reeeeeee-*shat*!"

The key to understanding another of The Coathanger's significant weaknesses lay in Bushy's dim living space. The servants' quarters in most Johannesburg homes were at the rear of the main house, in concrete courtyards where the laundry was hung to dry. Our house was no exception. The centrepiece of the courtyard was a rusty green rotating clothesline, which starred as a satellite floating in the outer regions of space in many of Carolyn's and my imagined adventures. I had painted 1980s cartoon characters on one of the courtyard walls—Garfield, Odie, Hägar the Horrible, among others. Bushy's room was to the right of this, and marginally larger than a closet. In it were a hotplate, a radio receiver, a small black-and-white television, a battered chest, and a single bed that stood several feet off the ground on a stack of bricks, a picture of the

Virgin Mary taped to the wall above it. The room smelled potently of the red floor polish that covered its concrete floor. A small window covered by a red curtain bled ethereal light into the room during the day, giving it the religious aura of a monastic cloister. By and large, this was how Johannesburg's servants lived.

A visitor would notice, with some incredulity, that the bricks under the bed legs made the bed almost as tall as Bushy. This was because of the *tokelosh*. Bushy told me about the *tokelosh* when I was young, and warned me of his fiendish ways. A Zulu folkloric boogieman, the tiny demon creeps into rooms in the dead of night, grabbing his sleeping victims by the throat and throttling them to death. This is best avoided by raising one's bed high enough to avoid his nighttime endeavours. Invoking this little devil inevitably made Bushy uneasy. If she was performing a coat-hanger massacre, I only had to raise the spectre of the diminutive beastie and her arm would halt mid-whip. She broke down entirely when I warned, "The *tokelosh* is coming to get you!" This she did not like at all. "Reeshat, never say the *tokelosh*! He will come for you also!"

Indeed, the *tokelosh* tack was something of a kamikaze manoeuvre. A frisson of dread ran through me as I spoke his name, and I knew I'd be seeing his shadowy form long after I'd fallen asleep. The *tokelosh* stalked through many an African nightmare. I often imagined him creeping from Bushy's dark slumbers, wafting over the courtyard and under the clothesline, then unlatching my window with thin, dexterous fingers to roost in the midnight crannies of my own unconscious. This *tokelosh*, this creature of the inky blackness, was the only dream that Bushy and I could possibly share. Our joint world was firmly anchored in the waking life, mired in the prosaic—a circumstantial intersection of vastly different lives. After that, and because of the *tokelosh,* our nightmares were the only thing we shared. At least Bushy had erected some (albeit Maginot line–like) defence; my mother vehemently refused to allow me to put my bed up on bricks.

I stumbled upon many such things about Bushy when I was young—some of which fascinated me, most of which mystified me. One of the strangest was a hint, a vision, of what the country could have become after Apartheid. I found it odd when I was eleven, but I didn't ruminate on it; I promptly tucked it into my utility belt, to be used during a Coathanger onslaught:

"Bushy," I said one day as she ironed a shirt in the scullery, "you're waiting for Mandela to come kill us, aren't you?" Nelson Mandela was an enigma to me (who was he, and what did he do to earn such elevated supervillain status?)—this dark fiend who lurked in a prison cell that could barely contain him. He was a Communist (whatever that was) and, in the only photograph the government allowed published, he looked, with his light beard and the hooded eyes of a pugilist, like little more than a portly thug.

"*Hiy ko-nah! Don't* say that man, Reeshat."

"Why not?"

"He will kill me. He will kill you first, foh shoh. But then me also."

It wasn't until much later that I came to understand this mystery. Bushy belonged to the Tswana, a small tribe of southern Africans originally from Botswana. The African National Congress (ANC) is predominantly a Xhosa party, and this was a cause of real concern for the fifteen or so other tribes that had significant populations in the country. Outside the South

African province of KwaZulu-Natal, the Xhosa made up the majority of black South Africans, and given the region's history, these others were understandably nervous about the future if the ANC was to be unleashed. This was a culture of tribes. Mandela was Bushy's Voldemort—another version of the *tokelosh*. "He's coming for you," I'd say. But he was coming for me, too. In this, I recall Falstaff's timeless advice to supervillains: "Heat not a furnace for your foe so hot that it do singe yourself."

In the 1970s and 1980s, Mandela's release from prison was somewhat unlikely, so we were safe for the time being. But later, I often wondered why so many of South Africa's servants didn't seem to want *any* change at all. Didn't they long for something that presented an alternative to the status quo? The answer seems obvious to me now: When you come from grinding poverty and extreme disenfranchisement, change of any kind is a dangerous thing. Basic survival depends on stasis. As bad as things may be, the situation could always get worse.

It was not unknown for Bushy to humiliate me in front of friends by twisting my ear if I was being cheeky or swatting my ass with a coat hanger if we strayed too close to the laundry on our way to the pool.

"Your maid's *mal,* man," my friends would say. "I'm *poep* scared of her!"

Yeah? Try living with her, pal.

When—and only when—the occasion warranted it, I would slowly make my way to the set of three drawers in my bedroom. Then, just as slowly, I would slide the bottom drawer open and peer inside. There, in a slick black tangle, lay vengeance incarnate: plastic snakes, three of them. This drawer was the cache of my most important weapons, and I opened it with the same gravity and respect shown by the captain and commandant in submarine movies when inserting the red keys into the nuclear torpedo system, prepared to blow up the world if they must.

Which snake I chose depended on the severity of the situation I was attending to. After picking a snake—or sometimes more than one, to block off entrances and exits—I'd head into the hallway, ready for battle.

I see Bushy's abject terror of snakes—plastic or otherwise—as a fear of karmic retribution for all the lizards she mutilated over the years. Then again, maybe it had something to do with the snake's deviousness in tribal stories, or perhaps its work on Eve in the Garden of Eden. A fake snake, thrown at the right moment, could elicit a harsh shriek, a "Reeshat! *Uswaba, wena!*" and a fierce coat-hanger pursuit. If the snake was lying on the linen in the scullery or blocking her passage to a part of the house she needed to access, she was incapable of continuing with her work. This made her, understandably, upset. Diplomacy was the answer, although negotiations were held grudgingly, on her part at least. They typically went something like this:

"Reeshat! Move the snake, boy!"

"I can't—I'm tired."

"Wake up, boy! *Uswaba, wena!* Move it *right* now. I have wehk to do."

"It's plastic, man. There's nothing to be scared of," I'd say encouragingly. "Move it yourself."

"Boy," and Bushy would raise that deadly eyebrow, her voice glinting in the light like highly polished adamantium, "I will *tell* your muthah."

This was Bushy's trump card—and it won every time. My mother was like most South African mothers. Scary. And Bushy knew this. She had countered one of her fears with one of my own, strategically breaking the deadlock. I'd quickly grab the snake, hoping to lower the eyebrow. No luck.

"I must tell heh. She must know what kind of boy you ah," Bushy would say, sauntering away as insouciantly as someone with one working leg can.

What was it about my mother? What was the source of her abundant power? Try as I might, I can't put my finger on exactly what it was about her that made me fear her so unwaveringly, though I can identify elements. Her right hand, for instance. It was nothing special to look at, a little bony perhaps. But a slap from that hand was the equivalent of ten coat-hanger beatings. This was my mother's secret weapon. It could find its way through clothing like a heat-seeking missile, locating a panel of chubby skin to inflame with red-purple agony. I still remember the sound it made, like a gunshot fired in a quiet, fog-shrouded valley. One of those slaps shut down an argument definitively. But my mother didn't rely exclusively on violence. Why bother, when you have Jewish Guilt at your disposal? Nothing, *nothing,* was worse than disappointing Mom. Her face would crumple, and she would age fifty years in an instant, her eyes flooding. Her body would cave in from the effort of having me as a son, and she would say something along the lines of: "*Ag,* I just don't know. I just don't..." before trailing off as she looked to the heavens for support and serenity. I couldn't handle disappointing my mother. It crushed my soul. Mom was a Dr. Spock mother (which, in South Africa, meant that she combined corporal punishment with bucketloads of TLC), and the warmth that could radiate off her cocooned me for my entire boyhood. There was nothing she would not do for her children. Disappoint this woman? No—that was not something I did without feeling that it *had* to be done.

Thus: Deadlock. I'd grab the snake, Bushy would sheath her coat hanger, and we'd go about our respective business, our own Treaty of Versailles to be broken another time, in another battle.

I remember the following incident clearly.

"What's this?" I asked. I was holding a tattered booklet that Bushy had left on the counter in the kitchen. Inside was her picture. She wasn't smiling in it.

"This my passbook. Be careful."

"Can I have it?" It looked suitably ancient, and I was sure it could be used in some kind of adventure story involving my sister, which would eventually result in her getting hurt.

"No, boy. Give it." Something in her voice told me that this was not a game, exceeding even laundry in tiers of importance. I handed it over without a struggle.

It was the summer holidays, which meant that Bushy had her three weeks off for Christmas. Back to Botswana she was going; she returned there for the holidays, once a year, at Christmastime. This always meant a discussion between my mother and me, given that Bushy had to be driven into town to the train station.

"Can I come? Please, please, please?" Town was dramatic. Town was exciting. Town was scary.

"Absolutely not!"

More often than not, my mother gave in, mostly because she did not want to make the trip alone. I pictured Johannesburg's core as a rough Afrikaner with a patchy haircut; buzzed sections of dry scalp showing through mangy sprigs of hair that pointed this way and that. The scalp was the dry, red earth of the Highveld rising in bumpy ridges on the outskirts of town, the hair sprigs the buildings that rose from that earth with no concession to city planning or aesthetics.

Does an immoral system breed immoral architecture? Think Albert Speer's Reichstag, or Vladivostok, or any Industrial Revolution–era urban environment in the United Kingdom. Johannesburg's buildings seemed an offence upon the land, like shards of metal and glass forced through epidermis and sunk right into bone. To me, Hillbrow Tower was a botched phallic symbol—the erect penis of a man with no testicles. Ponte, the circular tower that was the first sign of town for those arriving from the northern suburbs, was a hotbed of drug use and suicide. A fun thing for the residents to do was hurl themselves down the hollow centre of the building to land dashed against the mound of detritus (old tables, chairs, desks, lounge sets, televisions) that formed the growing core of the structure. John Vorster Square, the infamous police complex that nestled up to the M1 and another key city landmark, was more about *assisted* suicide. It was one of Apartheid's ground zeroes, a spot where dissidents and regular folks alike were brought in for a cup of coffee, asked a couple of questions, and then helped out the tenth-floor window. Driving through it, the city felt weary—too heavy to bear its own weight; the tremors we sometimes felt, tremors caused by labyrinthine mineshafts collapsing in on one another, made it seem as if the city itself were built on decaying foundations.

The centre of town, where the train station was located, was the only place I saw black people in any significant multitude—this in a country where blacks outnumbered whites eight to one. They thronged across the busy intersection with packages in their arms, large canvas bags striped with faded red, whites, and blues. Minibus taxis flew in at impossible speeds, discharging comical numbers of passengers; women supporting massive packages on their heads negotiated the crowds and traffic unconcernedly. People scurried furiously—a constantly renewed onslaught of humanity. I had a vague sense, sitting in the back of the car, my mother's hands tense around the steering wheel, that this is what we had to keep back, this inexorable tide that would wash over us and render us extinct. This is why the dam wall of Apartheid had been erected. And every Christmas, Bushy disappeared into this morass, an alien the moment she stepped from the car, faceless and nameless, off to Botswana laden with second-hand clothing, old toys, and packages of food, all to be taken to a home that might as well have been on the other side of the world.

What Bushy did in Botswana I have no idea, and I never asked. This world of hers was not one we shared. I find it hard to believe now that I never asked her what she did during Christmas vacation. In fact, I was uncharacteristically incurious when it came to Bushy's private life. This much I do know: Bushy had a husband who worked at Jan Smuts International Airport.[14] He was a tall, soft-spoken man named Jacob, and he carried the piety that I associated with that name; I only ever saw him in a white shirt tucked into black slacks, his black church sash pinned prominently over his heart. I know that Bushy had at least two sons. Her older son I met only once in all her years with us, and I do not recall his name. The other, Hendie, was born when I was about six or seven. I don't remember Bushy being pregnant, but one day, lo and behold, a black baby appeared strapped to her back.

"Where's the pickaninny from, Bushy?" I asked.

"His my son," said Bushy.

14. Now Johannesburg International Airport.

Okay, but how would this affect *me*? As it turned out, Hendie was preternaturally quiet. For my sister and me, he was a fleeting curiosity—fun to play with for the first couple of days but then slowly downgraded in entertainment status, eventually ending up somewhere between LEGO bricks and pick-up sticks. Dr. Poplak, however, was resolutely unimpressed. He was not a lover of small children in any capacity (his own he bore like pets forced upon him in a communal household—the odd rub under the ear, the odd bowl of food when the dish is empty, but general distance). Dr. Poplak glowered at the boy as he hopped around in strange froglike movements, and it didn't help that Hendie was nappy-free and prone to crapping on the shaded lawn by the side of our house. Although this drove my father partially insane, Hendie was a fixture until he was weaned off the breast and then, as abruptly as he arrived, he was gone, presumably back to Botswana to be brought up by Bushy's parents. He came back for holidays every now and then, but for the most part, Hendie grew up far away from his mother and could barely have known her, nor she him. This was the lot of Johannesburg's servants.

I wonder how badly Bushy missed her babies, and I wonder if Carolyn and I filled the void. The triumvirate of matriarchs who raised me—my mother, my grandmother, and my nanny—never flagged in their attentions. I was scrutinized, I was coaxed, I was encouraged, and I was babied. I was afraid of all three of them, but they also provided the warmth and security that were a hallmark of my boyhood. But I still wonder what Bushy got out of it; I wonder if our years together exacerbated the pain of separation from her own children or whether they assuaged it. After all, it was not all war between us.

For instance, my report cards were handed over to Bushy once my mother and grandmother had thoroughly inspected them.

"This is good, boy. Did you come fehst in the class?"

"No, Brian Reichman did. Then Bradley Rothstein."

"Maybe we go for a walk. Find them."

Bushy used me as entertainment for the few other local domestics who risked coming over to her quarters for a barrage of Sotho and maybe a cup of tea. There were two Bantu television channels, broadcasting programs in Zulu and Xhosa, and one of these ran the animated Spider-Man series. The show was dubbed into Zulu, with Spider-Man becoming Rabobi. The original theme song was catchy. You know the one: "Spider-Man. Spider-Man. Does whatever a spider can. Spins a web, any size. Catches thieves, just like flies." It was no less catchy in Zulu. I would be summoned to Bushy's tiny room, even smaller now because of the four enormous black women and little spidery Bushy stuffed into it. "Okay, Reeshat. Sing the 'Rabobi.' Come on, boy!" And there I was, in front of five women who were in real danger of laughing themselves free of their mortal coils, singing *"Rabobi, Rabobi! H'lau u Muna i Rabobi!"* Tears streamed down their shining black faces, their girth jiggling under their cloth uniforms, and I had 'em, folks, I had 'em! They loved me! Sadly, the life of a child star is at best the length of childhood, and when my voice broke and acne began to pepper my otherwise creamy white skin, the "Rabobi" shtick fell from favour. I have not sung for an audience since.

Often, I convinced Bushy to kick my soccer ball at me so I could practise my goaltending. Regardless of how accustomed to her disability she was, it couldn't have been easy kicking a ball with her good leg, her full weight balanced on her ankle. She'd grimace, but I think she got some satisfaction out of the enterprise, especially after I sulked off, having saved precisely none of her kicks. The ball screamed like a crashing Zeppelin as it tore through the atmosphere, shredding air molecules and practically catching fire as it roared toward me. Half of them I'd simply step out of the way of, thinking, dryly, "Pelé, my ass."

Hundreds of little things. I liked to give her a bottle of seawater and a jar of sand for good luck whenever I returned from a vacation by the sea. She would swallow a teaspoonful of seawater and grimace. "Is *very* good for you," she'd say. "But only for the blehck peoples." I wasn't too upset that racial lines were drawn for seawater *muti*—the few times I'd swallowed a mouthful while swimming were enough for me.

She would coach Leigh and me on our chalk drawings, the canvas the entire concrete courtyard of my house.

"Is this a li-yon?"

"Yes."

"He must be *big*gah. And more blood in his tith."

I liked the precise, slow way Bushy did everything—the reassuring *clob-shph-thnk* as she moved about doing her work, the vacuum trailing behind her like a faithful cur, a bucket of cleaning products never far away. She was a fixture of the house and my life—one more element of the security and stability that were my mainstay.

There came a point, however, when all this started to suffocate.

Our old war for territory, a game we played when I was a boy, ceased to be fun. Now when Bushy entered my room to vacuum it (and I happened to be doing something illicit with my Kylie Minogue album covers), those territorial claims seemed life and death. I did not want her in my space. "Jesus, Bushy. Get outta here, man!" To which she'd reply, "What yoh muthah say I not clean the room?" Why, for all the tears in heaven, could she not clean the room when I was at school?

"Because I clean downstairs fehst. This what I always do, boy!" I'd raise my finger in warning and say, "Bushy, don't call me 'boy.'"

By the time we shipped out to Canada, Bushy and I barely spoke. We never got over that bad period—that period where I was an insolent, hormone-addled teen blasting *Dark Side of the Moon* on his stereo and telling her to "bugger off, man" when she knocked on my bedroom door, thinking she was a pain in the ass who wouldn't get off my back for ten seconds so I could have a fucking wank in peace.

Slowly, we broke our ties.

The last time I saw Bushy was in 1995, the year I went to visit Gaga and Oupa after finishing university, five years after leaving South Africa for Canada. My friend Rozanne drove me to the meeting that had been organized the day before with Bushy's new madam, a polite woman with an Afrikaans accent. "She is very excited to see you," said the woman over the phone. The house was in Orange Grove, near my old primary school. It was May, and despite winter setting in, rich green creepers cascaded over the stocky outer walls of the house. The woman I'd spoken to over the phone let me in. She carried herself with rigid Afrikaner propriety, an affectation that mirrors elegance without quite capturing it. I was invited into the living room, where Bushy and I were to hold our reunion. When I was growing up, the help didn't hang with guests in the living room (Bushy had never sat in ours). I'm not sure whether this gesture was solely for my benefit, but it spoke well of brand-new attitudes in the brand-new South Africa.

The home was neat and cold, tiled in wall-to-wall ceramic. "She'll be coming through in a tick," said the woman. Bushy made her appearance from the kitchen, like the guest on a talk show. "Reeshat," she said quietly. "Look at you, boy!" I rose, and it was clear to me immediately that something was wrong. As we hugged, a chill ran through me—there was almost nothing left of The Coathanger. She was emaciated to the point of fright and small bumps covered her skin. Bushy's new madam withdrew to give us our privacy.

The bumps, Bushy explained, were fleabites. She sat on the edge of the cream leather couch uncomfortably, as if the plushness would sear her skin. She kept her head down and picked at her fingers obsessively. "Reesh, they don't trit me well he-ya." She kept her eyes lowered and her voice lower as she recited the litany of abuse she had suffered at the hands of these new employers. Her room was infested with fleas and other vermin, her employers were cold and unkind, and there was never enough to eat. This didn't quite jibe with my impression of the woman who had so graciously sat us down in her immaculate living room, but you just never know with people. And the little hand on my knee told a deeper story. The hand that had been, despite its size, so full of power and strength and terror when I was growing up now looked like the carcass of an overcooked quail. "Reeshat, I don want to wehk he-ya no more." This much was certain: The past five years had been very cruel to Bushy.

I remembered our first walks, when we dismembered the lizards of Fellside with such gusto. Life isn't really so different for us as it was for them. Every now and again, without warning, the great twenty-cent coin in the sky roars down and severs our tails as we innocently move toward the sunlight for our afternoon nap. For Bushy and me, the defining incident was my family's immigration to Canada. Basking in the sunshine and safety of my circumstances, my tail grew back big and strong. But in the dank shadows of post-Apartheid South Africa, Bushy's tail remained a withered stump. She was, simply, half the lizard she had once been. All the odds had been stacked against her—she was a tiny cripple from Botswana who had found employment in a country that had an abundance of cheap labour. She managed to school, clothe, and feed a family that she never saw. But eventually the odds that weighed so heavily were too much to bear. So there she sat—beaten—picking at her fingers and staring at the blazing white ceramic in this strange, cold house.

A surge of impotence washed through me like a wave of bile, and the gulf between Bushy and me was so glaringly apparent that this felt like an out-of-body experience. What was I doing in the same room as this creature? We didn't inhabit the same planet, and we never had. In the world I grew up in, no white person and black person ever did.

Directly after the reunion I called my mother in Canada, and she spoke to Oupa, who made some calls. Bushy was soon after employed in another job, and then another. We have long since lost track of her.

"Reeshat, my boy, eat everything on your plate," The Coathanger would say. "Then you can be beeg and strong like me." Bushy's superpowers, I now see, were her delusions. When I saw her that day in the bright white living room, those delusions were gone. I imagined Bushy looking in the mirror and taking her reflection at face value, which is never advisable at the best of times. Superhero stories aren't supposed to end like this, but that's how The Coathanger's seemed to. I often wonder where she is now, and if she is still using her weapon of choice in the name of goodness, light, and simple bad temper. After all, people's delusions are the only weapons they need. I hope she's still out there, wielding hers.

Manson

What's in a name? That which we call a rose
by any other name would smell as sweet.
—*Shakespeare,* Romeo and Juliet

My mother was the human resources department for our household. Her initial hire, Bushy, had her problems. ("Five girls I've taught to cook," Gaga would say to Mom, "and yours can't even make a cup of tea?") Manson, the affable man who worked in our garden for many years, was perhaps a far more egregious hire, if for entirely different reasons. Most people would at least think twice before handing over the garden shears to a man named Manson. I'd like to think that my mother was one of them. I'd like to think that she at least *pondered* the bard's famed aphorism. But I suspect my mother's failure to do a background check on a man named Manson stemmed from the facts that (1) she is trusting in nature, (2) he was such an impossibly nice guy, and (3) local African names come in two varieties—(a) Old Testament (Jacob, Rebecca, Johanna, etc.) and (b) weird and wacky (Tryfina, Bushy, True Love, etc.). My mother was probably inured enough to section 3, subsection b, that a fellow named Jack Ripper could have stepped into our house and been considered as fair a candidate for the position as a dude named Craig.[15]

Manson was a large man, hulking in his shabby, faded blue overalls. His head was shaved to the skin, leaving grey stubble that looked to me like tiny sparkling gemstones set into his skull. He was a deep chocolate brown and leathery from the sun; his enormous hands looked as though they were upholstered in elephant hide. Both his teeth were proudly displayed in a perpetual grin that rarely faded. At a certain point, Dr. Poplak outfitted him with a pair of dazzlingly white dentures, which added significant wattage to his smile. His was such an irrepressibly sunny disposition that you feared for his sanity; he gave the impression that his spirit was unbreakable and his happiness an immutable universal constant. His Malawian-accented English tumbled forth from his mouth in a musical jumble: "Me a-gonna mow-ee grass a-now," Manson would say. "Right-eo, Manson," Mom would say.

Our house had a smallish backyard that contained our swimming pool, a lemon tree (bearing fist-sized fruit), our *braai* and patio lounge, and an impressive hibiscus bush. But the main show was out front. Three large flower beds displayed a wide array of both indigenous and foreign flora. There were two oleanders, a variety of violently coloured petunias and pansies, a dizzying array of aloes, several species of rose, a massive evergreen that jutted into the sky at a dangerous angle, another hibiscus, and my father's bougainvilleas. Cicadas provided the constant soundtrack, with regular vocal contributions by grey

15. Incidentally, Manson's given name was Master. A black man named Master would perhaps run into a little flak in South Africa, so he elected to change it.

loeries, bokmakeries, and turtledoves. In the middle of the yard was a patch of lawn sizeable enough for a two-on-two soccer game, the far perimeter of which was marked by an old rusty swing set, the only blight on this natural wonderland. A brick driveway rolled through it all like a great river, a Nile or an Amazon. It took Manson several days to weed the drive, sitting cross-legged in his tattered overalls with his garden implements, slowly and meticulously working his way downstream. And deep within one of the flower beds, in the shadow of a jacaranda tree that stood outside our garden fence, was a small chicken-wire hutch that served as the home of my pet tortoise.

Manson had spotted the foolhardy creature in the veld one night. It was close to my eleventh birthday, and he figured it would make a good gift. "Madam," said Manson when he brought the little fella to our house, "I think the L'il Baas Reeshi will like this *very* mush." My mother agreed. Manson referred to me as either L'il Baas, L'il Baas Reeshi, or L'il Baas Reeshat, and the utter absurdity of this did not hit me until I went to university. I made the mistake of telling a room of drunken fellow students in my residence (this in icy Montreal) what I had been called back in the old country. They found it hilarious that someone, somewhere, had addressed me with deference. After the tears of mirth had dried, the harassment began. Those who I am still in contact with continue to drop the "L'il Baas" sobriquet whenever they get the opportunity. I am now less communicative in a room full of inebriated people.

Still years away from such harassment, L'il Baas Reeshi gratefully accepted his gift. The first sight of his new friend was of a mottled grey-and-brown shell nestled in Manson's weatherworn hand. For some reason known only to his eleven-year-old self, L'il Baas named the tortoise Houdini. What's in a name? In

Houdini's case, bucketloads. There was nothing the great illusionist could do that his namesake couldn't. Escape artists embody the restlessness of the soul, that desire to constantly be elsewhere, living another reality. Tortoise Houdini was a creature with a mission, as if his own escape made the escape of every caged animal everywhere at least a remote possibility. Did he have an assignment from Mother Nature herself? Consider the facts: His hutch was surrounded by chicken wire that Leigh and I had sunk a good two feet into the soil. One part of the fence was set against a large concrete cinder block that was difficult enough for an adult to move. He had lettuce leaves and carrots, rocks, and all manner of entertainment in his four-by-four habitat. Not good enough. He required all the space the Earth has to offer. This ingenious chelonian (I loved calling him that—it sounded like a word from *Star Trek*) always found a way out, without leaving any clue as to how he performed the feat.

When Houdini wasn't busy escaping he was, well, dull. The minutes would tick by as he slowly telescoped his wrinkled head out from his shell to look at the lettuce held in front of him. Then, he'd nip petulantly at the leaf with his beak, and if the slightest noise or movement alarmed him, his head disappeared, the whole process to start over again. This was about the extent of the fun to be had with Houdini and an exercise in extreme patience for an eleven-year-old. Despite that I could brag about him to Leigh ("*Ja,* no, Houdini was *lekker* fun last night. I don't think he likes you, 'cause he does *kiff* tricks when you're not there," I'd lie), he was probably the most boring gift I had ever received. Still, I stuck with him. He had no such attachment to me. The tortoise had magical abilities. Like most of his species, he was slow. But take your eyes off him, even for a second or two, and he moved much farther than seemed tortoisely possible. His brilliance was in establishing such an expectation of sluggishness that when you blinked and he was halfway across the garden, it seemed like time itself had shifted. Indeed, it did appear as if Houdini had access to a portal in the space-time continuum granted only to the slow and the meek.

It was this particular gift that led to Houdini's eventual fate—there was simply no hutch secure enough for such tenacity. Using his dark art, he extricated himself not only from the hutch but also from our garden, lined as it was with the split-pole fence, bolstered by a concrete block foundation. Manson found him dead as he did alive—in the middle of the street—and brought him back to my mother cradled in his hand. "I know L'il Baas will be very sad," he said, shaking his head. I can picture my mother's face as she told him to discard Houdini, cracked shell and all, anticipating the grief with which I would soon be wracked. Grief, it should be noted, that I had engineered by naming him after an individual whose life's work was the art of escape, thus fating him to a terminal case of wanderlust.[16] I was as shattered as Houdini's shell—and I took his death personally. Why had he so keenly felt the need to be free? What was so unendurable about life on Forbes Street? I should *never* have called him Houdini. "Shame," Mom said. "Whatever we called him, he still would have wanted to escape. They just don't like being cooped up."

What Mom also thought was a shame was that Manson was going to kick our asses one of these fine days.

---

16. Apparently, I still managed to ask Mom, through my tears, whether his "body oozed through his shell." The morbid curiosity of a preteen is boundless.

"You must stop it with Manson!" she'd yell. "He can't work with you two around!" Carolyn and I were fond of opening the bags of freshly cut grass that Manson filled as he mowed the lawn and spreading the fragrant contents all over the newly shorn area. As far as asshole moves go, this is pretty high up on the list, but I'd be lying if I denied the immense amount of enjoyment we derived from these pranks. My sister and I (our truces were rare and only in the service of making someone else's life more miserable than we could otherwise make it on our own) would lie in wait behind a clump of bushes. When Manson emptied the contents of the mower's rear grass catcher into a bag, we'd hold back until man and machine resumed their cutting. Then we struck, and the result was grass-bag carnage. Manson would shake his head and give a full-bodied chuckle. "L'il Baas," he'd say, "Caro! Heh, heh, eh-heh!" Manson did good-natured resignation better than any other human being I have ever encountered. Never once did I get the slightest indication that he was actually angry about these antics, but neither did I get the impression that he enjoyed them.

A clue to Manson's eternal affability may have come by way of his best pal, Paul. He was a short, garrulous fellow typically dressed in shabby slacks, shabbier dress shoes, and a garment that was a strange cross between a Mao jacket and a lab coat. Paul was always laughing, which was strange for a guy who inhaled about a page and a half of bad news every day. Never did you see him without a massive "cigarette" rolled in newspaper between his wet lips. These cigarettes had a smell to them, a smell an aficionado of cannabis would identify with a drool as Durban Poison. And Paul smoked an immense amount of the stuff. His eyes were so bloodshot that they looked like they spent the night beside his bed marinating in tomato juice. His smile made even Manson look manic-depressive, and he had a booming laugh that saw frequent action (a hearty "ha, ha, ha" to Manson's "heh, eh-heh"). He moved in a twitchy, dance-like manner, as if the ground beneath him were burning and he couldn't keep his feet on it for long. Paul was a stoner of monumental proportions. And to come within ten feet of him was to become stoned yourself.

In South Africa, there was tacit tolerance of the black population's marijuana use. Considering how obsessed the authorities were with all things law and order, this was surprising: The drug seemed to wander under the radar. For young whites from the burbs, smoking weed was one way we could experience a small, illicit aspect of black culture. It also made Pink Floyd rock even harder. The drug was remarkably accessible. Golf courses were an excellent venue for the prospective smoker to purchase a shopping bag full of *caddy gunj* (weed sold by caddies) for a handful of coins. Sure, sometimes you were stuck with a lifetime's supply of marjoram, but just as often you had enough weed to smoke you and your neighbourhood to kingdom come. If you were sharp—and lucky—you could get a matchbox of powerful stuff from any petrol station for just a few rand, or, if the gods of intoxication were smiling on you, a sizeable chunk of Malawi Gold (the manufacturing process of which is to bury Malawi-grown cannabis in a shallow grave, baking it under the African sun until cured).

I kept my stash (when I was old enough to have one) in the treasure hold of a toy pirate ship that I had received for my eighth birthday. It was a brilliant hiding spot, and I felt like a pirate myself whenever I fumbled with the plastic cage and dipped my fingers into the dark recesses of the hull. I had a baggie of the stuff nestled beside a pack of Rothmans cigarettes and several bullets I had accumulated with a friend. A Hells Angel member would've been proud, and the plastic pirates, with their swords and painted beards, looked on in smiling approval. "Marrrrr, me hearties!" I'd say as I rooted around for my baggie. My mother, however, did not approve. "Come here," she said to me one afternoon, in that special way she had. I knew I was doomed, but there was something else in her tone—a hint of embarrassment, perhaps—that suggested I might get out of whatever I happened to be in alive. "I found something in your boat."

I flushed crimson. "*Ja,* I'm keeping that for some chinas at school, Ma. I swear! *Jassis,* why you looking in my treasure chest anyway, man?"

"I'm asking the questions!" My mother, too, looked flushed. "Where did you get that grass? Did you, uh…" She hesitated. "Did you take it from *our* closet?"

Ah, my parents' closet! What a wondrous place that was. Like the wardrobe in Professor Kirke's house that opens onto Narnia, this humble closet also concealed a world of fantasy and excitement. Primarily, it was the hiding place for my dad's two pornographic magazines, and his gun. Possession of foreign dirty magazines was *streng verboten.*[17] You smuggled them into the country in among the clothing in your suitcase, and if you were lucky, you got to keep them. If you were unlucky, you were arrested and charged with indecency. More likely, the customs officer found them, confiscated them, and kept them for

17. There was a local soft porn magazine, *Scope.* It featured pudgy, *boerewors*-fed farm girls in one-piece bathing suits, staring up at you from the pages with reproach. If there was any nipple, it was covered by a black star.

"official use." These two magazines, an ancient *Playboy* and a *Penthouse,* were my introduction to the sexual universe. What hid under those copious pubic triangles I did not know, but I made it one of my principal missions in life to find out. I carefully tore several pages from both priceless volumes and bartered with friends also lucky enough to have fathers who had travelled abroad.[18] And so the onanistic arts proliferated in Johannesburg.

The gun was different yet disturbingly similar. I would stand in front of my parents' full-length mirror in my underwear (why underwear I do not know, and I'm afraid to dig too deep into the Freudian implications of that one), posing with the weapon outstretched in my arms in the manner of my favourite TV character, Magnum, P.I. The gun was a 1940s Italian nine-millimetre semi-automatic, and its size and mass gave a hint as to why the Italians had fared so poorly in World War II. How did an underfed, ill-clothed Genoese or Venetian heft this weapon level with a target, let alone pull the trigger and survive the recoil? It was a semi-portable cannon, not a handgun. Despite its failings, I took every opportunity to visit with the gun when my parents were out. I had seen a heavily cut version of *Taxi Driver.* "Are you talking to me?" I'd ask the mirror. Gone was Travis Bickle's psychotic Queens mumble, replaced with a thick, guttural Johannesburg drawl.

"Are you fucking talking to me, *boet*? Are you *chuning* me *kuck*? Coz I swear, man…!"

---

18. These pages made excellent material for bartering with other young gentlemen in high school. One page of premium *Penthouse* (showing bush, of course) could get you cigarettes, alcohol, and, most important, another *Penthouse* page of equal or better value.

My rib cage heaved with the effort, and a lactic acid burn soon rendered my arms useless. I'd have to lose the Bickle shtick and move to some other pose, maybe some Bruce Willis, or a little Stallone, until my biceps couldn't take it anymore. Those bullets in my treasure chest were meant for this gun. Thankfully, I never got around to loading the magazine. This was long before I understood the intricacies of calibration, and I'd hate to think what would've happened if, by chance, I had managed to chamber a round. There is many a handless Italian veteran unlucky enough to have been issued a similar model, I'm sure.

As for the dope, I had actually never come across it in the fantastical recesses of my parents' closet. It turned out that every Christmas, an appreciative patient gave Dr. Poplak a bag of Malawi Gold (why you would want your dentist to get that stoned is beyond me); consequently, my parents had built up a formidable stash. Burning it would've meant greenhousing the southern hemisphere in a thick purple cloud for at least a month. I have no idea why they didn't just discard it, given that they weren't the smoking type. So it gathered up in the closet, among old knick-knacks, pornos, and semi-automatics, vestiges of an alternate Hunter S. Thompson–like universe my parents never inhabited. I was not punished for my illicit treasure (my mother had found my contraband cargo when she gave the boat to my young cousins to play with), but my drugs were confiscated and, along with a small fortune's worth of Malawi Gold and the Rothmans, disposed of at the town dump. Mom didn't care about the bullets, of course. Those I could keep.

Both Manson and Paul hailed from Malawi, and it is a place where, by all accounts, you need intoxicants to get by. It was then, and by every measure still is, a desperately poor country. Nowadays it has twinned HIV/AIDS to its main export:

malaria. Manson, like most Malawians, had a nasty case of the notorious ague. When the fevers wracked him he would sweat more than usual, and his rich chocolate pallor would become ashen. He looked poisoned to the core, which meant that he was slower on the uptake during a Grass Redissemination Incursion (GRI). He never lost his laugh, though, no matter how bad the fever was. That laugh rose out of him like instinct, like a totem of his true self, fever be damned. Occasionally, my mother took him to a doctor to be fixed up with medication, but the only cure for malaria of that virulence is new blood, organs, nerves, muscles, bones, and skin. And lots of rest and liquids. None of which happened to be an option.

Like Bushy and so many Africans of the day, Manson came from an impoverished village in an impoverished country to work as a labourer in a workforce flush with labourers. And like so many black itinerants, he slid effortlessly into the economic machinery of Apartheid and was tacitly welcomed because more Mansons meant an abundance of ever-cheaper labour for factories, mines, industry, and homes. These itinerant workers, legally non-existent as they were, lived in the townships surrounding the great cities of the country. Home for Manson was Alexandra, a place that, if there were brochures advertising its delights, might be described as "charmingly pre-development, Third World rustic." Travellers heading due north from our house along Louis Botha Avenue passed the outskirts of old Alex, fenced off from the road like Houdini's tortoise pen. Ramshackle tin-roofed shanties were lined in infinite rows, low-slung wires zigzagging the sky above them. Dirt roads, the gutters of which ran with toxic sludge, broke clusters of huts into grids; this was the paradoxical epitome of organized chaos, both meticulously planned and capriciously random. Manson and millions like him moved to places just like this. The new South Africa boasts eleven official languages. The downside to this polyglot mélange is that there are also in attendance eleven different attitudes, viewpoints, cultural imperatives, and requirements. All this tension, mixed in with the poverty, the dust, the disorientation, and the booze, made for an environment that was not necessarily congenial.

My mother had often driven past Alexandra. She must have noticed that there wasn't so much as a lone, sorry-ass daisy within spitting distance of the township, and perhaps this is what stoked her belated curiosity. So it came to pass that my mother, out of interest, asked what perhaps should have been her first question of Manson. "Manson," she inquired, a full decade after hiring him, "where did you learn to garden so nicely?"

The garden was looking especially charming that afternoon, each and every stem standing stock straight to salute her, holding aloft a panoply of vigorous colour, all accented by the deep green of the freshly mowed lawn.

"Madam," answered Manson, "I learned to gahden in-na the prizun."

Now this was in and of itself no biggie, since most blacks were in and out of South African prisons as often as an octogenarian goes to the bathroom.

"Oh, I see. You must have been there a long time to learn to garden like this, hey?" My mother smiled.

"Yes, Madam. Many ye-ahs. Many ye-ahs. Heh, eh-heh."

"Many years, Manson? Shame, but what for?"

The sun blazed. A loerie chirped.

"For the mehdah, Madam."

Colour drained from my mother's face, and she became as white as the glorious oleander blossoms blazing on the bush beside her.

"Murder, Manson? *Murder?*"

It went like this: When Manson came from Malawi, he moved into a tiny concrete dwelling in Alexandra. His place was adjacent to that of a man with whom he had several disagreements. These disagreements escalated, as neighbourly disagreements do, and things started getting nasty, so nasty in fact that Manson in self-defence put a definitive end to the dispute. This he did by driving an axe into his neighbour's skull.

That afternoon, Manson related the regret of his life to my mother, whose blood pressure must have been off the charts. Mom, for her part, was more than a little uncomfortable given the litany of her children's sins against this convicted axe murderer. I bet she was downright queasy. But ever rational, Mom started doing some mental math, combined with a psychological evaluation of the man standing in front of her. One main thing stopped her from telling him to please leave her property right this bloody instant, besides the fact that he was an excellent gardener: Her children were still alive when they so clearly deserved to die.

So she said, "Shame, Manson. But what's done is done, hey. It's in the past now."

"Yes, Madam. Heh, eh-heh."

And then they turned their attention back to the hydrangeas, the petunias, the oleanders, and the aloes. After all, it wasn't really his fault—Manson was by sheer circumstance forced to change his given name, and he had picked a really, really bad one. So, our gardener the axe murderer grabbed the garden shears, wiped the crud-encrusted blades on his overalls, and went back to work.

Subedar Major

If my mother was not home, eating was a problem. Bushy did not cook. Dr. Poplak could not so much as open a tin (his one victual-related task was working the *braai* on Sundays, charring meat so badly that lamb chops were barely distinguishable from the coals). Like most white South African boys, I had never so much as considered how food ended up on a plate. Dr. Poplak, coming home from his surgery for lunch one day, found Leigh and me at the kitchen table, waiting for provender. My mother was out; Bushy was hiding.

"What?" asked Dr. Poplak as we stared at him with the wide, glistening eyes of starving children.

"Hungry," I managed. I batted a fly away from my lips. Leigh slipped in and out of a faint.

"Jesus bloody Christ," Dr. Poplak said. "This is Africa, you know." My father was the only person I knew who conjured up the continent we lived on. "You should be out there hunting. How old are you now?"

"Nine," said Leigh and I together.

"By the time I was nine, I was hunting and skinning my own buck." Indeed, by the time my father was nine, he had apparently accomplished a lot—worked down the mines, moved out of his parents' house, made a good living, never asked for a thing, and now, hunted and skinned buck. Muttering, he cobbled together two mangled, soggy sandwiches. They drooped sadly over our hands as we picked them up.

"I don't want to hear any criticism," said Dr. Poplak. "I just want to hear chewing. Every last crumb better be gone or I'll drown you both in the pool."

Dr. Poplak believed that when a child removed his or her shirt, the rib cage should be visible (through the skin, that is). Our fridge and pantry wouldn't have been out of place in the monastery of a fundamentalist sect of monks on a starvation diet. There was plenty of dried stuff in jars—lentils and rice—but nothing a kid considered nutritious. Even the odd takeout meal was banned after my sister threw up what she called "Kenfucky Fried Chicken" into our swimming pool when she was six.

This made Carolyn's and my secret trips to the Lido Café (pronounced *keh*-fee, which is what South Africans call a corner store) all the more special. We'd hoard the pocket money Oupa gave us and walk the two blocks to heaven like escapees from a Jenny Craig maximum-security compound. I was catholic to a fault in my tastes, but Tempo bars, Peppermint Crisps, and Jelly Tots held a lofty place in my affections. Occasionally, we'd buy a tin of condensed milk. I'd puncture two mouth holes with my penknife, and we'd slurp the tin dry even before reaching home. This was like doing four generous lines of cocaine after a daylong Jack Daniel's binge—we'd come close to killing each other as the sugar rocketed through our bloodstream, then fall into a deep, black depression that lasted the rest of the afternoon.

Given the state of our fridge and pantry, Lido was an oasis. With half-cent coins we bought a candy we called, unselfconsciously and without irony, "nigger balls"—round gobstoppers that turned from black to purple to red to orange as you sucked your way through them. And we never left without buying a handful of Chappies.

Chappies were individually wrapped waxy chewing gums that had a "Did you know?" quiz on the inside of the wrapper. ("Did you know hyenas have the strongest jaw in the animal kingdom?") We'd read the quiz out loud to each other, pop the waxy gum into our mouths, chew for ten seconds until the flavour disappeared, and move on to the next Chappy.

Along with being an educational tool, a major cause of tooth decay, and a level-two carcinogen, Chappies were also an important part of the Apartheid-era economy. When a black person purchased an item from a café, proprietors would not bother giving them their halfpennies' or pennies' change. Whether they liked it or not, black customers often received Chappies instead. Since Chappies could not be traded for like value, this was tantamount to theft. After all, a handful of change could get a black worker back home on a bus, or even a real food product, one that came without trivia questions.

I once saw such a transaction take place at the Lido Café. It was a small incident, but one of the most vivid moments of my childhood. While I was humming and hahing over whether to buy a Lunch Bar or a KitKat, a black man put a loaf of bread and a handful of change down on the counter. The swarthy Lido pusher scooped up the change, clanged open the till, and dumped a handful of Chappies on the counter. His customer stood there and stared at them. The proprietor pushed the Chappies farther toward the counter's edge. The black man made no move to pick them up. "Go!" shouted the café owner.

The black man's body slumped as if he'd taken a physical blow. He picked up the Chappies and left. Defiance was pointless. I paid for my chocolate, receiving my change in pennies rather than chewing gum—the Lido proprietor would not dare try that trick on a white nine-year-old.

To me, the Lido Café was never quite the same after that, but the fact remained that it dealt what my sister and I most desperately needed: stuff in bright packages that was bad for you.

Dr. Poplak was befuddled. "Where are your bloody ribs?" he wanted to know. We didn't feel bad about these clear contraventions of Dr. Poplak's (and, by extension, my mother's) strict no-sweets policy, mostly because we learned early on that Dr. Poplak himself was no slavish adherer to truth and propriety. This is not to say that the good doctor was dishonest—far from it. In fact, I have never met anyone as scrupulously above-board as my father. Let's just say that he had a colourful way of representing the facts and an imaginative way of reinterpreting past events. For instance, he most likely did not hunt and skin his own buck by the time he was nine. Also:

"When I was in India, you think we had a nice bed to sleep in, like you have here?" he'd ask me. Dr. Poplak steadfastly claimed that he had risen to the rank of subedar major in the British Army in India, and he had fought valiantly as an officer and a gentleman in the fading days of the Raj. His career varied greatly, depending on the requirements of the tale (one day he was with the fusiliers, another in the cavalry), but it was a halcyon time and he was forever wistful about it.

"*Ag,* they knew how to treat an officer in those days," said Dr. Poplak. "The sepoys would bring us a nice curry lunch in the mess, and then a gin and tonic at fifteen-hundred hours, just before tea. For the mosquitoes, you see. And then polo."

My parents, who had a reasonably busy social life, were used to their friends asking about Dr. Poplak's exploits in India. Even so, he was still able to get away with seriously inspired bullshitting when the occasion called for it. Once, when one of my mother's cousins asked him if he would attend her daughter's ballet recital, Dr. Poplak's face crumpled and he looked off far into the distance. He was close to tears.

"No, I'd love to," he said, biting his lower lip. "But ever since I buggered my knee back when I was a professional dancer, I haven't been able to look at ballet again. It's. Just. Too. Painful..." After he accepted a series of profuse condolences, he was off the hook. He used this one again, on my sister, to get out of going to her recitals (watching little girls run around on stage dressed as chicks or honeybees or African dancers constituted some of my childhood's most painful hours). I think Carolyn was in her teens before she learned that her father had not, in fact, been terribly injured in a botched *brisé.*

Dr. Poplak's obfuscations were not restricted to Forrest Gumpian cameos in war-torn places such as Angola and Calcutta, or to a quick-witted cock-and-bull story to avoid horrendous social situations.

"What's the chopped liver made from, Da?" I asked him one Friday night.

"Fox," Dr. Poplak said without hesitation.

"*Ag,* bloody rubbish," said Gaga, as I spewed what I assumed was a small forest creature's intestines back onto my plate. Gaga was unimpressed. "Phillip! I'll kill you!"

"Fox," repeated Dr. Poplak.

"Eat that bloody liver," yelled Gaga as I tried to disinfect my mouth with water and a napkin.

I did not eat that bloody liver, but I did consume a lifetime of elaborate confections served up warm by my father, whose powers of narrative invention knew no bounds.

"This is Africa," Dr. Poplak told people. "Where I grew up, I'd wake up to the lions roaring at dawn. No other sound like it."

Well, this *was* Africa, and Dr. Poplak *did* wake up to the sound of lions roaring at dawn. His childhood home was in the old suburb of Saxonwold, right around the corner from the Johannesburg Zoo. He left that choice piece of information out, of course—preferring to conjure the image of the Great White Hunter in the wilds of the Dark Continent, an addendum to his subedar persona. To white urban South Africans, Africa was as exotic as India. Nothing in Africa was less African than Johannesburg, and *especially* the leafy, oak-lined suburb of Saxonwold.

There is, however, one African-themed story Dr. Poplak has never recanted. He related it without his usual drollery, in a manner suggesting that it, or something like it, may actually have occurred. This does not make it any less improbable, fantastical, or unlikely.

He told us the tale on a stormy autumn night, when the wind and rain were ripping leaves from the trees, and the city was transformed, in a matter of hours, from summer to winter. The story took place where the suburb of Killarney meets the suburb of Houghton. Nearby is a gloomy park of some significant acreage, called The Wilds. Overgrown lawns are clotted with thick knots of acacia and wisteria, presided over by tall blue gums. The park's landscaping, never particularly meticulous (hence the name), had been left to nature. No one went into the park, and if they did, they were almost guaranteed to spend the day or so following their re-emergence lying on a cold metal slab, undergoing an autopsy.

The official story was that a serial killer was on the loose, preying on blacks from rural areas who had stumbled into The Wilds, unaware of the park's dark heart. Unofficially, the prevailing theory was that some sort of simian creature, something possessing great speed and dexterity—a being with monstrous strength and a heart of pure evil—inhabited The Wilds. Its cries were often audible to those who drove by late at night, their windows rolled up, their doors locked, fear a cold steel blade against the jugular of logic and reason.

There were sightings. A flash of an enormous beast as it leapt between bushes, a blur of a great shadowy thing in the rearview mirror. The brooding trees of Houghton Drive met like a series of clasped, bony hands—and there it hid, waiting to strike. The beast was looking for something more substantial. The stringy meat of the indigent had lost its zing; bluer blood was on the menu.

Long after the sun had set, with the winds sending the remaining leaves from the bent boughs of Houghton Drive skittering across the deserted roadway, Dr. Poplak made his way home. As he gently and instinctually pressed down on the accelerator to make his way past The Wilds, a dark shape swept through his peripheral vision, quick and indistinct. He looked over his shoulder. Nothing. But as he rounded the hill, heading east, his car headlights illuminated someone as they crossed the road. Except this was no someone.

"It was a some*thing*," said Dr. Poplak.

Hitting the gas pedal, my father swerved around the creature as it leapt into the trees above him. Perhaps this was a ruse, a trick to cause him to crash into a trunk of one of the immense trees lining the road. Then, as he lay stunned and bleeding, it would drag him from the wreckage and consume him in The Wilds, just as it had consumed so many others.

"That," said Dr. Poplak, who was as pale as moonlight when he arrived home, "was a close one."

You never knew with my old man. Perhaps he had a near collision with another car, maybe he'd almost hit someone and had fictionalized the tale so that he could (a) get some commiseration, (b) get the shock off his chest, and (c) remain essentially uncommunicative.

After he'd calmed down (read "had a large drink"), Dr. Poplak scooped coal into the anthracite heater, kicked the dog (as was his custom), and settled in front of the fire to read the newspaper. I'll never know whether his tale was in any way true (asking a South African male a direct question is inadvisable—lots of "*Ja,* no, but, *ja,*" and so on), but I do know why the story worked. At its heart was this point:

You never know when The Wilds will swing from the trees. You never know when Africa is coming for you. And there is nothing white South Africans were more afraid of than Africa.

Up to now, there had been nothing to be afraid of in my world. I had never thought that—besides the odd *tokelosh* nightmare or a bout of measles or a botched bedtime story from Gaga—life held any unpleasantries whatsoever. Or nothing the adults around me couldn't solve in a flash. But whatever had swung from the trees and tried to take out my father did not sound like an easily solvable problem. I imagined something dark, its red eyes burning, hiding in the ancient trees of Houghton Drive: a creature so hell-bent on murder that it made the *tokelosh* look like a mewling kitten. And I imagined it waiting with immeasurable patience for the opportunity to strike—and showing no mercy when it finally did.

"Do you think they'll get it, Da?" I asked.

Dr. Poplak snorted.

"Not on your life, boy." He flapped open his newspaper. "This would never have happened in India. The sepoys would have shot that bloody thing years ago."

C.H.O.M.P.S.

When I was about nine, I shot a bird. I used a school friend's BB gun, which was, according to him, enhanced with a spring from a pump-action shotgun, thereby allowing the ball bearing to travel with greater velocity, ensuring a deadlier shot. You don't need to be a lifetime member of the NRA for this to sound like bullshit to you—but nevertheless, young boys will tell each other such things. Mechanics aside, we had been shooting at birds for about an hour, my friend and I, when finally, and purely by accident, I hit one. It was minding its own business, cleaning a wing (its own) in the high branches of a large jacaranda when it was struck from its perch. The creature's head, at least the back of its head, exploded in a fine red mist and a *pooph* of tiny feathers. The bird fell to the ground with a thud, flapped its wings, and perished.

I didn't sleep for weeks.

What if the bird had babies to feed? What if its friends missed it? Great White Hunters do not ask such questions, especially not of their mothers. Clearly, I was not the killing kind. The inspiration for this Young Ernest Hemingway moment came from a book that was required reading for any South African boy, a tome called *Jock of the Bushveld.* It details the adventures of the runt of a litter of bull-terrier pups that grows up to be a legendary *bushveld* hunting dog and a faithful companion to his master, this in the early days of the Transvaal gold rush. *JOTB* doesn't even end as sappily as this genre often does. The book and its knighted author, Sir Percy Fitzpatrick, have a sentimental streak, but it's that warm, nineteenth-century kind of sentimentality, not the icy-cold manipulative version we've come to know courtesy of hand-drawn animated films and sitcoms starring children.

Anyway, *Jock of the Bushveld* had me pining for a puppy: a faithful four-legged companion and—until I had to give the pursuit up for, um, psychological reasons—a hunting partner. I'm not exactly revealing new truths when I say that there's a wide gulf between the ideal—so often rendered in entertainments such as *JOTB*—and real life. It's the *immensity* of this gulf, how badly and how quickly things go off the rails, that continues to surprise, long after anything else does.

The domesticated dog in Johannesburg is a unique strain of canine. Caged, ornery, and militantly opposed to visitors (invited or otherwise), the local cur is shot through with a viciousness not found in the dog parks of North America. These are not pets. They're employees.

In my parents' search for a watchdog and the typical childhood campaign for a puppy, Dr. Poplak, my mother, my sister, and I met in a rare confluence of need and want. Despite this, Dr. Poplak tried to pull it off as a favour: "You'll have to clean up after him. And take him for walks. I will not be responsible for that dog." This is how we found ourselves packed into the Passat Wagon, zipping along the M2 in the direction of Pretoria. In the 1980s, there was no earthly reason to go anywhere near Pretoria—it had the worst elements of colonial capitals such as Ottawa or Canberra (small, staid, conservative, dull), along with being the epitome of an Afrikaner Calvinist city, and therefore unremittingly boring. The broad boulevards were devoid of all life, giving the impression that the most fun to be had in the city was an extra-long church service, followed by a lynching. If Apartheid had a spiritual home, Pretoria was it. But on this day, we might as well have been driving to Disneyland.

The Highveld whipped by us, dusty with several years of drought and buzzing with unseen life. My sister and I squirmed happily in the station wagon's back seat. Usually, we'd be strangling each other by this point, but for short-term peace from the brats, nothing beats the purchase of a baby dog. The route to the farm took us up a long dirt road whose length and bumpiness threatened to break the informal truce. Before the first fist fight could break out, the rickety gate appeared before us, as did the farmer.

He was a real olde-timey Boer, his large belly straining to rip through threadbare dungarees, tucked as they were into absurdly large leather boots. His face seemed fashioned from clay cured in spittoon juice and then baked in a kiln for too long. Bloodshot eyes kept an intense gaze on his black farmhands as they swung open the rickety gates. *"Maak oop! Gou!"*—Open! Quickly!—he growled at them, waving us into his farm with a cracked, weathered hand. Despite the drought that had left his land parchment-paper dry, a cigarette dangled delicately off his bottom lip. Dropping it would have meant a conflagration of Biblical proportions. He seemed unperturbed, if not a little encouraged, by this possibility and lit another off the embers of the first.

The farm was dusty and red—a Martian landscape. Abandoned barns and dilapidated outbuildings suggested that there had been plenty of activity on the property before the drought rendered the Highveld barren. No more. Now, the farm churned out the Mercedes-Benz of watchdogs, the penultimate in canine technology, a dog that would keep your life and property as safe as Nazi loot in a Swiss bank account. This brand of dog is called a Boerboel.

Boerboel literally means "farmer's big dog" or "farmer's mastiff." The dog is supposedly part Doberman pinscher, part bull mastiff and part Rottweiler, but I have my own theory of its genetic origin. I believe it is a direct descendent of that famed mythological watchdog Cerberus, spliced from the three-headed demon dog's DNA and cultured in a laboratory deep in the caverns of the underworld. The only problem with this theory is that Cerberus was bested, and this could never happen to a Boerboel. Hercules would have stalled at his eleventh labour and faded from legend. As for the idea of lulling a Boerboel to sleep with a lyre, à la Orpheus—this would elicit but the driest of chuckles from any who have encountered the breed. Boerboels are not musically inclined.

What they are is alarmingly cute as puppies. The beasties, six of them in all, stumbled over each other in the enclosed yard, so young they could barely open their eyes, their clipped tails still raw, crusted wounds. They gave sharp yelps, staying as close to Mom, a sullen bitch dragging six well-used teats in the dust, as they could. Pops kept a wary eye on us, his leaden gaze taking in our every movement like a croc on a busy riverbank, making sure we didn't get too close to anything he considered of value. He stalked the perimeter of the enclosure as if he had a cigar in his slobbering jaws and a Magnum .44 holstered around his haunches. His stub of a tail didn't wag once. His testicles were huge. He was all business.

"Look how cute they are!" squealed my sister as she scrambled into the pen. "*Ag,* can't we take them all?" Carolyn was used to such pronouncements being met with smiles of pleasure from adults bewitched with her own dark-eyed, curly-headed version of cuteness. Not so our Boer. "*Passop,* hey," he warned. "They bite." Mom lifted my sister to safety. "Just behave yourself, please," she whispered sharply at a bewildered Carolyn.

I gazed at the animals in the enclosure as they went about their business. Typically, Boerboels are the size of pit bulls and Boston terriers, and their large heads fit their stocky bodies in a similar manner. Their coats are dusty brown, as if made from the very dust of the Highveld. Their haunches are muscular, they are not unattractive; they're mellow, watchful, and obedient. Perfect.

"We'll take this one."

He was a chipper puppy, and he scampered around the back seat of the car, sharp teeth gnawing at fingers, wetting himself (and us) with happy abandon. His small head nestled easily in the palm of our hands and his fur was as soft as velvet. He liked to play and to chew things—like shoes and the feet inside them. I came up with a kick-ass name for him: Chomps. Or rather, C.H.O.M.P.S. I borrowed this acronym from the movie of the same name, a movie my sister and I had watched on my grandparents' massive VHS machine and loved. Perhaps we'd feel differently if we watched it now. A posting on the Internet Movie Database describes it as "stupid, yet vaguely entertaining," a description I find more worrying than I would outright derision. C.H.O.M.P.S. stands for Canine Home Protection System, and the movie is about a teen genius who creates a robot dog with X-ray vision, dazzling speed, and incredible strength.[19]

---

19. Presumably, you need a magnet to pick up after it.

A businessman tries to swipe the dog for his own nefarious purposes, but our fearless protagonist and his robot charge end up giving it to the bad guy, doggy-style. But guess what, folks? You don't need a robot dog that sees through walls, jumps over houses, and pisses Valvoline. Just buy a Boerboel.

Chomps grew rapidly. He ate an enormous amount of food. Puppy pellets quickly became too expensive, so my mother took to buying a horrendous minced dog food concoction (with the stomach-churning name of Beefies), packaged in foot-long plastic tubes. Frozen Beefies were delivered once a week by a black driver who dumped them at our front gate and ran for it, as if he understood that the creature consuming the contents of the box was not to be meddled with at any cost. A mystery-meat *babotie* of gristle, bone, and innards, this foul mass would be defrosted and then warmed in a large pot and summarily served to the hungry pup in a scooped-out loaf of frozen bread.[20] This meal was gone in seconds. Three months in and Chomps was larger than his parents. Five months later he was larger than *my* parents. After that, his recessive genes really started kicking in. There was definitely Great Dane in Chomps's genetic potpourri.

Leigh and I loved playing with the critter, casting him as the star monster in our action-figure adventures. This stopped quickly. "Um," said Leigh. "He ate Mr. T." Chomps's teeth had become absurdly sharp, and his incisors showed no signs of slowing their growth. When he devastated the A-Team van—a feat no bad guy on TV had been able to achieve—he was relieved of his imaginary monster duties.

20. This is a variation on a South African dish called bunny chow, created by mixed-race gourmands from the Cape. Mom served the bread frozen in an attempt to get Chomps to eat slower.

A year into his life and Chomps had lost the gait and bearing of a puppy. His body was woven from thick cords of rippling muscle; his head was the size of a soccer ball. The ridge of fur along his spine resembled a buzzed-down mohawk and gave him a paradoxically punk-military appearance. He slobbered a viscous gloop, and he never lost the sprightly playfulness of a pup. Except that he weighed 130 pounds. His skull was four inches thick and he was impervious to pain. His bark started as a deep rumble from his belly, then ripped through the length of his torso to hit air as a blast of pure bass. Chomps was untrained and unhinged, as persuasive an example of the perils of inbreeding as ever walked on four paws.

I say Chomps was untrained, but this is partially untrue. He did attend two training sessions. Dr. Poplak, sensing that it would be a long road, decided it best to leave the training to nature. "These dogs train themselves," he told my mother when she asked why Chomps had missed five training sessions in a row. This very 1960s piece of "live and let live" ideology (the only piece of such ideology I ever heard my father invoke, which leads me to suspect it may have been motivated by indolence) proved to be severely misplaced. Chomps wanted to live and let *die.* That was his natural inclination, bred into him by twenty generations of Boers whose outlook in the 1980s was exactly the same as it had been in the 1780s.

In addition to those two training sessions, Dr. Poplak used a TV program called *Training Dogs the Woodhouse Way* in an attempt to instill some sort of discipline in our large charge. Barbara Woodhouse was a stately British septuagenarian who—and this was the charm of the show—trained *owners* how to train dogs. Dogs she was kind to; owners, not so much. "Walkies!" was her signature line, pronounced "Wahhh-kies."

"Sit-ahhh!" Dr. Poplak would say to Chomps, the Woodhouse way, which included an arm movement combining a reverse Nazi salute with a bicep curl. Chomps would slurp at the thick cords of drool hanging from his maw and stare at my father with a depth of puzzlement that was heart-rending. He wanted to understand—he really did—but he simply did not have the mental capacity, not to mention the early guidance. "Mr. Boerboel," Barbara would have said (she addressed owners by the breed of their dogs), "you must endeavour with greater intent." But like all old dogs, you can't train South African men of a certain vintage. They are what they are, and must be accepted as such.

I've mentioned that Chomps was big. I am told by caninophiles that large dogs are typically more docile than smaller breeds, assuming they are exercised appropriately. In that case, throw some Shih Tzu into Chomps's genetic jambalaya. Walking him wasn't an option; few people are strong enough to wrangle a 130-pound Boerboel on a leash, and none of them is a member of my family. If Chomps saw a dog in the distance, he was sniffing its ass five seconds later, while you sat on the ground with skinned knees and second-degree rope burns on your hands. So Chomps ran around the yard in circles, digging up great clomps of turf with his enormous paws. Banned from the front garden for ripping it into a state of desertification on one extraordinarily hyper afternoon frolic, the beast was relegated to the backyard, a space that, unhappily, contained our pool.

Lord, we loved that pool. I remember coming home from school on particularly hot afternoons to hear Mom say, "You look so hot and bothered. Poor boy! Go get into the pool." And get into the pool I did, sinking under the cool blue surface and letting the irritations of a tough day wick away with the sweat and grime. The pool was a refuge, a resting place, an aquatic playground. But that changed when Chomps came, because Chomps developed a condition when he was about a year old.

Typically associated with rabies, hydrophobia is considered the deadliest symptom of the illness. The wickedness of the disease is such that it forces the creature suffering from it to fear water, or liquid of any kind—resulting eventually in dehydration and death. Because Chomps did not have rabies (what the hell was going to bite Chomps?), a veterinary pathologist might say that he suffered from atypical hydrophobia caused by mental retardation. Specifically, Chomps hated it when any member of the family swam. He barked, whined, and finally leapt into the pool to "save" us, which usually meant a few puncture wounds and a tetanus shot. The beast became so distressed that we had to lock him in the scullery if we were considering a swim, and all hell broke loose if he so much as heard us in the water. He would try to scratch his way out, his talons leaving delicate curls of wood shavings in a mound at the foot of the scullery door. And so we swam silently and focused, like Green Berets crossing the Mekong River at night, equipped with nothing but a Speedo and a prayer. If you've heard kids in a swimming pool, you've done exactly that: heard them. It's just no fun otherwise.

Indeed, Chomps rendered many occasions less fun. Birthday parties were a pain because Chomps went crazy with so many people around. In his excitement he jumped on guests with both paws placed solidly on their chests. Adults would be looking directly into those addled Scooby-Doo eyes, but kids did not fare so well. After parties at our house, my mother often received angry phone calls from other parents—"Do you know what your dog did to my daughter? He bowled her right bloody over. She's in shock!" So for birthday festivities, Dr. Poplak tried sedating Chomps with prescription drugs taken from his dental surgery. The record was four Valium, concealed in a hunk of bread. But this did nothing to slow Chomps down; he tried mightily to bang down the door of the kitchen, where he was ensconced, and join the fun. Nothing could stop this behemoth.

Not even a speeding Alfa Romeo.

It happened in a flash. I remember returning from school, unaware that Chomps had managed to sneak into the front yard. As I opened the gate, he bolted for the street, barking merrily. "Chomps," I yelled, just as a white sedan rounded the corner and sped onto Forbes Street.

The accident unfolds in slow motion: The driver slams on the brakes, frying rubber against the tarmac in a screech; the right headlight explodes in a shower of plastic and glass as the car makes contact with Chomps's haunch; the dog yelps in anguish, whipped around by the impact; he limps toward me, his eyes wide with terror; I scream and cover my eyes. "Chomps!" I wail. Death's stygian shroud descends over the neighbourhood. Crows caw. Funeral bells toll.

As was the custom in South Africa, the car did not stop after the collision.[21] Tears welled up in my eyes (at this point in my life, I did want the dog gone, but not quite in that manner); no living creature could withstand a crash like that. The Alfa hadn't. I gingerly rubbed the raised spot where Chomps had made contact with the car. This was an *Old Yeller* moment—where did we keep the shotgun? As I tried to settle him into a lying position so that he could die with his head in my lap, Chomps

21. There is no local term for a hit-and-run.

playfully nipped my hand. My teary soft focus cleared—the animal appeared to have already forgotten about the accident. Minutes later, he was prancing about gaily as we tried to coax him back into his lair.

But as it is with any place where you must barricade yourself against what lurks outside, what protects you also imprisons you. Chomps was as much our warden as he was our guardian. Ours was one of the few houses in Johannesburg that had not been burgled, but Dr. Poplak had to *inject* the dog with tranquilizers if we were to have guests.

Chomps should have been a miner: He loved to dig. His googly eyes focused on the task, his torso heaving with effort, he would dig his way to the bowels of hell if we didn't drag him away from the hole and give him half a deer to chew as distraction. Once, Chomps dug his way under the fence and into our neighbour's vast backyard, which was decorated with faux Greek statuettes and massive earthenware pots holding ferns, proteas, and other assorted exotics. He went on a rampage, bashing the pots over, ripping away at the ferns, humping the muscled deities. My parents were unhappy.

"You wanted to get this bloody dog," Dr. Poplak said to my mother. "You go clean it up."

My mother glared at him. "If you had, for once, gotten off your arse and trained him, this wouldn't have happened!"

"They're supposed to train themselves, man! He's just no bloody good at it."

So my parents crawled through the hole under the fence, skulked into the garden of our neighbour (they were thankfully away on holiday), caught the marauding dog, righted pots, replanted ferns, and glued arms and heads and genitals back onto torsos. This took them an afternoon. They army-crawled back through the hole, covered it with bricks, and poured themselves sizeable alcoholic beverages, which they consumed rapidly. Watching them run around that garden like special-needs ninjas on a clandestine mission was a watershed moment for me. This was not only when I realized that parents are human too, but also that it is a real bitch to glue limbs back onto concrete statues.

But if there is any real tragedy to be mined from the life of the creature—and I believe there is—it was not Chomps's chronic stupidity or his costly impishness. It was that his good-natured playfulness was overridden by the dark coding woven into his DNA. Chomps had a complicated relationship with black people, which seemed the most sentient thing about him. Those glazed orbs in his bulletproof skull cleared when he was around black folks. He knew the score, as if this were his sole purpose of existence: to protect us from the dark menace. Indeed, since Boerboels were bred as pure guard dogs, they are simply incapable of anything other than guarding, and it wasn't their *white* neighbours whom Afrikaner farmers were particularly worried would nick the chickens or pilfer from the pantry. Knowing Chomps, it's not so hard to believe that his breed was developed over the centuries to hate. Did the breeders experiment, as with a recipe? "*Ag nee,* man, the ones with more Rottweiler in them seem to like the *kaffirs.* A sprinkling of whippet and a touch of red setter next time, hey?" Whatever the case may be, just as a cat stalks a bird in performance of a genetically programmed instinct, so Chomps growled and bared his not inconsiderable incisors when we came in too close contact with black people. He could handle us around one black person. This was okay, assuming everyone stayed calm (Bushy he was cool with—years alongside her in the scullery had taught him that she was probably not the greatest threat to life, limb, or property). But two black people? Or two black people and *water*?

I came to understand Chomps as a creature of his breeding one afternoon in the backyard when I was about thirteen. Manson was washing down the brick pavement with the hose. My sister and I were together at the rear of the house on a Harass Manson incursion. Bushy was doing the ironing. And slowly, Chomps's worst nightmare started to piece together like a Rube Goldberg puzzle. Carolyn and I headed toward Manson, with Bushy following close behind, heading toward the laundry line for a fresh batch of dry sheets to iron. Manson walked toward us, hose in hand. Then my mother unexpectedly appeared. Manson came closer still. And a supernatural growl emanated from Chomps, a ghostly *grrrrrrrrrrrrrr* that travelled via generations and generations of Boerboels to land here, now, with all of us heading toward one another, a chance assembly of random characters in a one-act tragicomedy. Chomps's body snapped like a whip as he lunged for Manson with focused ferocity. His jaws clamped onto the hand holding the deadly hose. Manson desperately tried to keep a regular expression on his face—one of good-natured obeisance—but his ashen pallor and the sweat breaking out on his brow gave the game away. "Is okay, Chompy," he said. "Good boy." Chomps bit harder.

Imagine this scene rendered as a Rodin sculpture: two kids stepping back, frozen in surprise; a woman with Caucasian features looking on in shock, gravitating toward her babies; a smaller woman with African features, arms full of laundry, locked in a backward step; and a dog, contorted with inbred rage and fear and hatred, locked onto a man's hand as water falls from a hose.

Manson heroically kept his smile. We eventually extricated Chomps's slobbering jaws from Manson's injured hand, and Manson was rushed to the doctor for a tetanus shot (whoever makes that vaccine owes Boerboel breeders stock options). Pink flesh glistened through the worn leathery skin around his thumb, but he laughed it off. "Heh, eh-heh, Madam. Is okay," is all he said. A couple of stitches, and that was that.

And so it was that the velvety pup that had so happily peed himself in our Passat some years before turned out to be a 130-pound slobbering hydrophobic racist with the temperament and energy level of a speed freak on a massive dose of ephedrine. With his sunny nature subjugated by eons of inbreeding, Chomps was a metaphor for the South African condition writ in fur, muscle, and slobber. Toward the end of his life, my sister was the only one who could bear him. Too slow to realize that he did not live with people who loved him, he was always ecstatic to see us come home from school or work. "Fuggoff, man!" my dad would say to the creature if it came within a mile of him, clearly disappointed that Chomps had never trained himself appropriately. "Piss off, man," my mother would say if the beast drooled on her while she was feeding him his daily bunny chow. "Bugger off, man," I'd say as I stepped over him on my way to the pool, preparing myself for a half hour of silent, furtive skulking in the water. But Carolyn loved him still, and he would curl around her as they sat by the anthracite fire in the wintertime, she rubbing his great head, he too dumb to realize that he was so close to the heat that his fur was smoking. "The dog's on fire," Dr. Poplak would say, barely looking up from his paper, his glasses halfway down his nose. Carolyn and Chomps would scoot a little bit away from the hearth and continue the cuddle.

When we immigrated, my parents assured my sister that Chomps ended up "on a farm." Sure he did. I'm sure he came in very handy. But after his tenure there, I have a pretty good idea where he ended up. There's a spot in hell called the Gates of Acheron. It is here that Hercules wrestled über-dog Cerberus to the ground, thus successfully completing his labours. I'm guessing that there has been an ongoing (in)human resources head(s)hunt for a replacement. And I'll bet that Chomps stands alone at the gates of the underworld, chasing away even the most fearless of souls with one deep growl. This can be only very good news for black people.

'Cause there's no way in hell they're getting into Hades.

Early Days

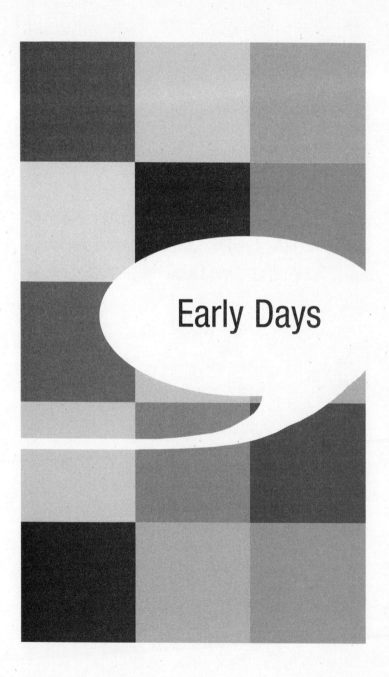

In which we Play Huggy Bear; Go to School and Flourish; Encounter a Supervillain named The Whistler; and Catch the Uhura Syndrome.

"I'll Be Hutch"

My mother ran a strict household. She had all sorts of rules we were to abide by, and to step outside the bounds was inadvisable. Bedtime was bedtime. Half an hour of TV a day. No sweets or pop in the house. No playing until homework was done. Dr. Poplak liked to claim he was strict, but he never really had the chance to put his alleged strictness into practice, because, like most South African fathers, he didn't have much to do with us when we were small. Besides, strictness is a process. As a parent, it's not as simple as making a statement like, "Eat those vegetables; otherwise, there'll be no TV for a week." You have to be prepared to follow up on the threat and withstand the tantrums, the saucer-eyed pleading, the door slamming. My mother was more than up to this. So was Dr. Poplak's brother, my uncle Percy.

Uncle Percy's rules were non-negotiable. He believed firmly in the adage "Children should be seen and not heard," except for the "should be seen" part. We visited with the other Poplaks every Sunday afternoon for a *braai,* either at our place or at theirs, and this meant that every second Sunday we were at Uncle Percy's house and subject to the same set of intractable rules as my cousins Lewis and Janine. The rules were legion: No gum chewing. No hands in pockets. Whisper when in earshot of adults. Wash hands before, during, and after meals.

No hyperactivity. The very notion of eating at the same table as the adults was patently ridiculous, but at Percy's house, we ate in the *backyard*! Percy was, by anyone's standards, strict.

This troubled Dr. Poplak, who had two questions for me when I was a boy.

"Who's your Lord and Master?" he asked. (It took me almost two decades to get used to my father's sense of humour.)

"You are, Da."

"Louder!"

"*Jassis!* YOU ARE!"

"Good boy."

His second question without fail made me feel sorry for him.

"Who's stricter? Me or Percy?"

"*Ja,* no..." I stumbled.

"Who, boy?"

"Um..."

As it turned out, all this strictness was good preparation for the school system, which, for me, began at a nursery school in the nearby neighbourhood of Norwood. Like most people, I remember only a few things about nursery school. Like swallowing a watermelon pit at lunch one day, and an officious four-year-old informing me that a watermelon patch would soon start growing in my stomach. I remember the burning shame of having to run through the sprinklers naked for splashing juice on another nursery school inmate, who responded in kind. Also, I remember being Huggy Bear.

This was a result of my mother's strict television-watching policies. Like I said—half an hour a day. No matter how much I begged, that half hour would not be extended to an hour to watch *Starsky and Hutch,* nor could my bedtime be adjusted to allow for the show's 9 P.M. start time. When all the kids played

Starsky and Hutch on their scooters, I had to pretend to know the details of the show. "I'll be Hutch," I said. "You can't be him, *doos*!" said Warren, nursery school's chunky bully. "Your hair's not yellow enough." Mortification, thy name is Hutch!

So, because I tanned darker, Warren cast me as Huggy Bear. Huggy Bear, for those who don't know, was the black street informant (read "drug-dealing pimp") with a heart of gold, who occasionally assisted the titular heroes in the solving of crimes. Huggy Bear's role, under Warren's direction, was to coordinate the scooter traffic. Because I had no knowledge of the content of the show, I had no idea that Huggy Bear was black. When I found this out, I hid behind the bushes so that I would not have to play that role any longer. If I'd just known to say "Starsky"! This was entirely my mother's fault: Why did she have to be so strict?

By the time I was six years old, in the lead-up to primary school, I had learned some hard lessons: Someone is always your Lord and Master. Strictness stinks. Watch as much TV as you can. And always make the right call on the character you wish to play, or you'll be assigned the minority role. Which, among white South African preschoolers, was already understood to be a grievous insult.

Floreat Quisque—Let Each Flourish

WOLRAAD WOLTEMADE[22]

"The man who lost his life saving others from drowning."

As lightning crackled over Table Mountain, rain lashed the sea into a foaming rage. It became clear that the *De Jonge Thomas* was doomed. The cargo ship was floundering, and desperate sailors were leaping into the roiling waters, only to be instantly drowned or dashed against the craggy rocks, or both. Suddenly, on the beachhead appeared an old man on a large black horse. This was Wolraad Woltemade, and he was not about to idly watch men drown. He stripped off his coat and shirt and rode fearlessly into the raging waters. He bore a heavy rope and threw it to the imperilled seamen, hauling them to the shore two by two. When five desperate sailors grabbed the line, both horse and horseman were dragged down into

---

22. I have adapted the five stories you'll read in this chapter from a textbook that was standard reading for (white) children throughout the country during my school years. It is called *Bravery in South Africa* and was written by Kay Schroeder. I've kept the tone, the style, and the content, and abridged for space. I should add that the first edition of *Bravery in South Africa* was published in 1980 (yes, *1980*!), which corresponds with my enrolment in primary school. This was not some hoary old text—it was a cutting-edge educational tool.

the depths along with them. Wolraad Woltemade saved fourteen men that stormy day in June 1773, and gave his own life in the process. The people of Cape Town have never forgotten his act of selfless courage.

School life conformed to a simple, terrible physics: (In)Action = Reaction. I learned the hard way that when the bell rang, it was not ringing idly. It was best to think of it as a starter's pistol. *Dring-a-ling* rang the bell. As a wide-eyed six-year-old still lost in the immensity of his new surroundings (and, admittedly, unwilling to return to the confines of the classroom), I loitered on the stairs leading up from the playground to the school. Several other boys were also there, giving this informal huddle the look of an organized gathering, which was forbidden in the country, never mind the school. With an awful suddenness, a dark creature swooped from his perch among the gargoyles, gathered us under his dusty hawk wing, and guided us into the school's warren-like northern end.

This creature's name, I found out once in his darkened office, was Mr. Peterson, and he was the school's headmaster. A pair of thick, black-rimmed glasses perched between the two shocks of dark hair on his otherwise bald head, and he had the whiff of a crypt about him. Peterson said little, which is far scarier than if he had said a lot. Tersely, Mr. Peterson told us to bend over and raise the back flaps of our safari suits. I had the sense that I was about to be injured in a way that would be both surprising and unpleasant. *Crack!* I jolted my head upright, and it took a second or two to realize that every nerve ending in my butt was in agony. The dark bird creature had whipped me. Who did he think he was? Only my mother whipped me, or, perhaps, Bushy. But Peterson wasn't interested in the punctilios of who could and couldn't physically abuse the six-year-olds in his charge. My body, I was being told, was no longer just for the eating of sweets and playing of games. It was now a palimpsest on which laws would be written in a criss-cross of welts. Mr. Peterson didn't speak because he didn't have to. His association was Pavlovian: Late for bell, sore butt. His message was clear: Behave. The safety and sanctity of your ass cheeks depend on it.

I woke up every morning with a lump in my stomach, wishing to God that this school business was all just a bad dream—a punishment bestowed on me for being a naughty boy. If that was the case, God and my parents could expect only good behaviour from then on. "Wake up, boy," said Bushy. "Beeg boys go to school. And you are a beeg boy."

Who the hell made me a big boy without asking if I was up to the task?

I still remember the smell of my brand-new school uniform. It had the alloy-tinged smell of fear. On the ninth of January, 1980, my neat green Ridgeview Primary safari suit was laid out on my cowboy-patterned comforter, along with a pair of shiny black Clarks and a woollen zip-up sweater. I had tried the uniform on at School & Sport, the chain that supplied Johannesburg schoolchildren with their educational finery.[23]

23. South African schools were exceedingly precise about uniform specs. They gave orders for seam length, sock height, shoe brand, and underwear colour. According to the rules on the uniform handout my mother received, "Ties in the school colours are to be worn throughout the school day in the winter. They should be neat, clean, and unchewed … No jewellery of any kind. MedicAlert necklaces must not be visible." (That second directive led, no doubt, to some hurried Hail Mary ephedrine injections.)

"*Ja,* you're a big boy now," my mother had said, tears welling in her eyes. The rough material scraped against my skin like sandpaper. My knees knocked against each other, and my bottom lip wobbled dangerously.

In the annual first-day-of-school photos my mother insisted on taking, I wear the same expression on my face—as though I've just received a proctological exam from a veterinary intern who forgot to warm the speculum. Of my very first day, I have only snippets of memories: the older children, Francis Bacon–like jagged impressions of shiny teeth, glittering eyes, grasping fingers, quivering noses, all disjointed and massively out of proportion; the teachers on the stage of the assembly hall, seated like marble colossi; someone trying to press an ice cream cone into my hand, which I intuited to be more for my mother's benefit than my own and duly refused. (Oh, the primal Freudian rage toward she who births you and abandons you to face the world!) The school was a terrifying maze of dark nooks and deep, chilly corners where unimaginable horrors lurked. The open-balconied corridors echoed eerily. Bad things happen here, I said to myself. Very bad things.

Leigh was also a new Ridgeviewer, but he was placed in the other Grade One class—a decision made by our parents so that we could "develop separately." This was of great concern to me—would he find another best mate?—but I was encouraged to see that even he, who lived so firmly in a dreamy alternate universe, was mired firmly in the here and now and therefore terrified of this new place. Our after-school games those first few months were glum affairs. Our parents called it a phase. I think of it more as traumatic stress disorder.

My class—Grade One A—under the tutelage of the unbending Mrs. Brown, was for the most part assembled of second-generation European immigrant stock—predominantly Greeks, Italians, and Portuguese. To Oupa's great consternation, I was not going to the local Jewish day school. No amount of coercion could get Dr. Poplak to pay those school fees. Still, there were at Ridgeview Primary enough Jewish kids—and one Jewish teacher—to run a small, early-morning cheder class, which assuaged Oupa's disappointment somewhat. This cheder would end up providing one of the greater lessons I was to learn at Ridgeview. But that was, thankfully, some years away yet.

Because I went to school with kids named Albano and Mirco and Sancia and Margeritha, I learned to curse in Italian before I could recite the blessings in Hebrew. *"Vafancoolo stronso!"* I'd say happily, revelling in the expressive qualities of my new Mediterranean lexicon. My mother, who had spent enough time in Europe to know a bad word when she heard one, was unimpressed. "You can swear in Italian, but you'll be crying in English," she warned. Cheder reminded me that I was Jewish, and I learned "Hava Nagilah" before singing "All Things Bright and Beautiful" at Wednesday morning hymns.

Social life quickly organized itself along sectarian lines. Jeremy Diamond became my best at-school friend. From a wealthy Jewish entrepreneurial family, he was a kid who never really seemed to be a kid. With a long, wise face and a permanent stoop, Jeremy, at the age of six, could comfortably have been installed as the CEO of a Fortune 500 company. He was constantly presenting business ideas, and I'm not talking lemonade stands: "*Ag,* you can draw *lekker,*" he'd say to me. "Let's build a spaceship to take people to space—and make some bloody money." Jeremy was Richard Branson in a green safari suit.

The Italian kids had a sophisticated organizational infrastructure and quickly formed a gang, led by an immense boy named

Gabriel. His large head sat on a missile-shaped torso, which sprouted two muscular arms that ended in big bunches of fingers dusty from being dragged behind him. He sat at the back of the classroom, never saying a word—he led only by example. Example meant—mostly—kicking the asses of kids who somehow offended whatever sensibilities were buried deep inside his head. Birthday-party photos show a wide range of children eating birthday cake at my house, but never Gabriel—I think my mother was scared of him. But before Jeremy and I established an intractable enmity with the Italian kids, they received birthday invites from my mother, as I did from theirs.

I was not an unhappy boy, but that first encounter with Mr. Peterson made an impression that never left me. It set the tone. Rules everywhere. Sitting on the patch of carpet at the front of the class while Mrs. Brown read about admirable feats of derring-do performed by South African heroes, I understood that I'd have to be brave to make it through school. I would have to be very brave indeed.

ELIZABETH SALT

"The woman who walked through raging Xhosas to fetch gunpowder."

The little village of Grahamstown was surrounded. The Xhosa witchdoctor Makanna, wearing a terrifying skirt of monkey tails, had assembled ten thousand warriors to drive the settlers into the sea. Their black bodies glistened with sweat and the *muti* they wore to turn bullets to water. While the initial Xhosa attack caught the intrepid villagers off guard, they hastily formed a defensive line and started firing away at the savages. Soon the ground was thick with black bodies, but waves more kept descending on the town. Sergeant Salt noticed that his squad was getting low on gunpowder. "What shall become of us?" he wondered aloud. His daughter, Elizabeth, who was nearby loading muskets, did not hesitate. Knowing that the gunpowder stores were housed across town, she strode through the throng of Xhosa warriors. They froze, dumbstruck by the vision of this stately, porcelain beauty. Elizabeth returned with a barrel of gunpowder. Replenished, the settlers redoubled their efforts, decimating the Xhosa ranks. Never again was such a sizeable Xhosa army assembled—all thanks to Elizabeth Salt's selfless act of bravery.

Floreat quisque—Let each flourish—rang the Ridgeview School motto. Flourish we did. Mrs. Brown ran her Grade One classroom like a military training camp during mobilization for an apocalyptic war. We sat at our double desk in pairs—boy/girl, boy/girl—pencil cases neatly laid out, canvas sacks draped over our chairs holding reading books, crayons, Pritt Sticks, medical kits, and flak jackets. We were taught to greet in unison: "Good. Morn. Ning. Miss. Izz. Brow. Winn." We stood up in unison. We sat down in unison. We lined up in single file—boy row, girl row, shortest to tallest. When a teacher entered the classroom, we stood and greeted in unison, then sat down again as one well-oiled, finely tuned machine.

The full-grown white South African female can affect a manner of speaking that turns words into whirling blades of sharpened steel, like shrapnel from an exploded smart bomb. Either you obey or you're torn to shreds. Mrs. Brown was a master of this dark art. "I'm talking," she'd bark if someone was dumb enough to speak out of turn. She did not explain her decisions. "May I go to the bathroom, Mrs. Brown?" was met with a simple yes or no, the reasoning for which she assumed you'd be intelligent enough to figure out for yourself. If little bums were getting restless in little seats, she'd fire off a "Quiet!" that was uranium-tipped in its devastating efficiency.

Mrs. Brown defined our early years at Ridgeview Primary—and that's because she was a redoubtable disciplinarian and an uncompromising educator. Ours was, according to the Powers-That-Were, a Christo-centric education system. George Orwell said that "all tyranny begins with the abuse of language." He hadn't met any Apartheid-era bureaucrats. They didn't bother with waffle or doublespeak—"Christo-centric" is as it sounds. This did not refer simply to prayer (which we had every morning before class). Rather, it was a systemic ethos. Calvinism was intricately woven into not only what we learnt but how we learnt it. It was the very fabric of the system: The reward of good work on earth was an indication of God's pleasure, and a sign of things to come in heaven. Smart children were intrinsically good; dumb children were intrinsically bad.

We learned, we learned quickly, and we learned well. We scrawled our names into our notebooks, saw Dick and Jane run, added one and one to make two, learned how ice became water, water became gas, and gas became water. All the while, Mrs. Brown added colour and nuance to the spare outlines of Mr. Peterson's first concise lesson. She was superb at engineering scenarios in which we would be fooled into misbehaving and then punishing us for our indiscretions. One such trick was leaving us under the charge of her quisling, a quiet boy named Harold whose facial features sloped far enough to the left that he looked like a slightly melted wax model. We weren't about to listen to Harold, and Mrs. Brown knew that.

"Did I not ask you to be quiet while I was out of the room? Did I not?" she'd ask on her return, her scowl deepening.

"Yes. Miss. Izz. Brow. Winn."

It was raining hard that day, and the school was shrouded in gloom, water running from the upper balcony in constant rivulets. She lined the boys up (we were to sacrifice ourselves corporally for the girls), grabbed a thick plastic ruler, and worked her way down the ranks, slapping our now wet legs one by one. In the curious acoustics of the school, the crack of plastic meeting skin sounded like the report of mortar fire. I remember waiting my turn with terrible anticipation. I looked over at Harold, who was an Example, and wished him dead. Finally, it was my turn. My leg shivered mightily, and the *crack!*, when it finally came, brought the sting of tears to my eyes. We boys looked at our polished black Clarks and pretended our faces were wet from the rain.

Despite the hard love, as we made our way through the alphabet, or followed Mrs. Brown's pointer to the charts dotting the classroom ("c-a-t spells 'cat'; d-o-g spells 'dog'"), we somehow absorbed the belief that we were the chosen ones. Precious. The black people in the texts we read were savages—or they didn't exist at all. There was no mention of any way other than the European way of doing things (in our texts, whites were referred to as Europeans). If we lived in Africa, you could have fooled me—even our world maps placed Europe front and centre. It was clear, though, that we lived in the perfect *manifestation* of Europe, rather than in Europe itself. We lived in an *ideal*. And we had our prescribed roles in this utopia. We were the scions of the ruling class, and we would be trained as such. But it felt strange to live somewhere that wasn't really anywhere—cut off from our people by a big chunk of nothingness. I'm not the first to point out that *utopia* means "no place"—and when Mrs. Brown pointed to the map, her rod drifting over Rhodesia and Zaire and Morocco and landing on Europe, that's exactly what she was saying. We were adrift. We were no place.

This no-place, I realized early on, had rules, rules linked inextricably with a school system that seemed as labyrinthine as a termite city that extends miles below the ground. And nothing embodied this more than The Eye.

Every time the ancient intercom system crackled to life, I'd sit straight in my desk and wish frantically that I was elsewhere. It was never, ever, good news. The Eye, my name for the intercom speakers installed front and centre in each classroom, looked like the orb of a massive fly—and I firmly believed that those in the administration office (and perhaps beyond) could see us—see right into the darkest nooks of our subconscious. "*Boet,* they can *see* us from that thing," I'd tell Jeremy.

The Eye had its subalterns—and no group of individuals represented the essence of The Eye better than the Inspectors. They visited us on the semi-annual Inspection Day: men and women fashioned from the same formless gloop as the politicians I saw on TV, sent by the Transvaal Education Department to lean over the teachers' shoulders and make sure they were educating according to the system. We knew when the Inspectors were due because props suddenly appeared—stuffed toys, new charts, and fancy coloured handouts. Also, it took about a week to prepare for the inspection, and the teachers were understandably more worked up than usual. "The Inspectors will be here tomorrow, so we will be on our best behaviour," Mrs. Brown would say. Even the most hard-core miscreants came to school spit-shined and silent on inspection day.

"Okay, children! If three of these monkey toys leave for Boksburg four minutes before these nine rabbit dolls..." Hands were expected to be held straight when in the air, the answers precise. But the Inspectors, who sat at the front of the classroom writing notes in their notebooks, were there not just to see that we were learning but to remind educators that the walls did indeed have eyes. Teachers were docked points for failing to adhere strictly to the syllabus, but they also could be penalized if kids were not using regulation-length pencils. From the sublime to the ridiculous and back again, the Inspectors leafed through our textbooks, sniffed under desks, checked for regulation panty colour, and nibbled at urinal mints, making sure that everything was just so, and that we were developing into upstanding members of the volk, just like the fearless Elizabeth Salt.

DIRKIE UYS

"The boy who would not leave his father to die alone."

"Can I come? Can I please?" begged fourteen-year-old Dirkie Uys. His father, the great Boer soldier Piet Uys, was assembling a commando unit to punish the treacherous Dingaan and his Zulu warriors for the murder of Piet Retief. Uys the Older was reluctant at first, but eventually he gave in. "Oh well, come along then," he said. "But be sure to be careful!" The party soon gave chase to a gaggle of impis. But the commandos ran into trouble. "Ambush!" cried Piet Uys. The fighting was fierce—hundreds upon hundreds of Zulus fell on the Boers. As the commandos fled the Zulu assault, Mr. Uys was hit square in the back with an assegai. He yanked at the dreaded weapon and a fountain of blood poured from his wound. "Ride for your life, Dirkie," urged Mr. Uys. But Dirkie would not. "I'd rather die here with you, Pa, than flee!" Just as those words passed from his lips, the Zulus rounded on the injured Boers. Dirkie Uys perished alongside his father, choosing certain death over his own safety. We commemorate his incredible bravery on the eleventh of April, and have done so since 1838.

Little boys adapt, and I was no different. The first thing to learn as a schoolboy was how to talk like a schoolboy. In this, I had an advantage: my older cousin Lewis.

I saw Lewis every weekend, but because he was a year and a half older than me, and a year and a half bigger, he used a mixture of violence and mental abuse to enforce his status. He acted as a hormonal weather forecast—whatever he was going through, I could expect to go through shortly. Once, he spent a Sunday afternoon insisting that I tie his shoelaces. He was wearing loafers.

Because of his age, Lewis had access that I didn't to slang—slang imperative for navigating the maze of schoolboy power games.

"What does *graunch* mean?" I could ask Lewis over the phone.

"That's when you put your tongue in a chick's mouth, and she puts her tongue in your mouth," he'd say.

"*Jassis!* Who does *that*?"

I made him promise that he'd supply me with the latest slang from the upper grades, and he was pretty good about doing so. Young South African males from Johannesburg spoke in a patois that was all but incomprehensible to anyone other than local schoolboys. Thanks to his two older brothers, Jeremy possessed slang that was highly advanced. A conversation between us might have sounded something like this:

"*Huzzit,* china."

"*Lekker boetie. Huzzit* with you?

"No, man, *lekker. Jassis,* hey, math homework was a *lank graft* last night."

"*Ja, boet.* But *The Golden Girls* was a *lag*!"

As with the arcade games I played at the Lido Café, school became more dangerous the further one advanced. I quickly realized that if I wanted to stay on the good side of the Italian posse, I had to act bigger than I was. "*Huzzit,* chinas," I'd say as I sauntered past them on the way to play marbles at break, Gabriel's heavy-lidded eyes following me. Jeremy was not so conciliatory toward the gang. Maybe this was because he had the advantage of being a good foot or so taller than me and had his brothers to tutor him in the art of schoolyard fisticuffs. My mentor—Lewis—was a lover, not a fighter.

Every break, after eating our lunch (a peanut-butter-and-jam sandwich in Tupperware is my Proustian madeleine—the smell is enough to transport me back through that pinhole in time to Ridgeview Primary), Jeremy and I stuffed our pockets with marbles and gathered on a dusty patch in front of the playing fields for a game of *marlies.* Our enmity with the Italian boys solidified here: Competition for the big, clear marbles with the colourful swirls inside was intense and tempers often flared.

"China," Marco would say, "don't *choon* me that you hit that *marlie*!"

"*Boet*—I hit it fair and square!"

"*Jassis, boet,*" Jeremy would say to me later. "One day, those *okes* are gonna get it."

"*Ja,* china. You telling me," I'd say with false bravado. I didn't see how hammering my head against their fists would constitute their getting it, but Jeremy seemed resolute. He was eight months older than me, and the attendant extra wisdom accounted for something. I hoped he knew what he was doing.

After school, I was with my mother, off to judo or art class. When these activities were over, it was glorious freedom. Leigh and I would busy ourselves in our gardens or in the pool, enacting complicated, long-running adventure narratives based heavily on American cultural exports. Or Jeremy and I would hop about in the sprawling rock garden at the back of his house, leaping from boulder to boulder while he tried to figure out how he could make his first million by the time he was eleven. On Sunday afternoons, after the *braai,* Lewis, his sister, Janine, Carolyn, and I assembled ourselves at our pool (with Chomps safely locked away) for a sporting activity we called the Olym-Pops. This was a derivation of the Olympics, with a variety of swimming styles and race distances. There were sleepovers and birthday parties and skateboard challenges down the hill toward Patterson Park and ten-speed races along Forbes Street—all under the bright, benevolent Johannesburg sun, which rarely burned too hot or too cold. The great Johannesburg clouds looked down on us like centurions as we frolicked. In this walled, forbidden city—where the rabble could not roam—we lived a life of adventure, of pleasure, and of innocence. We grew up slowly. After school, we middle-class white South African children enjoyed the best childhood that has ever existed in the history of humankind, bar none. It was bliss.

So when Sunday came around—and especially Sunday evening—I was hit with what Mom called the blues. There was nothing else like the feel of a Sunday in Apartheid-era South

Africa. Everything—and I mean everything—was shut: One didn't so much as dare have a heart attack on the Lord's Day. The feel about the city was less religious than funereal. Those huge clouds hanging in the afternoon sky became brooding and melancholy, their punctual afternoon deluges signalling the end of freedom and the packing of the school satchel for the next day's classes. My first taste of depression was on those Sunday afternoons, when the sun seemed like a heat lamp, keeping a stale buffet warm.

If I had any inkling of how to make a sandwich, or any notion of how to look after myself, I would have packed a bag and fled for the hills.

RAGEL DE BEER

"The little girl who froze to death to keep her brother alive."

Frikkie was missing! The De Beer's favourite calf—more of a pet, really—was lost in the snow. "Pa," said Ragel, a very pretty and well-behaved young girl, "we must try to find him!" Her younger brother, Jamie, nodded in vigorous agreement. Anton De Beer reluctantly agreed. "All right, but that storm is fierce. Let's be quick about it." The De Beers headed into the vicious Drakensberg blizzard. The wind whipped away their cries, and soon Mr. De Beer had lost contact with his children. Frantic, he searched the snow for them. The night turned to day, and he and his neighbours gathered to intensify the search. What they found elicited a great heartrending cry from their lips. In a hollowed cave of snow lay an unconscious Jamie, wrapped in all his sister's clothing. Next to him lay the blue, frozen corpse of Ragel, wearing only her shoes. "She said God would keep her warm, so she gave me her clothes," explained Jamie. "Indeed," said a stricken Mrs. De Beer, "she is warm with God now."

If there were a dossier on me in the staff room, it would probably have read: Restless. Loud. Enjoys attention. Regard of own intelligence not in step with actual abilities. Occasional problem with authority. Always hungry. Small bladder.

The years wore on; I still couldn't bear school. I hated opening the textbooks, with their lifeless illustrations and faded photographs. I loathed my exercise books, wrapped neatly by my mother in regulation brown butcher paper and then carefully again in plastic. I rebelled in small ways: I chewed the contents of my pencil case ("Poplak, if I see you eating your pen again, I'll have your teeth removed!"), I let my socks fall below my knees, I chewed my tie, I kept my hair dishevelled, and I spoke out of turn.

Our world was stratified and competitive. If you were a dunce, you wore a dunce cap. If your homework was garbage, you stood in the garbage can. Stupid was as stupid did, and it was called as such. "You're an idiot. Go stare at the wall and think about that for the rest of the class." (How ruminating on your own stupidity leads to intelligence I will never know.) Tests were handed out in order of score—from highest to lowest. End-of-term grades were read out in class, this time beginning with the lowest-rated student, eventually arriving at the highest—like a top-forty countdown. I always, without fail, came third. Nevertheless, my heart would thump each time the teacher read out the results. What if I had slipped up and come last for some reason? What if I had overnight become a *doos* and would have to stare at the wall, sitting in a garbage can, wearing a dunce cap? Coming third was central to my self-identity. If I came third without trying, I must be an unequivocal genius. Coming tenth would not do. Besides, my grandmother and mother could live with my coming third. Any lower and life at home would change for me.

Not all the teachers at Ridgeview Primary adhered slavishly to the system, but those who did believed in it utterly. There was, for example, my Standards Four and Five Afrikaans teacher, *Mevrou* Du Toit. What impressed me most about her was the stout right forefinger she wagged, or pointed, or tapped against the blackboard to bring our attention to something. It was immaculately tipped with red nail polish, suggesting fresh arterial blood. The finger was attached to a large arm further joined to a body, heavy of bosom and topped with a head surrounded by chin. There was a rhinoceros-like truculence to her bulk that was an exact manifestation of her mind. She was corporally and psychically unmoveable.

I wish I could disassociate the language of Afrikaans from *Mevrou* Du Toit, but I can't. To me, Afrikaans seemed to be a culture inculcated under threat of extreme violence. The gum jar, for instance. If she caught you chewing gum in her class, the piece in your mouth went into the gum jar, and a piece from the jar went into your mouth.[24] (*Mevrou* Van Vrede, another Afrikaans teacher, took a more conservative approach—the gum ended up on the downy fluff at the back of your neck.)

---

24. Here's my thing with the gum jar: There should, by dint of mathematical logic, have been only one piece of gum in the gum jar at any given time. But this was not the case: There were, in fact, far more. So, at some point, *Mevrou* Du Toit must have got someone (or ones) to *chew gum specifically for the gum jar.* That, I'm sorry, is just sick.

"I have given you," said *Mevrou* Du Toit a couple of weeks after I broke my arm in a typical act of boyhood stupidity, "more than enough leeway. I can't look at work this messy. Must we cry for you for how long? Get someone else to write it for you, or fail this class."

By contrast there was Mrs. Toberman, my Standard One teacher, who also did duty as the extracurricular drama teacher and as the cheder teacher. There was the school librarian, Mrs. Rademayer, who encouraged us to read anything and everything we could get our hands on—"Nothing written on paper is bad if you're willing to think about it," she'd say. There was my mathematics teacher, Mr. Billups, ex-hippy and cynic supreme, who sneered every time he mentioned the government. These people were more in line with my mother, who was a hardliner over nothing except TV watching and nutrition. These people were the cracks in the system.

If the frustration I felt at school coalesced in any one person, it was in my Standards Two and Three history teacher, plump, sandy-haired Mrs. Kramer. Meek and soft-spoken, she had trouble disciplining the class. Her credulity strained the patience of even a mildly intelligent ten-year-old. In fairness to her, history was a minefield for South African educators. It had been rewritten in a way that soft-pedalled the brutalities, made credible characters out of heroes (white) and villains (black), and steered well clear of anything post–Boer War. We did not learn to list our prime ministers, in chronological order, as a Canadian or an American student would. Recent history (the establishment of Apartheid, for instance) was nowhere present in our texts. Rather, our gaze went far back, to a sepia version of the olden days. From Jan van Riebeeck's triumphant landing at Table Bay, to the pernicious influence of the British, to the

Great Trek (the central event of primary school historical education), to the current state of political perfection, our textbook compilers had devised a timeline that began with the building of the pyramids and ended with the landing of Van Riebeeck: the beginnings of civilization to its apparent peak. Sure, we learned about the bongo-beating, chest-thumping savages, occasionally noble in their own way, but we also learned that they were destined to be churned under the wagon wheels of the great civilizing push forward. What was their place in things now? That's hard to answer when "now" didn't exist.

We learned about the incidents and values that built our society, but we did not learn what sort of society those values and incidents had built.

"Mrs. Kramer?"

"What is it, Richard?"

"I don't understand why…"

"*Ja,* but there's nothing to understand, Richard. Learn the dates of when Piet Retief met Dingaan; that's what you'll be tested on."

Mrs. Kramer had a point. I couldn't take understanding home to my parents. I could take only a report card. But little boys see weakness clearly, and I saw it in Mrs. Kramer. Her bemusement whenever we asked a question, her wide-eyed stumbling through the curriculum, seemed like the warm-up for a slapstick floor show. To run a regime like the one we lived under you need everyone in a position of authority to commit. The doubters and the cynics are easy to locate and eliminate, but it's the credulous fools who make Swiss cheese out of the most elaborate fictions.

We questioned. We did. In the same way a North American student will wonder why the hell he's learning calculus when his

$4000 Mac laptop is perfectly capable of doing a sine/cosine calculation by itself, we wondered why we were learning about girls who were dumb enough to give up their clothes during a snowstorm (what snow, where?), all on account of a lost calf named—of all things—Frikkie. The veracity of these stories—these fairy tales, more like—is highly dubious. No one has ever confirmed Ragel's act of sacrificial idiocy, and the Dirkie Uys story plays out a little differently in other (official) versions of the tale. So why did we sit on the carpet in the front of the classroom at storytime, listening to tales of heroic bravery that, if you shine the light on them a certain way, look like acts of wanton stupidity?

At first blush, the architects of Apartheid seemed at a loss when developing a curriculum for us English-speaking kids from English-speaking families. They outfitted us with the tools to think critically about everything we were learning, providing us with not only an education but also the social armour to survive, and indeed thrive, in a competitive universe. They allowed the odd liberal to float about on the fringes of the system, at the same time fortifying our education with the essential vitamins and nutrients of Afrikaner nationhood, even though they knew we were culturally distinct from it. It appears paradoxical and self-defeating—creating this über-class of potential enemies and dissenters.

It didn't (and doesn't) pay to underestimate those grey-suited inspectors and their superiors. They created the conditions in which we could thrive (entirely outside normal standards of competition, given that such a small minority of the population had access to the spoils). They created a stable of capitalist/Calvinists, necessarily depoliticized and accustomed to wealth and comfort, with an entirely justifiable—considering our level of education compared with that of the black population—sense of superiority Yup, they made us Master. *Baas.* And it was a long time before any of us—L'il Baas Reeshat included—took to questioning the status quo. They knew we could think critically, but they hoped we wouldn't. For the most part, white South Africans didn't. In the sixteen years I lived in South Africa, we never had a full-blown political discussion at home. I never had a full-blown political discussion at *anyone's* home. My uncle Percy, who had been a radical at the University of the Witwatersrand in his student days, didn't discuss his past. He was, like most white South Africans, cut off from the present. What the regime did early was kill our imagination. There were no other possibles. This was it.

And that's why nobody screamed bloody murder when our cheder class was ripped to shreds.

RICHARD SIMELANE

"The man who tunnelled a way to safety for himself and his trapped companions."

Quick as a flash, the mine tunnel collapsed around the miners. Once the thunder and the dust had settled, the men took stock of their situation. "The white boss!" the Bantu men cried. "He is gone! We will surely die!" The young Swazi boss-boy, Richard Simelane, clicked his tongue sharply. "There is enough oxygen down here for some hours. We have water in the furrows, along with lamps and tools. We will dig our way to safety." There were murmurs of dissent from the Bantu, but they reluctantly agreed. Digging with his bare hands, Richard would not give up. Bleeding and exhausted, he inspired the

Bantu with his determination. They finally broke through, and Richard went to find help—promising to return. In the tunnel, he came across a rescue party. Tired as he was, Richard returned with the rescuers for his friends—just as he had promised. He was awarded the Chamber of Mines bronze medal for his acts of bravery.

Every time The Eye crackled to life, bad things happened. For instance, after it ordered us to "Make your way to B block immediately," we would—on a bad day—be met by a terse, barked, "Take off your pants." My heart would constrict, my forehead would turn icy cold.

Not *this* again.

Because of our elevated status as deities-in-training, white South African schoolchildren were subject to constant examination. One ritual was particularly unendurable. I knew it was coming whenever the pallid, cataract-ridden relic of the Hippocratic arts, carrying an instrument bag lifted from a triage tent *circa* the Crimean War (he still, I'm sure, regularly prescribed bleeding), entered the room. My genitalia turtled their way through my abdomen, nestling somewhere around my lungs. I looked over at Jeremy in terror, and he'd look at his shoes. Ol' Saw Bones would make his way down the line, laying his ice-cold stethoscope against our chests while cupping our scrotums in his wrinkled hands.

"Give me a big cough," he'd say, looking into the middle distance.

"Merph."

"Bigger, please."

"Galorph!"

"Thank you."

What, I ask you, is the connection between the respiratory system and the testicles? These checkups were buttressed by sixteen-millimetre films about disease, germs, amoebas—with the distinct message that cleanliness was next to godliness. Which is all well and fine, but how do you scrub the cells inside your body as well as the skin outside? Those films, with the droning voice-over and scratchy images, had a way of separating you from your body. It was a war. Keep the vessel clean, or else.

The vessel also, we were reminded, was not to be used for rampant enjoyment, especially not venereal. Other films, presumably made by the same joyless filmmakers, described to us the ovaries, the testes, and the manner in which babies grew in a mother's stomach. They did not tell us how those babies got there in the first place.

I did have a girlfriend in my final year at Ridgeview. We hooked up at a spin-the-bottle party—the kind where you slow dance to the soundtrack from *An Officer and a Gentleman* and *graunch* in the closet. I was in love with Anna Bella, but she was saving herself for Tom Cruise, so instead, Vanessa and I united. Here's a typical phone conversation between us:

"Hello, *huzzit*?"

"*Huzzit.* No, good. And you?"

"*Lekker.*"

"No, *lekker.*"

Long pause.

"*Huzzit.*"

"No, *lekker*. How you?"

"*Ja,* no. Good."

Although we lads stuck our tongues into girls' mouths at birthday parties and discussed the relative merits of the incoming bulges beneath checked dresses, we were curiously stunted in sexual maturity. Those "health" inspections and the attendant movies helped skew our normal adolescent sexual growth.[25] As well, growing up under the skirts of so many matriarchs (mothers, teachers, maids, grandmothers, aunts) had rendered us South African boys terrified of female sexuality, if we even knew what female sexuality was, that is.

My involvement with Vanessa put me in with the Italian crew, and this soon became complicated. I didn't blame her for the cheder incident. Indeed, I think we still dated—if you could call it that—for some months after. It had nothing to do with her, I was sure.

According to the official line, it had nothing to do with anyone. It just happened—an occurrence unrelated to any causal relationship in the known universe. On the morning of the incident, as we stood waiting for our teacher, Mrs. Toberman, under a bright winter sky, I had a feeling in the pit of my stomach that something was wrong, that things were about to change.

I heard Mrs. Toberman gasp, then saw what would be called, if it were a reality-TV show, *Classroom Makeover: Neo-Nazi Edition.* Swastikas were painted everywhere. These were not the most artful of renderings of the Nazi emblem—most were ungainly red shapes but they were big and garish and did the job. And just in case they didn't, the scrawled "Fuck Jews" got the point across. Prayer books lay in tatters across the floor. I looked at Jeremy, who sputtered in impotent rage. No one said a word. Mrs. Toberman closed the door and started weeping.

---

25. As if there is such a thing as normal adolescent sexual growth, but what I mean is that a firm notion was inculcated in us that boys and girls were very, very different, and we should be scared of one another. South African kids in the 1980s did not lose their virginity at thirteen. On their wedding night, more likely.

The enmity with the Italian boys had spiralled out of control, and even my sister, who had come to Ridgeview three years after I started there, was harassed mercilessly for being Jewish. (This began after a row between Carolyn and her fellow classmates over a chocolate-banana sandwich.) Mom, understanding that pressing the issue would lead to only more harassment, pulled Carolyn from the school, but in many respects, this is how things were in South Africa. We expected it. It was normal. I don't think the incident was even much a point of discussion at home.

"*Jassis,* they fucking hate us, *boetie,*" said Jeremy. It ate at a guy like Jeremy, whereas I could absorb it into my daily experience, mostly because it didn't feel out of place. After all, wasn't this normal? Jews hated Italians, who hated Afrikaners, who hated blacks, who hated whites, who hated Jews, who hated blacks—that's how things worked, wasn't it?

Neither Jeremy nor I, nor anyone else, could prove who defaced our cheder class that day. But Jeremy never let it rest with the Italian boys. The final straw was our fetching classmate Susan Gilbert. When she became embroiled in a love (read "hand-holding") triangle with Jeremy and a member of the Italian contingent, it was on.

Jeremy and the Italian faced off in the dusty marble-playing area, encircled by a group of yelling boys—twelve-year-olds locked in some typical act of South African sectarian violence. The fight came down to coaching, and Jeremy's brothers had taught him well. He went in at a slight angle so that his opponent's blows fell harmlessly on his back. Then he turned and clobbered the Italian in the face, felling him to the ground. Better Jeremy than me, though. I could never have gone through with something like that. All the tales of bravery we'd been force-fed over the years had done little to bolster my fortitude. I was no Dirkie Uys; if Dr. Poplak was jumped by a bunch of blood-lusting impis, he was on his own. I would not fetch gunpowder, and I would not dig my pals out of a tunnel with my bare fingers. I hadn't seen much bravery on the part of others, either. And even when I did—well—the cheder incident wasn't resolved by Jeremy's courageous pummelling of our Italian classmate.

That's the funny thing about the South African education system. It created true-blue believers or full-blown skeptics (who did nothing with their skepticism)—but very few in between. No, if they were to write a story about me, here's how I wanted it to end:

And to this day, they have never forgotten his incredible act of cowardice. And he lived happily ever after.

The Whistler

Mr. Billups, my Standard Five math teacher, appears to have lost the plot. "Wipe," he yells at me, his thick moustache clotted with spittle, "that supercilious look off your face." I'd love to comply, but I have at hand neither a mirror nor a dictionary. My face freezes. Billups turns from bright red to fuchsia. "Right! You won't wipe it off?" he spits. "I'll have it wiped off for you." He leaps from his desk and in one bound has me by the scruff of my safari suit. The class is silent, as it usually is when a teacher has a breakdown and does something he'll probably regret when he sobers up the next morning.

"I cannot take you anymore!" Billups says, his chest heaving. He leads me down the open-air corridor along the second-floor balcony, where a vista of Johannesburg's northern suburbs spreads out before me. I seriously consider making a jump for it. We make our way down a dark, cool stairwell, where pigeons coo and spiderwebs hang in the high corners. Then, straight toward the bowels of the school: the headmaster's office. It dawns on me that this could end very badly.

"You know what he'll do to me, right?" I ask, my voice trembling like a septuagenarian torch singer after several whisky sours.

"Poplak," says Billups with a weariness and disappointment that deflate his wide chest and shoulders, "I just don't bloody care anymore."

With his big mitt, he heaves me into the administration office and pushes me toward a door whose sign reads: "Mr. Edward H.I. MacMillan, Headmaster." Billups knocks twice. I've been a student at Ridgeview Primary for seven years, and I'm so close to getting out of here I can taste it—a thirteen-year-old version of a 'Nam vet about to be riddled with enemy fire on the last day of his last tour.

From within the office I hear a high-pitched, cheerful whistle. Something bouncy—*Boston Pops Does Huey Lewis and the News.* Footsteps. Then the door swings open. A face, a big pink pudding with two raisins for eyes, looks down at me. The pudding's whistled ditty rises an octave. He's been waiting for this.

"Mr. Poplak," says The Whistler, a huge grin cleaving his pink visage, "what a lovely surprise. Do come inside."

I remember being in Mrs. Brown's class, a six-year-old in a safari suit, looking with trepidation down and across to the north block of the school. That's where the big kids went to class. If I listened carefully, I could hear the low murmurs of Afrikaans, the scrape of their chairs, the occasional barked instruction from a teacher. Often, I'd hear something else, something far more ominous.

The sound would rise up slowly, and from no particular direction—the echoes of a ghost-ship whistle rising and falling from across the way. It was both cheerful and lugubrious—a bagpipe dirge played by a clown. Every time I heard it, the hairs on the back of my neck stood on end. Now and again, if I was sharp enough, I'd catch sight of a large man in a brilliant white coat that fluttered around him like the wings of a dread angel.

I developed a theory. My mother, although she refused to read my *Batman* comics to me as bedtime stories, did occasionally as a treat explain the words inside the bubbles. I knew of Batman's nemesis, The Joker, and I suspected that whoever was doing that whistling was cut from the same malevolent cloth.

I dubbed him The Whistler.

I didn't know it at the time, but he was to become a significant part my life, and a hallmark of my younger years. I found this out shortly after receiving some very good news.

"Children," said my Grade Two teacher, Mrs. Erasmus. "Mr. Peterson is no longer with us. We have a new headmaster now." The dusty old crow had flown the coop, eh? I'd never forgiven him for that first caning, and I wished him the worst in his new endeavours. "*Ja,* that *oke* can flip right off," I'd whispered to Jeremy on more than one occasion.

"Let's all rise and say hello to our new headmaster, Mr. MacMillan," said Mrs. Erasmus.

It took me a few seconds to put two and two together. I heard the whistle approach and caught a flash of white through the window just before the door opened. My heart did something funny in my chest. The whistle stopped outside the classroom, the door swung open, and we broke into a salutary chorus of "Good. Morn. Ing. Mr. Mac. Mil. Lan!"

He'd sauntered in, grinning. "Excellent." (His voice had a way of lilting merrily at the end of a word such as *excellent.* If he had kept going with the lilt on its sonic trajectory, the word would have ended in an insane-asylum scream: "Excel-eeeeeee*eeahhhhnt*!") "Do be so kind as to be seated," he said. We sat warily, as if our chairs were now in league with our new principal, able to direct pain to our backsides at his orders. MacMillan took a seat in the teacher's chair, leaned back, and observed. Wisps of hair blew over the plains of his enormous pate; his fingers were the size of bratwursts, his limbs the mass and pallor of hocks hacked from a hog. But it was the little eyes set into that big pink pudding face that did it. Have you ever looked a chicken in the eye? There is nothing there, just a deadened singleness of mind: Must. Peck. For. Grain. Must. Peck. For. Grain. This, combined with his grin, gave MacMillan a look that reminded me precisely of The Joker, right before he throws Bats in a shark tank or tries to bury him alive.

MacMillan's black eyes scanned the classroom, reading us one by one. This man had a preternatural understanding of children. Once he had slotted us into a narrow range of personality types (wallflower, smartass, genius, moron), that's where we stayed for the duration of our time at Ridgeview Primary. He knew each and every one of us by name and reputation, which was not that much of a challenge since he kept the school small—enrolment was limited to 180 children. He conferred with the teachers in the staff room, built mental dossiers on each of us, and went slowly (but painfully) about the business of correcting what he saw as our flaws.

He referred to me as "Mr. Poplak," according me a respect he did not believe I was due. Did he size me up that first day? Did he see from the way I squirmed in my seat that I had the restlessness of all reasonably bright children? That I liked attention and was noisy? Regardless, it didn't take him long to make that assessment, and I was immediately slotted into the smartass category. He'd seen the likes of me before, and he'd see the likes of me again. He had six long years to work with me, and he'd make good use of every one of them.

"Oh, we'll get you right, Mr. Poplak," he'd say. "Don't you worry. We'll get you right."

The Whistler's omnipresent, sinister melodies became the soundtrack of my life at Ridgeview. As I moved up through the grades, I understood that he was both everywhere and nowhere. I would hear that whistle behind me, turn around quickly, but there would be nothing there except the play of the breeze. Or I'd hear it far off in the distance, and my lunch would lurch in my stomach as the fluttering white lab coat bore The Whistler rapidly toward me.

I think we started our enmity, The Whistler and I, in my third year of primary school. It's almost impossible to articulate how much I loathed school—I still woke up every morning with that lump in my stomach—but Ridgeview Primary had become more navigable over the years. I soon learned that if you wanted to make those glorious creatures—your female desk partners—light up with a giggle, you needed a store of antics, and those antics were often met with official censure. "Richard, if I hear another word from you, it's off to the office," my Standard One homeroom teacher would threaten. There was, sadly, no other way to get the attention of blond, fine-boned Sancia. It was a trade-off.

There was a process to keeping children in line. Teachers were not allowed to cane the children themselves. Many were squeamish about corporal punishment, so they ignored in the name of discipline any moral conflict they may have harboured by unceremoniously booting us from class. What happened to us "out there" was not their responsibility. What they didn't see, they didn't know.

"Out there" was a death trap. A lone child in those empty halls during classtime was about as safe as an Afrikaner showing up at an ANC Youth League rally wearing a "Robben Island Rocks" T-shirt. I remember sitting outside class on the cold tiles and waiting. And waiting. Time moved in agonizingly slow increments. Birds chirped, traffic lapped at the distant shores of the neighbourhood streets, the glorious Highveld cumulus massed in legions, turning progressively greyer in preparation for that afternoon's thundershower. And then I'd hear it. At first I'd think my ears were playing tricks. My heart would start thumping, an arrhythmic *ga-ga-thlunk, ga-GA … thlunk.* The sound was by now unmistakable.

Seconds (hours? eons?) later, an efflorescence of light cuts through the gloom at the balcony's far end. He emerges, the sunshine reflecting off the impossible purity of his lab coat, a terrible power moving in slow motion toward me, preceded by his aria. He doesn't even look down as he passes. He stops whistling mid-bar. "Be so kind," he says, "as to visit me in my office, Mr. Poplak."

Would absolutely love to. You brew the Darjeeling; I'll bring the shortcake.

There were several portraits of MacMillan dotted around the school, including one pastel creation in the staff room and one hanging beside the portrait of P.W. Botha in his office. Something about those portraits bothered me. It takes an immense self-regard to hang a portrait of yourself at the office, especially when you're the principal of a school in a Johannesburg suburb. That meant MacMillan's notion of himself was outside all reasonable proportion, and more ominously, that he was building a small but well-articulated cult of personality—a way of asserting authority not only over his students but over his employees as well.

Yet, the portrait was not the creepiest thing hanging in MacMillan's office. Not by half. Nor were the framed quotes from the Bible. Predictably, one was Proverbs 13:24: "He who spareth the rod hateth his son; but he that loveth him chasteneth him betimes." (He whom battereth my bum, may he burneth in deepest hell, I'd think to myself as I gazed at the framed aphorism.)

No, the most sinister thing was mounted on the back of the closet door. Here, his canes hung—about eight of them—arranged in descending order of thickness. This is akin to a great hunter displaying his guns, but instead of the accompanying stuffed stag, buffalo, or leopard heads, Mr. MacMillan would have had to mount[26] the ass cheeks of preteen boys as his trophies.

There was, according to schoolyard scuttlebutt, a policy that governed caning. Paperwork had to be filed after a buttock was marked with the angry tiger stripes from the stern disciplinarian. According to official corporal punishment procedure, after the deed was administered, it had to be logged in a book for the Inspectors' perusal (presumably, the principal got docked points if he wasn't caning *enough*). The flagellator was not allowed to lift his or her elbow higher than the shoulder, which had to be kept at a thirty-seven-degree acute angle to the longitude of the buttocks, and the cane had to have a tensile flex of about four pounds per inch squared, and so on. There were legions of such theories. They amounted to approximately zero once you were in that office. Once you were in that office, you were in his world, and all bets were off.

"Huzzit," we'd say to each other in the hushed tones of death row as we awaited our fate outside the oak office door. From within, whistling. A phone would ring. He'd answer it. More whistling.

---

26. C'mon, you know what I mean.

"No, *huzzit.*" We'd look at our shoes.

"*Ja.* What you here for, *boet*?"

"*Ag,* I snapped Lisa Reading's training bra. *Boet,* why's she wearing a bra in the first *blerry* place?"

After an interminable wait, the door would swing open. "Come in, gentlemen," Mr. MacMillan would say with mock politeness but genuine cheerfulness—as if we were about to commence the dispensation of a million-dollar bursary among ourselves. He herded us into a line, from shortest to tallest, and began the pre-game show.

"I presume you all know why you're here. I suppose I don't need to remind you that when you wear a Ridgeview Primary uniform, you are subject to the rules and regulations that I have laid out. You have broken those rules. That was unwise, and you will presently feel the consequences of doing so."

The younger among us, first-timers especially, typically started sniffling at this point.

"Spare the rod and spoil the child, eh? Have wiser words ever been spoken? Poplak? Enlighten us."

"Never, sir."

"Never, indeed."

And here's where The Whistler's dark genius—at least equal to that of The Joker—manifested itself. He'd open his cupboard with a flourish, beckoning the youngest among us to come forward and take his pick. The veterans crossed their fingers and exhorted their gods, while the tiny fellow pointed to the thinnest, most innocuous-looking cane he could see. "Interesting choice," The Whistler would say, his face almost entirely cleaved by a grin.

The grunt had made a tragic mistake.

There are major differences between types of canes. The natural inclination for a cane virgin is to pick the thinnest cane he sees. Yet, thin canes travel through the atmosphere at a greater velocity, concentrating their impact on a smaller surface area, than do thicker canes. They're closer to a whip than a cane, really. The effect is almost a tincture of pain—platonic pain, pain so pure that it is akin to clarity, to beauty. Thick canes don't exactly tickle, but they are nowhere near as painful.

MacMillan knew that the poor boy who had picked poorly, he who had caused us far more agony than necessary, would be roundly punished by us for his lack of experience when he left that office. The grunt had made enemies. And that was part of the grand plan.

"Gentlemen," The Whistler would say by way of closing, "let's hope never again to meet under these unpleasant circumstances."

The fact is, most of us in that office *would* meet again under these unpleasant circumstances, because no one who was jacked was ever jacked only once. A caning was the punishment for asserting our personality, for rearing against authority—a pathology some of us had, with the net result almost always a sore ass. But a thorough jacking did have a macho cachet—six of the best could raise your profile inestimably in the eyes of your peers. It could make you a legend. And those who remained uncaned—well, that was worth eternal citizenship in Pussyville, which was no place to live if you expected to go unwedgied in the South African public school system.

A central truth is at work here: Caning did not work. Humans don't remember pain. We can gauge when something is good for us or bad for us (for instance, we know not to put our hand on a hot stove element), but we can't actually recall the sensation of pain caused by something like a cane, which left—at least on any of the schoolboys I knew—no real physical or psychological consequences. But we can remember boredom. There's nothing I feared more than an afternoon disappearing under the interminable fog of a detention. And at home, there was one surefire threat (and my mother did not make idle threats) that instantly brought me in line: "If you don't behave, there'll be no television for a week." Beat me, by all means, but don't *break* me. Not that. Never that.

"Oh, Poplak?" MacMillan would say as I made for the door, rubbing my throbbing ass cheeks.

"Yes, sir?"

"Don't test my patience, boy. You'll find it as lacking in volume as your intelligence. And when it goes, so help me God, I don't hold myself responsible for my actions."

Who was there to hold MacMillan responsible for his actions? Try as I might, I can't think of anyone. In South African schools, headmasters had an enormous amount of autonomy. So long as they stuck to the syllabus and didn't battle too much with the Parent-Teacher association (these organizations were quite powerful, because a school relied on private money for the upgrade and maintenance of amenities such as swimming pools and cricket pitches), a headmaster's school was his to run.

Newspapers reported more egregious corporal abuses—and it was rumoured that MacMillan badly beat an Italian kid he'd had it in for—but part of the reason we were at school was for the discipline. As children in South Africa, we had no advanced understanding of our rights, and that's because we didn't have any. In short, there was nobody to hold Mr. MacMillan accountable for his actions because his actions were well within the bounds of accountability. Our parents knew he was a maniac, but, after all, the country was run by maniacs. As a society, we were inured to nutcases in positions of power.

Nowhere was this better epitomized than in MacMillan's science class. The science room was on the east side of the second floor of the second block—too remote for my liking. Inside were the tools of nineteenth-century scientific inquiry—Bunsen burners, beakers, dead things bobbing in jars of formaldehyde. God alone knows what had been embalmed, dissected, and bottled in that room. I just hoped it wouldn't—at some point—be me. The smell in that room summed up MacMillan—a combination of musty papers, butane, old wood varnish, chemical compounds, and death—a sense of age-old menace and an arcane yet incomprehensible reasoning. I had no clue how the combination of three things made one thing and why water evaporated yet also made ice. I could not fathom how the elements on the periodic table stood in relation to one another. This is where the dark, stern, and unbending rules of the physical universe merged with the dark, stern, and unbending rules of a big, cheerful Scottish arsehole. Our experiments were not experiments, given that we knew exactly how they'd turn out. We were proving rules.

"Mr. Poplak is bored, everyone. We're tiring him here—he has better and bigger things to think about. What is on your mind, Mr. Poplak?"

"Nothing, sir."

"'Nothing, sir' is exactly right, Mr. Poplak. 'Nothing, sir' is the correct answer. What makes up the compound CO_2, Mr. Poplak?"

"Calcium and a couple of oxygens, sir."

"You, Mr. Poplak, are an idiot."

The room whirred with projectiles—he'd throw chalk and blackboard dusters with remarkable accuracy. *Ding,* you'd hear, as a long piece of chalk bounced off your head.

Once or twice, though, I saw the cracks in his studiously maintained facade. When MacMillan became angry, he lost the loquacious banter and turned a furious shade of pink. The grin never faded, though—not once. Not until the last time, anyway. I suppose I should have known better, and perhaps I shouldn't have pushed so hard.

I never, ever should have had that supercilious look on my face.

Mr. Billups, my math teacher in Standards Four and Five, was as much a child of the 1960s as any white South African during the Apartheid-era could be. That placed him in a very small ideological pickle jar. His ideals mashed under the wheels of the regime, he was left with precious little—a constant sneer, jokes sans punchline, sarcasm wielded as if it were a heavy scabbard he could barely raise above his head. Oh, the brutal paradox that was the South African hippy. The Man had won. Resoundingly. Billups believed in no future because he was no longer capable of even imagining the future that lay in wait for the country a scant five years down the road. He had given up, idealism replaced by an impulse for violence that manifested itself in outbursts in his classroom. Perhaps decades of playing Crosby, Stills, Nash & Young on his guitar while simultaneously aiding in the physical abuse of young boys got the better of him. But he shouldn't have felt so bad.

In South Africa, the hypocrites were the good guys.

The roots of Mr. Billups's self-loathing are clear to me now. He was a teacher in a country that paid teachers nothing yet subjected them to a scrutiny far more invasive than that given to pilots, or police officers, or brain surgeons. He felt the boot of the regime on his neck, because he stood at the fulcrum of the machine: He was complicit in creating the minds of those whose fate it was to perpetuate a system he loathed.

Regardless of the risks, Billups sneered at the Powers-That-Were, hissed when he said "P.W. Botha," reminded us as often as he could that "there are people nowhere near as fortunate as you in this very country. And they're suffering. And we have to think about that." He was one of the key people who placed me inside the context of Apartheid—a context to which I had previously been blind. At the age of twelve, I understood, through Billups's acidic commentary and the tendrils of smoking rage that wafted from him, that this country destroyed everyone who lived in it. I largely understood this because Mr. Billups was a ruin of a man.

In his classroom, I started to understand the implications of Apartheid as only a child could—by analogy. If I hated that The Eye knew exactly what I was doing, and that because of people like The Whistler I was physically punished for doing things that didn't seem a matter of life and death (chewing gum in class, telling Jeremy that I wanted to see *Top Gun* that weekend), then how would I feel if someone told me that I couldn't live where I wanted? Or that I wasn't—God forbid!—allowed into a movie theatre to see *Top Gun,* no matter how badly I wanted to see it? I learned at Ridgeview Primary that I didn't like people telling me what to do. And that's how I came to have an early kernel of empathy with those who suffered under Apartheid. Perhaps it was true that blacks weren't as clever as whites and shouldn't do *everything* we did. After all, my schoolmates and I parroted the invective we heard at home and in the schoolyard—blacks were *kaffirs* and *shvartzes* and coons. But banned from the Ster-Kinekor cinema? No, that just wasn't right.

Despite the more enlightened aspects of Mr. Billups's character and the empathy it engendered, there was his temper to deal with. He was a big man, with a wide chest, a furiously unmanaged head of brown hair, and a thick moustache that made him seem unkempt, dangerous. He was still an authority figure, and I was still acting out my smartass role. "One day, Poplak," he used to say, "we're gonna have words."

And one of those words was *supercilious*.

I don't remember how the incident flared up, but I do know that I was twelve years old and consistently desperate to impress my classmates. Don't get me wrong: In a South African classroom my means were far more limited than they may have been elsewhere on the planet. Here, a comment whispered out the side of your mouth was insurrectional, as was surreptitiously chewing a piece of gum or passing notes.

Maybe I caught Billups on a bad day. Maybe he acquired a genuine dislike for me over the years. Maybe he saw in me a superbly articulated version of what he hated—a boy on the verge of understanding who didn't yet have the maturity, or perhaps the faculties, to truly understand (or to try to understand) the scope of the horrors around him. No clue. I do know that Billups *believed* in children, and he believed that we, as privileged white kids, had responsibilities. So we were bound to disappoint him year after year after year.

"Poplak," he said as he dragged me down those stairs, "you'll remember nothing else I've said or done, but you'll remember this." I felt so terribly betrayed. Billups and I were by no means pals, but I felt that he was trying to get through to me. But now he'd snapped.

"You know what he'll do to me, hey?" I said, panic welling up in me.

"I just don't bloody care anymore," said Billups. He sounded like a man completely defeated. I couldn't figure out how a look on my face could do so much damage. It must've been quite a look.

The Whistler and I. Alone in that office. His big, pink face looking down at me from the walls, alongside P.W. Botha and quotes from the Bible. "Ah, Mr. Poplak. I knew it would come to something like this. But it ends here, boy. I believe I'll make an impression today. I shall give you my best. I owe you that." He was enraged, and the grin, for once, was gone.

"Sir..." I started, but I knew there was nothing to say. I was nauseated with fear. This was what reckoning felt like. Because of a look, life slips out of control, and you step into hell.

He pushed me down roughly, so that I was bent over, staring at the carpet. I'd lost count of the times I'd been in this position. I sucked in my breath. "Here we go, Poplak. Here we go, my boy." One, two, three, four—four! Then five. Then six! Six of the best! Through the pain, I understood that this was legendary. The lashings hurt like hellfire, and you can be sure the official elbow-to-ass ratio was resoundingly contravened. My knees shook and tears ran freely from my eyes. My chest was so constricted that I could barely suck in air. I was genuinely scared that the beating would not stop there.

The Whistler grabbed me by my shirtfront. "How was that, Mr. Poplak? How did we enjoy *that*?" Then he launched into a tirade, spittle flecking my face in a light drizzle, the stench of his coffee breath wafting over me so that I smelled it for weeks afterward.

The hero status I would have earned from my six of the best was mitigated by the fact that I returned to class blubbering, barely able to sit my flaming arse on my chair. Billups didn't make eye contact with me. I don't believe he ever did again.

And after the pain and the humiliation died down, I was left with one burning question. What the *fuck,* I wondered, does *supercilious* mean?

Seven years. That's a long time when you're thirteen. I have no idea how many safari suits I went through, or how many pairs of black Clarks, or how many green canvas satchels. Jeremy and I shed no tears on leaving. "*Boet,* we're finally getting out of this *kuck*-hole," he said to me. That pretty much summed it up.

I can't recall if I felt any nostalgia or sadness on my final walk around the school. "Don't disappoint me," said Mrs. Brown, sniffling as she said goodbye. "I know you'll do well—you're going to be a doctor. I'm sure of it." When we hugged on that December day in 1986, I saw that Mrs. Brown was not actually a monster. She just played one for money.

It is now seventeen years later. When I walk through the eerily quiet Ridgeview Primary courtyard to research this book, I feel no nostalgia whatsoever. None. Just the feeling that I've fallen through a pinhole in time. Nothing has changed—not one alteration to the school property is obvious from this angle. Loeries flap in between the fronds of the massive palm that centres the school like an axis, just as they did when I was in Grade One. Believe it or not, I hear a "Good. Morn. Ing. Miss. Izz. Brown" emanating from the same classroom she's occupied for nigh on forty years. It is one of the strangest feelings I've ever encountered. It's like being a ghost in your own life.

Then it hits me.

Peer Gynt. That's it—*that's* what The Whistler whistled. Grieg's *Peer Gynt Suite.* Which, in turn, jars loose another memory: Fritz Lang's *M.*

Maybe it's because the sky is a thick slate grey, the precise colour of the sky when the red balloon (don't ask me how, since the film is black-and-white, but you just know it's red) gets stuck in the power lines in the famous montage sequence. *M*'s antagonist—a child murderer played with a surfeit of bottled creeptitude by Peter Lorre—has a sound signature, a leitmotif cueing his presence in a scene. This is a chilling, a cappella whistled version of a theme from Grieg's *Peer Gynt Suite.* In the sequence of which I speak, we are treated to a series of cuts of a children's playground, culminating in a shot of a balloon trapped in the power lines. Implication: Innocence is further obliterated; another child snatched by the predator; the wolf is among the sheep.

Not for the first time, I ponder *M*'s central premise. The film holds at its core a fascinating idea: an equation between brutality to children and fascism (and, by extension, any immoral system). In the makeshift trial sequence that closes the film, a gathering of vigilante Brownshirts put the Lorre character under the klieg lights and a strong parallel is drawn. Lang is saying that they are of the same universe—accusers and accused; products of one another; Siamese—or in this case, German—twins. He is warning us: Live like this, believe like this, and you will end up eating your young.

Sadly, this insight sounds many leagues deeper in the swamp of Apartheid-era South Africa than just Ridgeview Primary School. It comes to rest somewhere else entirely. During my research, I spoke to Pauline Carr, a forty-year veteran of the South African education system (she taught at the primary school my cousin Lewis attended). In 1994, the new ministry of education took her to visit a township school. I suppose the ministry was trying to show white teachers why it was so urgent that black children—even though their levels of literacy might be considerably lower than those of their white counterparts—should immediately be integrated into white schools in the suburbs. In 1994, the Apartheid regime was officially dead, but its legacy was not. Pauline was about to witness exactly how the Powers-That-Were constructed the education system. After all, she and I had seen it from one side only. As bad as the inspections, the corporal punishment, and the invented history lessons were—from the other side it looked much, much worse.

What Pauline saw, instead of twenty kids to a class, was close to a hundred. The unheated classroom was divided in two, as was the blackboard, with a chalk line delineating class A from class B. Two teachers, barely past their teens, yelled out the lessons. Three kids sat at each desk. At first, Pauline couldn't figure out why the kids stood up to write—then she realized that their desks were way too big for them. Their pencils were not regulation length—they were worn to nubbins—and there was only one for every three children. Posters were made on the back of cardboard boxes. In white schools, the supply of chalk, textbooks, Bristol board was infinite. The horrors of the Apartheid regime hit Pauline like a bus.

She went home after the field trip and slept for a week.

In the townships, the young were consumed, churned up, and destroyed. It's no coincidence that the Apartheid worm turned on the student Soweto protests of 1976, when black students refused to take their education in Afrikaans. Something snapped. The Powers-That-Were pushed too hard.

And something pushed back. Thirty years later, and balance has still not been restored.

The revolutionary journalist Stephen Biko put it nicely: "The most potent weapon in the hand of the oppressor is the mind of the oppressed." The Inspectors and those they worked for—they were in the mind-creation business. In black South Africa, they created the minds of the oppressed; in white South Africa, the mind of the oppressor. Another favourite of The Whistler was Prokofiev's *Peter and the Wolf*. He loved that tune. And while he was indeed the wolf, I should never have assumed that we white children were the little lambs. We were not that.

We were wolf cubs.

Arooooooooooooooooooooooooo!

Test Pattern

On a particularly magnificent Johannesburg day in 1977, a platoon of deliverymen hoisted a cold, lifeless television set out of a massive box and placed it, with much groaning and grunting, atop a shelving unit in our sunroom. It was one of those enormous jobbies that may have looked futuristic for about four minutes in 1972 but even to a four-year-old looked ridiculous in 1977—as if designed by someone stricken with a paradoxical fascination with space helmets and Louis XIV armoires. Still, I was as impressed with the contraption as I had been the first time I'd seen one, one year earlier when my grandparents took possession of an even grander version of the same species. Theirs had been purchased in anticipation of the first televised broadcast in South African history, which was to happen in early 1976.

We South Africans ever so slightly behind the times.[27]

My sister and I were fascinated by my grandparents' set, perched as it was against a large picture window looking out onto a row of impossibly tall, swaying blue gums and the golf course beyond. We loved walking toward the large convex glass

27. To place things in context, Sony released the Betamax on the market the same year television was introduced in South Africa. The delay was partly because of the Powers-That-Were's belief that TV would rot the fabric of society. You gotta give them that one.

of the TV and watching our bodies contort into outrageous shapes; we were obese midgets and then, with just a step forward, Silly Putty giants. Yes—early TV in South Africa was a glorified funhouse mirror. I also enjoyed the wooden crate my grandparents' TV had arrived in; I clambered inside merrily and pretended that it was a car. Here I'd love to say something winsome and elegiac about the loss of childlike imagination wrought by the advent and subsequent ubiquity of television, but that would be a tad disingenuous. I am not writing this chapter on the cultural impact of wooden crates.

It is perhaps fitting that the first time I saw a television actually do what it's supposed to do was on the Sabbath. The First Turning-On of the Television was an event. Oupa proudly pushed the silver button and stood back a respectable distance. A thin white line of electrical current slowly gave way to an image that would become seared into my cerebral cortex like a brand on a cow's rump: The South African Broadcasting Corporation's, or SABC's, test pattern. South Africa skipped straight past the whole black-and-white era,[28] and the test pattern was a barrage of furious colour. With its concentric shapes and brilliant primary blues and reds and greens, it looked like a puzzle that would never be solved in our lifetime. I touched the screen and static electricity fizzled at my fingertips—coils of potential energy, gaining steadily in power and ferocity while simmering away inside the box. This was some new magic—an alchemy that would turn a dark piece of glass into a bustling wonderland. All it required was patience.

For months, the test pattern was an electronic promise. "Stop looking at that bloody TV," my mother would shout when we

28. C'mon, you know what I mean.

asked Oupa to turn it on. Whatever drug television exudes, whatever signal it emits through the airwaves to enslave us all, it did its dirty work within the first few seconds of exposure. And when the SABC started broadcasting fish swimming in an aquarium—well, could it get any better than that? We were hooked.

Every time an image crackled across the giant glass of our TV screen, we were enchanted. Residing as it did in our sunroom, which was ringed in glass and looked onto our patio and the glittering pool beyond, the television seemed like a natural extension of the fun and games we engaged in outdoors. TV was not considered a right—it had no time to assert itself as such. It was not a babysitter—we had one of those living with us. In the land of corporal punishment, we did not need TV to keep us quiet (which is not to say that a ban from TV-watching for a week or two wasn't incorporated into one of the overall, intricate punishment stratagems my mother devised to keep us in line). It took TV a while to get a hold on us South Africans as a cultural force. By a while, I mean at least several months. And as a cultural force, TV in South Africa took on a nasty edge: Television was state-run.

Let's just say the government had itself a lovely new toy.

Despite this, in those formative days, TV was a novelty, plain and simple. Plain and simple is, in fact, an excellent way to describe the initial years of South African broadcasting. In those early years, one had a choice, and that choice was English or Afrikaans. This rigid fidelity to bilingualism caused each television broadcasting day to be divided between the languages, something like this:

Monday, Wednesday, Friday: English 4–8 P.M., Afrikaans 8–11 P.M.; Tuesday, Thursday, Saturday: Afrikaans 4–8 P.M.,

English 8–11 P.M. Sunday programming lasted but a few hours, and this only for televised church services, hymn recitals, and readings from the Good Book. The bridge between the English and Afrikaans services was the "late" news at 8 P.M., which was when the television room became Dr. Poplak's domain and we were told, in no uncertain terms, to get the Good Christ out and let him enjoy the house that he had bought and the stuff inside it that he had slaved for, working his fingers to the bone while we sat around staring at the TV until our bloody eyes went square.

There were, of course, no debates about channel surfing, or what shows to watch when. The very idea of a remote control was superfluous—mostly because there were no other channels to change to. Besides, we simply didn't think of smart gizmos to minimize manual labour in South Africa. Manual labour was our one abundant resource, and minimizing manual labour (or any labour at all) is, arguably, the driving impetus for all technological innovation.

Dr. Poplak would roar back from his surgery in Friday-afternoon traffic, his Alfa Romeo farting its way down Louis Botha Avenue, tires squealing around the appropriately named Death Bend, to make it to the sunroom for the weekly 5 P.M. broadcast of *Pop Shop*. "Switch that TV on," he'd yell to me as he stripped out of his blood-splattered safari suit. He washed his hands and his face, depositing himself dripping wet in front of the set. *Pop Shop*'s format was simple—five music videos interspersed with VJ gabble[29]—all this in the days when the music

29. The best of which was by a gentleman named Alex Jay. He wore a large feathered earring for the duration of the 1980s, which made him, in my opinion at the time, the absolute coolest person on TV. He also used the word *unmitigated* in relation to Sting. It's not often you have to look up a word when watching a music-video show.

video was in its infancy (which is to say, exactly the same as it is today, except with more clothes). There were no commercial breaks during shows on South African TV, so we had one half hour of unsullied 1980s pop to enjoy. I don't know what attracted Dr. Poplak to *Pop Shop* with such religious ardour. What did Cyndi Lauper, Culture Club, and Duran Duran mean to him? He had a tin ear and was pathologically allergic to "noise." Noise was defined as, but not necessarily restricted to, yelling, loud talking, music over a certain decibel (which varied depending on mood), scratching, sniffing, coughing, chair scraping, and the inhalation or exhalation of breath. Even silence bothered him. "Why are you so quiet?" he'd ask us after successfully shushing a conversation.

Unless you count four long sweaters and a pair of ripped jeans over neon fishnets, videos held little prurience in those days, so you can't even accuse Dr. Poplak of that. I'd love to posit a theory as to his *Pop Shop* mania, but none comes to mind. We live in a post-Freudian world, where we believe that each and every behavioural quirk can be explained by some deep-seated, untapped desire within us. Did my father dream of a life of pop stardom? Were his musical ambitions thwarted when he was a youth? Or did he just like the bright colours and bouncy tunes? I know I loved *Pop Shop* because pop was life and death to me. I tabled out the videos I'd seen in my music scrapbook (there were no repeats—a video played once and once only) and meticulously cross-referenced them with *Casey Kasem's Top-40 Countdown.* I dismissed anything that was South African in origin, and if any of our local pop stars, such as Johnny Clegg or David Kramer, took up valuable video slots, I'd get genuinely upset. I could tell before I heard a bar of music whether a video was local or imported. On the rare occasions when two South

African videos were played in one episode, I felt completely ripped off, as if my room had been burgled. That especially applied to Johnny Clegg videos. He was a local pop star who enjoyed limited international success in the wake of Paul Simon's *Graceland.* He dressed in traditional Zulu outfits and performed traditional Zulu dances while singing Africa-infused pop. That he was white made this seem absurd to me. Boy George dressed as a woman made perfect sense, but Johnny Clegg as a Zulu dismayed me. "C'mon, Alex," I'd yell, "no more of this *kuck*!"

"This isn't the news," Dr. Poplak would say, "so I don't want to hear an opinion."

From *Pop Shop* to *Star Trek.* This was the distance travelled by my father's disparate taste in television programming. *Magnum, P.I.* was the median at which he paused to get his bearings. *Star Trek* was the only show that we were allowed to watch during dinner. Because of its rarity, the practice took on ceremonial importance.[30] *Star Trek* played during wintertime, which meant we would carry ceramic mugs of thick soup with us to the sunroom, given that it was the spot farthest from the (relatively useless) anthracite heater and therefore a tad chilly in July. There we would watch the shenanigans on the USS *Starship Enterprise,* a mere nineteen years after the show aired elsewhere in the developed world. I liked the show well enough, but I remember being vaguely disturbed by Captain James T. Kirk's proclivity for pussy, regardless of what star system it came from.

---

30. The SABC did not rerun shows. If you missed one, you missed it. A season was thirteen weeks long, and that was it. In the case of *Star Trek,* there were only three seasons. Which means I ate dinner in front of the TV a total of thirty-nine times during my childhood.

In one episode in particular, I recall getting edgy at the intimation of carnal relations between Kirk and a green woman with a beehive hairdo. As a South African lad newly interested in those slight bumps appearing under the shirts of my female classmates, I couldn't conceive of the mixing of races never mind the mixing of intergalactic species. If you had told my ten-year-old self that there were couples out there in the wide world consisting of one black person and one white person, I would have called you a crazy person (the government, on the other hand would have called you a criminal and charged you under the Immorality Act). The one time I encountered such a phenomenon did not allow for my parents to elucidate. We were on the London underground during a short trip to England and, lo and behold, before us sat a black man with dreadlocks and his affectionate white female companion. I was eight or so, my sister six, and we stared our eyeballs dry. My parents tried to distract us as best they could, pointing out the brightly coloured advertisements and promising to buy us *anything,* but the situation was clearly becoming embarrassing. It became excruciating when Carolyn pointed at the couple and started to inquire loudly as to the precise nature of their relationship. She began with the words "Ma, why's her garden boy…?" That's when my red-faced mother clamped a hand over Carolyn's mouth and shuttled us off the tube. My parents were so traumatized that there was no quiet explanation for the fact that in other countries, blacks and whites can be mommies and daddies together.

My understanding of mixed-race coupling took a long time to formulate, but it was hastened by the release of the top-selling female-artist sophomore album of all time—the eponymous *Whitney,* in 1987. I remember staring unblinkingly at the cover of the LP while listening to the record, captivated by those shockingly white teeth, those copious brown locks, and the hardest-working tank top in showbiz history. I loved the sensual way *Whitney* was written in that 1980s cursive font, I loved the jaunty way her shoulders were thrown back, and, God help me, I loved the music. I made the mistake of outing my lust for Whitney to my peers—and the verbal abuse was unrelenting (for a week, I was a *kaffir*-lover—and a week is a long time for a schoolboy). Nonetheless, at least the inkling of mixed-race sexuality had been raised, even if it was via 1980s album-cover art.

Before all this, before my libido took the driver's seat, what was I to think of Kirk and his alien belles? Clearly, *Star Trek*'s thematic underpinnings of universal tolerance did not quite jibe with the local ethos. And what of Lt. Uhura?[31] For the uninitiated, Lt. Uhura was the black woman with the oversized earpiece (I loved the way she put two slender fingers to her ear when a particularly troublesome call came through) who acted as the ship's de facto intergalactic communications officer, directing calls from distant planets or spacecraft to the appropriate *Enterprise* crew member. In North American pop cultural lore, the casting of Nichelle Nichols, a young black woman, for the role of Lt. Uhura was a first in many respects. Nichols was the first black actress in a starring role on a network show, the first positive black female role model on television, and the first minority to engage in an interracial kiss on television. Martin Luther King Jr. himself, when he got wind of Nichol's decision to quit the show after the first season, personally encouraged her

31. *Uhura* is derived from the Swahili word for freedom and was the resounding cry of the Kenyan Independence movement in 1963, thereby giving South Africans a double scoop of the subversive in our *Star Trek* sugar cones.

to stay on the *Enterprise's* bridge, such was the importance he placed on her breaking of the colour barrier.

In the United States, Lt. Uhura represents a small, beautiful moment in the history of that country's civil rights movement. A full two decades later, *Star Trek* crossed galaxies and came to South Africa. There was barely a single black woman in the country at the time working as anything other than a domestic servant, let alone a communications officer. If Lt. Uhura's relationship with North American audiences was complex, it was infinitely more so with South African viewers. Gene Roddenberry's daring act of progressive casting was entirely lost on me. The very thought of a black woman working alongside whites was so outlandish that I simply couldn't process it.[32] Lt. Uhura must have been from outer space. My South African brain worked *around* the problem: I figured they were saving on green face paint.

Let's call this phenomenon the Uhura Syndrome. I define this as the viewing of pop culture through the refracted lens of racism—where an audience is challenged by an inherently racist institution such as Hollywood to confront its own inherent racism, which subsequently overrides any of the potential positives associated with minority casting. The Uhura Syndrome works by binding onto the narrative of an entertainment product and literally reworking the character histories and relationships while the show is in progress. It is a form of delusional psychosis, a dazzling, paradoxical act of imagination—paradoxical because it arises from the inability to imagine, in Lt. Uhura's case, a black Earth-woman in a position of responsibility on a spaceship in the year 2266.

32. Spock, with his humourlessness, his dour sensibility, and his soporific drone, I thought was from Pretoria.

Television from the outside world routinely made the mental gymnastics associated with the Uhura Syndrome a necessity. *Magnum, P.I.,* for instance. We loved the show, but T.C., Magnum's long-suffering 'Nam buddy who flew a helicopter, posed another example of the Uhura Syndrome, albeit from a different angle. Just as there were no black communications officers in the country, I can say with absolute authority that there were no black helicopter pilots in South Africa at the time. For a black South African, applying for a driver's licence was an exercise in frustration. I can only imagine what obstacles would have confronted the aspiring black whirlybird operator. Did I view these characters as outside the entertainment experience—as sidebars to the overall show? Did they have other tasks on set that made their appearance in acting roles a mere convenience? Did T.C. wax the Ferrari? The answer lies in the corollary to the Uhura Syndrome, one I'll dub the T.C. Factor. Black characters with white-collar jobs existed, for South Africans, within the hermetically sealed, tightly prescribed universe of pop-cultural product—and nowhere else. They didn't challenge assumptions, because here many of us tightened the grip of fiction and forbade our suspension of disbelief to enter everyday working consciousness. And if that—the idea that this was just a fiction, a story—failed, there was always the old fallback (and one I heard many, many times): "*Ag,* but the blacks are different in America."

An even more sinister relationship existed between black characters and white South African audiences. This is nowhere better explored than in the three seasons of *The Cosby Show* that played on the SABC prior to the establishment of trade sanctions. Like a surprising amount of Hollywood entertainment, the show had no resonance with local black viewers. *The Cosby Show* was not broadcast on Bantu stations; Bill and family never achieved anything near icon status among local black Africans. Township life or domestic servitude was so inalterably different from even a basic American existence that, regardless of the colour of the characters, there likely was no point of common reference for the two cultures. (Humour has an especially difficult time making it across culture barriers.) Among the white population, *The Cosby Show* was as popular as it was in North America. I have no idea how the show played in Pofadder or Bloemfontein, but I suspect it was just as heartily enjoyed in those *dorps* as it was in cosmopolitan centres like Johannesburg or Cape Town.

I believe that there was a fundamentally disquieting reason why *The Cosby Show* was so well received in South Africa, and it is incidental to the show and its star's easy appeal. And this reason is the same reason why people enjoy watching poodles dressed in tiny facsimiles of human clothing roll a ball about in a circus. It's the incongruity—the unlikely convergence—that acts as the entertaining principle ("as edifying as seeing a dog in a parody of breeches," as Joseph Conrad put it). Watching black people act like white people was intrinsically compelling. I heard this more than once in relation to *The Cosby Show:* "*Ja,* no, man! They're just like us, hey!" The very thought of "them" being "just like us" was so ridiculous that it was entertainment in and of itself.[33]

---

33. One show that did resonate with local blacks, and that was incorporated into the resistance movement, was the extraterrestrial invasion miniseries *V,* because of the way the human characters fought an insurrection against the alien invader. In town, and especially in the townships, the big red V insignia was daubed on concrete walls. This was an iconic case of North American pop culture being appropriated by those opposed to Apartheid.

I sometimes wonder why it was sanctions and not the SABC and their co-conspirators, the Censorship Bureau (officially known as the Directorate of Publications, or the DOP), that terminated *The Cosby Show*'s run on South African TV. Surely, if the producers had allowed the show to play its entire eight seasons, one or two South Africans might have thought twice about the role of black people in society, and the Uhura Syndrome, along with the T.C. Factor, might have been somewhat (in the words of Alex Jay) mitigated. Indeed, some might have come to the conclusion, given that the characters resembled whites in every way except colour, that there was indeed some intrinsic similarity between the two races. But the SABC needed content. A network that refuses to rerun shows runs out of options quickly, even if broadcasting for only eight hours a day. Thus, the DOP waved through just about anything, so long as it didn't explicitly criticize the South African government or come off as overtly tolerant. Meanwhile, entertainment companies in the United States and Britain engaged in cultural sanctions, denying South African audiences the very shows that could potentially motivate *some* diversity of opinion. *All in the Family* aired, though it was eventually pulled (not by the Powers-That-Were but by its distributor). Archie Bunker may have been one of the most ingenious comedic characters in the history of American television, but this was probably lost on most South Africans—especially those employed by the DOP. In the show's standout episode—twenty-six minutes of the most potent television ever produced—Archie is horrified at the idea of Sammy Davis Jr. becoming his next-door neighbour. The Group Areas Act made such concerns in South Africa unnecessary, and Archie's rants were probably met with sincere nods of agreement throughout the country—the satire completely evaporating in the face of the world's elite class of racists. There may, however, have been a few—just a handful—of audience members who *got it*—who had their doubts about the status quo validated (and, of course, there *were* South Africans who got it, in the same way that there were North Americans who didn't). Sadly, sanctions denied us the controversial content that the DOP was too daft to ban.

If censorship is a key practice of any patriarchal bureaucracy—the stern father who has our very best interests at heart—then the DOP was a bumbling, cataract-ridden paterfamilias. For one thing, most of those sitting on the board were Afrikaners who, because of the language barrier, routinely missed elements such as satire, irony, and humour. Their criteria for slicing and dicing were difficult to fathom—if there were any criteria at all. They were very, very squeamish when it came to sex, and they would, of course, ban outright anything that alluded to the emancipation of or freedom earned by black people anywhere. Otherwise, you never really knew what they would do. This was particularly true of the movies, where the censorship czars were at their most uneven.[34] For one, they

34. There is the peculiar instance of Richard Attenborough's controversial (in South Africa, anyway) biopic of the murdered black South African journalist Stephen Biko, entitled *Cry Freedom.* The de Klerk government allowed the film to screen uncut, but two small bomb blasts at 10 A.M. screenings on the first day of its release "forced" the authorities to pull the film, to save us corporally if not spiritually. The blasts were small and innocuous, prompting the overriding suspicion that the government had rigged the whole exercise to make itself look both liberal and cautious. The blasts, you see, were blamed on "terrorist elements." This was an allusion to the ANC and its ilk. No one of any intelligence could figure out why the ANC *wouldn't* want a film about a famous anti-Apartheid crusader screened. But it does stand as the most intricate case of state censorship on record.

neglected to censor the previews. We would watch, slack-jawed with awe, all the footage we would not get to see in the full-length feature. In fact, I went to the movies largely for the previews—they were as close to liberal-minded soft porn as South African culture came.

Our censors were poor editors. They would sever away an offending chunk of celluloid with garden shears and then join the reel back together with a bandage or a half roll of duct tape. The visual and aural jump was the unmistakable tip-off that we were denied some choice but illicit section of the movie we had just paid for.

Surprisingly, the grey-suited men of the snip-happy DOP handled art films with delicacy. These were often shown in small theatres, the audience mostly made up of young men sporting goatees and Lennon glasses, old men in raincoats with shopping bags on their laps, and a smattering of teenage boys. I went to see Stanley Kubrick's *A Clockwork Orange* at one such theatre. I had heard that the filmmaker did not skimp on the boobage, and that information turned out to be reliable to a fault. However, when presented with such a film, the censors used the age-old concept of the fig leaf to obscure offending body parts. In their case, they slapped black rectangles in front of [redacted]s, [redacted]s, and [redacted]s. This was an immense disappointment. However, I was slightly touched by the DOP's respect for films of the canon, if somewhat damaged by it: In my late teens, far from the shores of *Afrique du Sud,* confronted with the bra of a real live female for the very first time, I half expected to see a large [redacted] where her [redacted]s were.

Like the blundering censorship folks, the SABC needed time to get up to even a low level of professionalism. The local broadcast service had been developed in the 1930s to provide radio for what was a large and, at the time, isolated and sparsely populated country (that refers, of course, to the white population). Radio culture still permeated the SABC when it first turned on the cameras. I think the SABC was only dimly aware that we could now see it as well as hear it. Severe, humourless, and utterly subservient to the ruling party—all this made for some interesting television.

The evening's festivities began promptly at 4 P.M., with *Die Boek.*[35] In this show, an ancient Afrikaans gentleman, resembling a corpse that has lain for three days in state, read a portion of the Lord's Bible in both official languages, Afrikaans and English. Believe me, you needed a good prayer for what was about to come. Local kids' programming was as wholesome and exciting as fortified Pablum soaked in powdered skim milk. The flagship in this rustbucket fleet was *Willie Wallie,* our version of *Sesame Street.*[36] The show's theme tune was so obnoxiously catchy that once it was in your head, only a .44 calibre bullet could dislodge it. I have heard that enemy captives at Guantánamo Bay, when not forced to stand in human pyramids and jerk off on one another, are treated to the loud blaring of Western popular music to loosen their stubborn lips. Substitute the *Willie Wallie* theme and they'd be yelling directions to Osama's six-bed, three-bath, south-facing cave within seconds. *Willie Wallie* starred an Afrikaans hostess who was menacingly condescending, as if she had access to key pieces of information

35. *The Book.*

36. Which never played in South Africa, a decision this time made by the SABC rather than the DOP. There was no way that the Powers-That-Were could handle the explicit theme of tolerance, and especially all the cross-racial mingling. Big Bird didn't stand a chance in South Africa.

that we would forever be denied. Her glassy eyes bored into our souls, and those freakish orbs gave the show a quasi-religious flavouring, thus smearing the proceedings with a patina of extra ickiness. Her sidekick was a puppet centipede named Bennie Boekwurm, who looked like a section of diseased intestine wearing spectacles and a tie. He lived in a library and loved to read.

In the same vein was *Cheesecake*.[37] This was about the adventures of a dog-type creature that resembled a shag rug someone had recently used as toilet paper. Cheesecake and his pals were constantly harassed by an arch-villain named Reginald, the Theatre Cat. I hope Reginald was better at theatre stuff than he was at bad-guy stuff—every episode culminated with his declaring, in plummy, stentorian tones, "Curses! Foiled again!" Reginald was the ultimate villain for a South African audience. First off, he was English. He was cultured, and he worked in the arts. "Culture" was shorthand for "morally bereft." "Worked in the arts" is something children did, like playing with action figures or making tea for dollies. It's something one outgrew. Now, I'm not saying that South Africa in those days was anti-art, oh no. Our artists were often winning free overnight stays in government-owned facilities and complimentary one-way trips to England, where criminal activity, including culture, proliferated.

Much later in childhood than most of my North American contemporaries, I was immersed in the world of animated bees, talking sock-puppet frogs, lovable witches (*Liewe Hexie*—or

37. An Afrikaans education expert named Louise Smit produced both *Willie Wallie* and *Cheesecake,* among others. She might find herself the first children's programmer prosecuted for war crimes at The Hague.

Dear Little Witch—was another local standard), singing vegetables, and all the other creatures that flickered their way through a cathode ray tube to nestle forever in our consciousnesses. I am eternally thankful that the SABC made no (or none that I watched, anyway) forays into proprietary adult drama—the potential results of that are too frightening to imagine. Watching shows such as *Miami Vice* (renamed *Misdaad in Miami*—or *Misdeed in Miami*) dubbed into Afrikaans has skewed my pop-cultural universe enough already.[38] I can picture Sonny Crockett and Ricardo Tubbs only as Afrikaners, and I was mildly disappointed during my first visit to Florida to find that Spanish is far more prevalent than Afrikaans. No, the SABC's adult-programming department stuck to doing what it did best: the graphic and unedited portrayal of ultra-violence in a news context.

Our version of *America's Most Wanted* was *Police File,* hosted by Michael de Morgan. Now, this was reality TV. Michael would start off by recapping recent crimes that the show had been instrumental in solving—those where viewers had helpfully passed along tips to the cops, resulting in the subsequent (and invariable) murder of the murderer. Arrests in South Africa rarely culminated in the use of handcuffs. More like tweezers, a few pints of Lysol, and a wet 'n' dry vacuum. And *Police File* was happy to show us the results of such operations. We were treated to black-and-white photos of the cops, cigarettes in hand, standing over the mangled remains of an individual who only last

38. *Miami Vice* was the first show in SABC history to try out a simulcast. The English soundtrack was broadcast on the old Springbok Radio frequency, while the show was dubbed into Afrikaans. The timing was about five seconds off, making it one of the silliest experiments the SABC ever engaged in.

week, we were told, was running happily free from the law. Indeed, *Police File* was like a photo montage of those who had met garishly ignominious ends. The producers never doctored the photo of a victim, regardless of how he or she ended up, or how long he or she had been ended up for. A photo of a head with a gunshot wound would flash on screen, the noggin distorted into what looked like the rushed work of a drunken trainee at Madame Tussauds, and Michael would ask, "If you recognize this individual, please call us at..." My parents were persuaded that perhaps it was best if I no longer watched the show by the photo of a suicide victim who had leapt from the top of Johannesburg's Ponte tower to a very definitive end. "If any of this individual's friends, family, or acquaintances..." If they what, Michael? Given that the victim resembled a half-finished plate of spaghetti bolognese, the only call they were gonna get was from Chef Boyardee.

But for unadulterated, unedited, and often live violence, you could do no better than the nightly news. The SABC news service's primary responsibility was to keep us in a state of panic, and this it did by capturing as much township violence as possible and broadcasting it as news. Sectional violence between blacks was the predominant motif of local 1980s news broadcasts, the implicit message being if they did that to one another, what the hell would they do to *us*? Typically, the newscaster opened a segment with the qualifier "The following footage is not suitable for all viewers." That statement raises a question. Who, exactly, is footage of a corpse with a flaming tire around its neck,[39] blades poking from its torso, crazed crowd peppering it with kicks, suitable for? In the deadened tones of the typical

39. This procedure was termed "necklacing."

South African anchorman (and, very occasionally, anchorwoman), we were warned of the great variety of bugaboos lurking in wait for us. The mélange the SABC cooked up invariably included (depending on the day) a Crock-Pot bubbling with Communist, Soviet, ANC, Zulu, un-Christian, anarchist malcontent. In this, the SABC has a lesson for news broadcasters everywhere. South African television newscasters never got excited. They never frothed at the mouth, spewing invective at the Commies, darkies, Russkis, or anyone else for that matter. If you wish to make the insane sound rational, simply read information—suitably editorialized, of course—off the teleprompter without having an apoplexy. This makes it sound less a point of view than inalterable fact.

If the news was the malaria-infested valley of the South African cultural experience, what then was its windswept peak? That's easy. Commercials. Every last smart person in the country worked in the advertising industry. Adverts, as we called them, were the central part of the South African popcultural vernacular. Movie adverts were the best thing about going to the movies—better even than the previews. Fuck Ewoks and bullwhip-sporting archaeologists. We had cigarette commercials!

These were dazzling, multi-million-dollar productions filmed all over the world, starring the most gorgeous people on Central Casting's roster. They didn't just encourage smoking, these adverts, they made smoking imperative. I still consider the Chesterfield man to be the finest single evocation of masculinity in the history of the moving picture. The campaign's tagline said it all: "Chesterfield—for a man's kind of man." Regardless of the adventure, this nameless, bestubbled cipher sauntered into the world's hotspots with nothing more than his 1950s

Land Rover, a tarp, matches, and a lifetime's[40] supply of Chesterfield cigarettes. He proved that there was no excuse, and no situation (flash flood, leftist Bogotá cartel, felled redwood), too inopportune for a man's kind of man *not* to be smoking.

Not to be outdone, Peter Stuyvesant set all its commercials on high-end water-borne vessels. The typical *mise en scène* involved three gorgeous couples, delicate champagne flutes, and—you guessed it!—a lifetime's supply of cigarettes. This genre was discreet about its ultimate purpose—no one lit up until the end of the commercial, sort of like the ejaculation shot in a porn movie. Still, the sight of those yachts cleaving through the Mediterranean with bikini-clad honeys on the deck took my breath away—breath I have yet to get back given how effective these commercials were in getting teens to light up. At least these commercials upheld the art of cigarette smoking—that it was a social practice *as well as* a deadly habit. I smoked in the style of the Chesterfield man—cigarette between the thumb and the forefinger—pulling it contemptuously from my mouth after a drag, like the nipple of a loose woman. In the deserted boys' bathroom at King David High School, you could tell a guy's favourite commercial by the way he held his cigarette. There were lots of Chesterfield men down there.

If commercials were the high point of the movie-going experience, they were doubly so for television. Since there were no commercial breaks during shows, a five-minute commercial block ran between programs. You *had* to keep people watching. And watch we did. This was because South African ads of that particular era have no equal. Perhaps it's because our culture was

40. Suitably attenuated, I'd imagine.

so cloistered that we knew how to speak to one another with an almost telepathic clarity.

In this, South African adverts were often less than politically correct. One egregious example was a commercial for Omo, a leading brand of laundry detergent. This depicted a typical domestic scene, with slight differences. Madam and "the girl" are unpacking shopping bags. We're not quite sure why Madam is looking over the purchases so carefully—didn't she just buy them? She removes the detergent from the bag. Hmm? She's skeptical. Cut to the laundry room. Here, the girl has done the washing, and Madam is doing an inspection. She's impressed. "*Ag,* Sophie," she says, "you should do all the shopping." The twist here, you see, is that *Madam had allowed Sophie to do the shopping.* This was an incongruity that would be lost on no South African madam. You can't trust them with money and the spending thereof, now can you, *skattie*? What's more—and here's the real crackerjack—*Sophie hadn't fucked it up! She'd done good!* The racism involved in this knee-slapper wasn't lost on even the most racist of us—it had the unintentional effect of turning a looking glass on the entire culture and making us look ever so slightly bad. After a brief period of introspection (I remember one or two op-ed pieces in the newspapers about the ad), the catchphrase was employed as a catch-all for when someone did something unexpectedly positive. The guy with two left feet on the soccer team somehow manages to score a goal? "*Ag,* Sophie, you should do all the shopping." The neanderthal at the back of the class manages a B on the math exam? "*Ag,* Sophie (*all together now*), you should do all the shopping."

That was the SABC—a healthy admixture of banality, racism, violence, and American television. As the 1980s wound down, so too did the golden age of Apartheid-era SABC. As more channels were introduced and more choice entered the landscape, we opted to get our daily dose of cathode crack elsewhere. I believe that it was the launch of the pay-channel M-Net that freed our eyeballs and our minds from the icy grasp of the intractable bureaucrats running the SABC. M-Net broadcast two hours a night of free crappy entertainment, rather than crappy entertainment *and* crappy propaganda. This was refreshing. Canadian taxpayers will be thrilled to learn that their hard-earned Canuck bucks contributed to my watching such cultural cubic zirconia as *The Littlest Hobo* and *Adderly* in the comfort of my Johannesburg home[41]—M-Net's speciality (necessitated by its almost non-existent budget) was C-grade television from countries other than America.

Did M-Net help bring Apartheid down? A massive assertion, surely. Let us take some time to examine it properly. Those who purchased transponders and subscribed (such fiduciary extravagance was unheard of in my family) were no longer under the sway of the SABC. M-Net made its debut in 1986, and Mandela was released in 1990. Could it be that those who gorged on Canadian or Australian TV shows, the occasional sitcom that barely lasted a season, and nine-year-old movies were more amenable to change than those still watching the dirge that was the SABC's nightly news? Or perhaps they became so indolent, slothful, and drugged up by all this by-product television that they didn't know or care when the world outside did start to alter somewhat. If it is a stretch to say that M-Net contributed to the downfall of Apartheid, there are no

41. Adderly was a gumshoe who solved crimes, rarely getting paid for the trouble. The show's sole gimmick was that Adderly had lost his hand. Yup, he wore a black glove on his left paw. That was it. Black glove. Not much else to it.

such contortions required in saying that the SABC was essential in keeping it propped up. It kept us hopped up on the Calvinist ethos of our ruling gerontocracy and made sure we were treated to a steady diet of misinformation (a bitter pill made all the sweeter by the entertainment bracketing it), violence, and brutality.

Despite all this, TV in South Africa remained a thrill, and that's because of its late arrival and its being parcelled out in small doses. In a land without twenty-four-hour programming, where most of what was on was genuinely unwatchable, TV was simply not the same experience it was elsewhere in the developed world. In Canada, where you could watch *Cheers* nine times a day or *Star Trek* until your internal core facilitator collapsed, TV was perhaps less of a novelty and more of a liability—another layer of fat added to mental and physical waistlines. Now, I look at my TV and wonder how this contraption could once have elicited any wonder at all.

TV's ultimate if unintended function is that it's a feedback loop, a nostrum for the march of time. Just as Sam Malone is the same age every time you watch him sling cocktails behind the bar, so it is with the viewer. We are transported back to the same state of mind, the very same age we were when we first watched a particular show—dosed with high-grade nostalgia into a type of trance, a catatonia that provides its fair measure of comfort. In small increments, this is probably no bad thing. But it doesn't have the same resonance for a South African once stricken with the Uhura Syndrome and its corollary, the T.C. Factor. Sadly, I can't indulge in harmless nostalgia—there's always a tinge of something else—a bubble of horror at assumptions once held, maybe? As a result, I have never quite been able to surrender to reruns. In many respects, the SABC ruined television for me. Across infinite space and time, whenever I see Lt. Uhura place earpiece to ear, I'm reminded that I once thought she was an alien.

Frankly, I'd rather read a book.

Awakenings

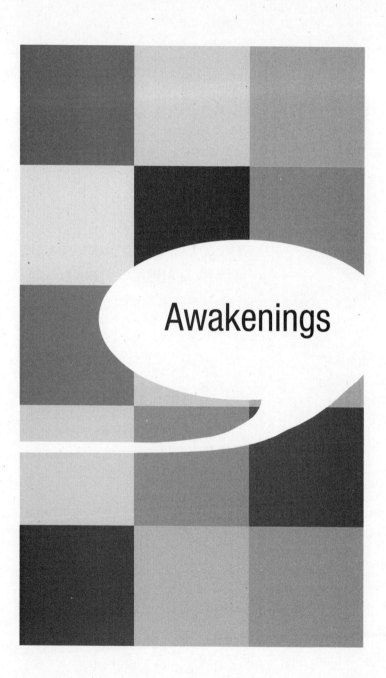

In which we Learn of the
Dangers of Communism; Take the long
Journey from ABBA to Zeppelin; and,
while Losing God, Get a Taste for Rebellion.

Waterval Boven

Veldskool is a very nice time, and I recomend [*sic*] it to everyone if they want to know more about the veld and also about other things.

—*from the official* Veldskool *scrapbook of Richard Poplak, age 12, May 1985*

It's two o'clock in the morning. I'm lying in three inches of mud, and something is chewing my face. I am hidden deep in tall grass, looking through a gap in the swaying stalks up the slight rise of a hill. A late harvest moon is rising—so big and so close that I can almost see the Stars and Stripes fluttering in the Lowveld breeze. The face chewer chews some more. I cannot scream, as much as I'd like to. This is because I am on a mission, an important one. After more than a week of hard-core training, I am ready to Stalk the Lantern. And stalk it I shall. Disregarding the creature that has decided my face would make a good entrée, I quietly wriggle forward, ignoring also a sharp burst of pain from my injured shoulder. Must. Stalk. Lantern. Said lantern, blessedly, comes into sight. It is, however, heavily manned. I'm just gonna have to wait it out. But that's okay. That thing eating my face has moved on. To my arm.

Welcome to *veldskool.*

A literal translation of *veldskool* is "field school," but that doesn't wash even as a basic descriptor. If there were an operating manual, it would read like a cross between Baden-Powell's *Scouting for Boys* and *Mein Kampf. Veldskool* was essentially the week-and-a-half-long rite of passage in which the twelve-year-old South African male leaves a boyhood of mutilating lizards and frying insects under magnifying glasses and graduates to performing the same and/or similar on real people. The process was, by design, rigorous pre-military training without the safety and comfort of live ordnance. The physical torment associated with military instruction was, sadly, only one aspect of the *veldskool* syllabus. There was also a spoken-word component, in which we were informed—in no uncertain terms and in no particular order—who our enemies were, what we could expect of them, and what it would take to overcome their unfailing, and largely unprovoked, aggression. There is a technical term for this. It is called indoctrination.

Most South African primary schools had as part of their standardized curriculum mandatory school trips, the exact specifics of which were up to the school's administrative staff. My cousin Lewis, for instance, went on an extensive bus trip around the country, following the picturesque Garden Route to Cape Town, where he spent a week with his classmates exploring the environs. He rode an ostrich in Oudshoorn. He analyzed rock samples and animal spoor and dried foliage. His scrapbook read like the travelogue of a Victorian gentleman botanist-geologist. I was not to be so lucky, and it must be said that you had to be *very* lucky to avoid *veldskool* altogether; this happened only in schools where the teachers themselves refused to chaperone the trips. When we were given the handout inscribed with the details of our excursion, I learned that our destination was not, as I had hoped, Paris or New York City or London or even Pietermaritzburg. No. We were going to Waterval Boven.

The name was redolent of abstemiousness and boredom and pain, suggesting that my own scrapbook would be a significantly different literary affair from Lewis's. So did the curt, ominously short list of requirements:

Long Pants. Clean. 2 pairs.
Short Pants. Clean. 1 pair.
Shirts. Clean. 5.
Underpants. Clean.
Socks. Clean.
Raincoat.
Torch.
Eating utensils.
Sleeping bag.
Malaria pills.
NO FOOD OR SWEETS.

I hypothesized that unlike Lewis, I would not be ambling up the face of mountains, crumbling dried shit betwixt my thumb and forefinger, saying, "Magaliesburg jackrabbit spoor, sir."

Where I was going, Magaliesburg jackrabbit spoor was not so much a specimen as it was cuisine.

"Ma," I asked upon handing her the sheet to sign, "do I have to go?"

"*Ag,* it will be fun," lied my mother. "Besides, you'll be with all your friends." This was faulty logic—I was with my friends every day at school, but that didn't make school fun, did it? Besides, *veldskool* had a reputation. Boys with older brothers had passed along tales of woe heavy with portents of doom and personal injury. I had heard of the maniacs who ran these places, the insane levels of discipline they implemented, and the brutality we would be forced to suffer. I had heard of broken arms, shattered femurs, fractured skulls, and Afrikaner men who had so perfected corporal punishment that when they caned you, they did so in the presence of a paramedic. "My *boet*," said Massimo Castelletti, a redheaded school friend whose brothers were renowned badasses, "told me that Waterval Boven is the worst!"

I wasn't so sure that this was typical schoolboy hyperbole.

Oupa promised that *veldskool* would make a man out of me, but I didn't want to be a man without the pubic hair to back up my credentials. Frankly, I missed my mommy already. Thus, leaving day was an emotional one—the principal emotion being fear. The entire Standard Five class gathered in the courtyard near the school parking lot[42]—fifty boys in clean uniforms, school caps firmly on heads, sitting in neat rows with our pathetic, refugee-like possessions forlornly beside us. It was a sombre crowd, and to judge from the trembling voices during roll call, I was not the only one expecting the worst.

Headmaster MacMillan's eyes were especially refulgent with the combined glint of madness and *schadenfreude* that May morning. His smiling rendition of the Lord's Prayer and his wishing us the best in what was pretty much a gleeful cackle confirmed without a doubt that we were in for a time of it. "Remember," he said, "you are ambassadors for Ridgeview

42. By "entire" I mean the male element. The girls were on their way to a female *veldskool,* where presumably they learned to cook, clean, sew, and, in general, behave as the perfect companions to the train wrecks of men that we would be after returning from our own *veldskool* experience.

Primary School. You represent me and everyone here. Do not do anything to disgrace us." *Ja,* right. When staying alive becomes a genuine concern, saving your primary school from disgrace is not a top priority.

Several classmates disgraced themselves by quietly weeping in fear and early-onset homesickness as we flung our paltry possessions into the cargo hold of the bus. The non-weepers, who according to tradition should have attacked these weaker creatures like a pride of lions takes down a three-legged gazelle, left them to their tears. This was no occasion for schoolboy mockery. Indeed, it was clear that the bus trip was to be a quiet affair. I sat at a window, watching my mother alongside the other waving mothers. How could she let me go so easily? The trip represented one of the longest periods I would be out of ear- or eyeshot of either my mother or Bushy. Eleven days is an eternity for a twelve-year-old. And even Jeremy and Leigh's presence on the bus offered little solace. We had been made to understand that we would be separated from our friends upon arrival and divided into groups with boys from other primary schools. My comrades-in-arms would in effect become my enemies.

Because we were ordered to keep a meticulous scrapbook of our trip (the equivalent of asking each infantry soldier in the trenches in World War I to write something at least as definitive as *All Quiet on the Western Front*), I can refer to my scribbles to guide us through the *veldskool* experience. This book—stuffed with leaf samples of which only gossamer veins remain extant, yellowed dog-eared brochures that crumble at the touch, and flower petals reduced to dusty shadows—resembles after so many years the ancient tomes of a troubled warlock under siege from the forces of darkness. Reading between the lines of the official, school-issued prose, there is ample evidence of a child under great emotional and physical duress. This scrapbook would break your heart.

"I think we are quite far from Johannesburg."

Each wheel revolution of the bus represented further separation from hearth and home as we chugged our way steadily down the N4 toward Nelspruit. I dared not look out the bus's rear window for fear of realizing how far from home we had travelled. My schoolmates and I only half-heartedly slapped each other's bare legs in that ritual native to South African school bus trips. Our chaperone, the moustached Mr. Billups, sat at the front of the bus, the slight up-curl of his lip suggesting that he, too, knew all too well what we were in for.

Waterval Boven is a hamlet located where the escarpment forms the dividing line between the Highveld and the Lowveld—and is thus, very reasonably, called the Middleveld.[43] In geographical and topographical terms, the area is one of the most varied spots on earth. Flat grasslands give way to rolling hills pockmarked with stunted acacia. Those hills terminate at the lip of the escarpment in sudden cliff faces that fall off into nowhere, delivering cascades of crisp water into the valleys below. The Elands River, running thick with trout and black bass, flows icy cold with snowy runoff, winding farther into the Lowveld, where it is transformed into an entirely different ecological smorgasbord within just a matter of miles. This riot of natural diversity stands in stark contrast to the region's cultural orthodoxy. In 1985, Waterval Boven and the few *dorps*

43. *Waterval Boven* literally means "Above the Waterfall."

dotted around the area made the village in *Deliverance* look as cosmopolitan and libidinous as Manhattan during the disco era. Here, they would never make you squeal like a pig *before* marriage.

This was territory where the Afrikaner Weerstandsbeweging (or AWB), a fiercely nationalist Boer movement opposed to anything resembling social progress, found a receptive constituency. The AWB, led by the invective-spewing Eugene Terreblanche, was characterized by the press as a bunch of bumbling fools—and they were indeed something of a national joke.[44] (Bearded and sporting an impressive paunch, Eugene loved to show up at rallies on horseback. He was often so drunk that he didn't manage to stay *on* the horse for the duration of his public appearances.) The organization's logo, a three-cornered derivation of the Nazi swastika, suggested National Socialism, but it was more Fanatically Racist Nationalist Libertarian. The AWB had a decent following, especially in the mid-1980s, and especially in the Middleveld. Many of these followers could be found in the charming burg of Waterval Boven.

I wasn't thinking about this as ominous cliff faces, clotted with vegetation, cast chilly shadows over our bus as it wound through the lower Drakensberg. Our only stop was at Pilgrim's Rest, an old pioneer village that once formed the base for miners foolhardy enough to scour this land for treasure. Pilgrim's Rest is now transformed into what the tourism wonks

44. Eugene and the boys loved a good drink (klippies and Coke, *ouens*!). Their headquarters, in the dusty town of Ventersdorp, was apparently a great place for AWB drunken-accident watching. Kids would take a detour home from school to see if the on-duty guard, patrolling the HQ roof with a high-powered assault rifle, would slip off and spray bullets into the air, yelling obscenities as he fell.

dub a "living museum," but in those days you couldn't beat it for authenticity. The seat of one of the most significant alluvial gold rushes on the continent, it was what the real Wild West must've felt like—hard, lonely, and heavy with dread. Before the place was sanitized, it was a real lesson in prospecting—a graveyard, in every sense of the word. My twelve-year-old imagination bustled with the town's ghosts: men in search of gold who had instead found malaria, yellow fever, or the wrong end of a pickaxe. The cemetery formed the literal and figurative centre of town, crawling stubbornly up a slope that disappeared into the low cloud ceiling. "The dead robber's grave," I penned didactically, "points in the other direction from the others." Indeed, Pilgrim's Rest's lone *gunnif* was buried facing east, perpendicular to his victims. This damned him to an eternity of hell, an infinite addendum to the hell he most likely experienced on earth.

With my peanut-butter sandwich clinging desperately to my esophagus ("I felt quite sick," I noted in my scrapbook), we wound our way through the foothills to the pride of the Middleveld—Waterval Boven. Upon arrival, before I could click my heels together three times, we were summarily dispersed among the refugees of three other Johannesburg-area school buses—a gaggle of about 150 dazed schoolboys and their chaperones. This—the mixing of schools—seemed to be one of *veldskool*'s main tenets. It added immeasurably to the disorientation and the competitive spirit—school pride being a supposed motivating factor. So, the cast of characters of my *veldskool* tour consisted of the Standard Five classes of three other Johannesburg schools, from suburbs far enough away from one another that our paths had never before crossed.

The Magaliesburg jackrabbit spoor hit the fan almost immediately. Several Afrikaner men in khaki safari suits, socks pulled up to just below their swollen, wind-chapped knees, yelled through their moustaches, "*Maak gou!* Hurry!" We were wrangled harshly into a courtyard, the focal point of which was a flagpole boasting a large Republic of South Africa flag fluttering gloriously under a quickly fading sun. These were strong white Africans—tough, hardened men of few words, lovers of the land and of stout, resolute, child-bearing women. These men were the Ooms.[45]

They herded us into neat, seated rows in front of the flagpole. We Ridgeview boys glanced nervously at the strange boys glancing nervously at us. I took the opportunity to look over my surroundings, which were basic to a fault—brick dormitories stretching the length of the property, a scattering of outbuildings presumably housing faculty, a threadbare garden stretching to the Elands that flowed some hundred yards from the dorms, and the large concrete courtyard where I now found myself. "It looks like a jail should look like," I wrote in my scrapbook in a rare moment of unguarded honesty, suggesting that the architects of W.B. Veldskool had reached a sort of platonic ideal of penitentiary design. There was, however, little time for architectural ruminations. Class was in session.

"Stand! *Maak gou!* Quickly!" Two hundred wobbly-kneed boys stood in unison, the bowel-loosening barks of our wardens—sorry—teachers inciting us unthinkingly into action.

"Atennnnnnnnnnn-shin!"

We snapped to, a reflex learned from school assemblies. Dead quiet descended—the loeries clamped their wings to their

45. *Oom* is an Afrikaans word meaning *uncle,* but it's generally attributed to an older gentleman as a sign of respect.

sides and shut their beaks, while the cicadas performed the entomological equivalent.

Around the corner he strode—a cross between Clint Eastwood and Archie Bunker, his steel-grey hair smeared into a perfect Hitler hairdo. His safari getup was as starched as a funeral suit, his socks yanked up to full mast and planted in pristine *velskoene.* A comb was tucked into his right sock to ensure he was able to maintain that wispy, sideways coif that spoke so clearly of his ideological affiliations.

"At ease." His voice, barely louder than a whisper, was audible as far away as Asia.

"I am Oom Piet," said Oom Piet, English words burbling in his thick Afrikaans accent like goldfish stuck in rapids. "You are now here to learn. You will learn the following things." He counted points off on stubby, well-worked fingers. "How to love your country. Respect for the flag. How to identify your enemies. How to combat them." To me, that seemed like a full week. When would we find the time for parachute drops and proper torture techniques?

Oom Piet jabbed his fingers in the direction of two boys. "You and you!" With a barely perceptible flick of the head, he guided the jittery lads to either side of the flagpole. There they stood, knees knocking together like castanets worked by a flamenco dancer with the DTs. One of the ooms blew on a bugle. Oom Piet stood up straight, eyes cast heavenward, and broke into the first few words of "Die Stem," our national anthem, in a surprisingly pleasing voice.[46] We followed suit—a

46. "Die Stem" is still an official South African anthem, although "Nkosi Sikelele, Afrika," or "God Bless Africa," is the more widely sung ditty at official functions and the like.

cacophony of prepubescent falsettos and counter-tenors. Oom Piet, to his credit, winced perceptibly. Following the singing of the anthem, two of Oom Piet's minions barked orders at the boys tasked with removing the flag from its perch. Clearly, the ooms had a thing about the flag. A big thing. It was folded and presented to Oom Piet, who gazed at it with reverence before tucking it smartly under his armpit. Then Oom Piet snapped to. We did likewise. He turned on his heels and returned from whence he came, and we were left contemplating his aura in the dying seconds of twilight.

"There is plenty of food for everyone and many items are very interesting to have for dinner."

As the sun went, so did the heat; the Middleveld can get chilly after dark. Stars glimmered mockingly in the sky, their cheerfulness a harsh contrast to the cuisine standing in rusty vats before us. Thankfully, I am partial to food in vast quantities (I subscribe to a maximalist, bulk-is-better philosophy when it comes to victuals), so I was more impressed by a twenty-gallon tub of raspberry jam or margarine than I was appalled. The same cannot be said for my comrades-in-arms. "What is this kuck?" whispered Jeremy. (None of us had spoken to each other since our arrival in W.B. We communicated with wide-eyed stares that pretty much said it all.) Jeremy had grown accustomed to his maid Johanna's exceptional roast chicken and potatoes on weeknights. *"Jassis!"* I said, gazing in wonder at a congealed mass of greying matter smouldering in a cauldron. "I think that's *eggs*!"

Two flavours of fortified Pablum completed the repast, while lubrication was provided by tubs of sweet tea or coffee.

This was pretty much the menu for the duration of our stay. I noticed black servants walking plates of roast beef swimming in arterial fluids toward the faculty buildings for Oom Piet and his henchmen. "Fuckers!" spat Jeremy, glooping a shovelful of banana mush onto his mess plate.

Before we bowed our heads to say grace, a small boy from one of the other schools walked over to a khaki-clad oom, an official-looking envelope gripped in his shaking hand. The oom opened it and read its contents, a look of confusion descending over his manly features. His moustache twitched.

"What's this?"

"A doctor's note," squeaked the boy.

"What's glut-ton?"

"Gluten. Gloo-ten. I'm gluten- and lactose-intolerant. I can't have the bread or the milk or the porridge."

The oom stared at this small piece of Johannesburg—his suspicions about city living once again confirmed—and gave a contemptuous snort.

"What must I do about it?" asked the oom, losing patience quickly.

"Um, my mother sent me with some…" At this the oom waved his hand dismissively—he was done with the conversation. Little Gluten/Lactose sat down to a meal of cold chicken and salad (he had a cooler full of grub installed in the refrigerator) and won no friends that night. In fact, I still harbour intolerance for the gluten- and lactose-intolerant, their very real disabilities notwithstanding. We stared hungrily at him and he wide-eyed us back, as if to say, "Chaps, if my constitution could handle it, I'd be right there with you. But meantime, this chicken is scrumptious!"

There were further indignities, such as rotating kitchen duty. I had never been inside the working part of a kitchen before. My task, among other things, was to help transfer jam from the enormous tank into a marginally smaller one. Furthermore, we had to wash our own mess kits. Troughs of soapy water were provided, and two hundred white South African boys, creatures whose hands had never encountered such labour, winced as the hot water stung their virgin pores. Many a knife, fork, and plate were lost to the depths, and most of us were cleaner than our mess kits by the end of it.

After being subjected to a post-prandial roll call—just in case the dinner menu had incited any of us to make an escape into the darkened veld—the ooms divided us into fifteen or so groups. It was made clear that this was a competition: Each group would be assigned points for tasks performed in the next eleven days, tasks ranging from the mundane (cleanliness of shoes) to the flat-out boring (neatness of bed sheets) to the somewhat interesting (Stalk the Lantern). It was a second-rate version of *Survivor,* except without the possibility of getting voted off the island. Thus, friends from school became enemies, and boys from the other end of Johannesburg—boys we would normally have pelted with orange peels and obloquies at intermural cricket matches—became fast friends. We were assigned to our dorm rooms, put on all the clothes our maids and mothers had packed for us, and crawled into our sleeping bags, shivering with cold. An icy breeze from the Elands blew in through open windows, and a half moon reflected off the open, glistening eyes of the strangers in the room. In a bunk across from me lay Little Gluten/Lactose. Evidently, gluten- and lactose-intolerance makes one sleepy—the bastard was the only one of us getting any kip. Homesickness nestled up beside me like a spectral bride and we drifted off into a field of nightmares, fuelled by the otherworldly animal cries from outside, where the African veld was an infinitely vast expanse separating me from my mother.

"I slept very well, and it is nice to make the room so nice and neat."

Have you ever been awakened by the sound of a bugle? It is unpleasant. Also unpleasant was uncurling my frozen bones from under the seven layers of clothing and the sleeping bag that had kept precisely none of the cold at bay. Even further discomfort was provided by the presence of Little Gluten/Lactose, who, it was clear, would be a liability for my group members and me. Surprisingly, we were passed over for showers and instead ordered to polish our already gleaming shoes. Punishment by association was a classic South African disciplinary technique—the ooms trusted that we'd take care of L'il G/L in our own Lord of the Flies fashion.

Their understanding of human nature was uncanny. It wasn't long before he was cuffed hard on the back of the head. "Can't you just eat the bloody bread?" asked a heavy boy named Dimitri.

"*Ag,* leave him alone, man." This from Derek, who was from a primary school on the far side of Johannesburg. Derek was one of those preadolescents who seemed much older and wiser than his years; his bearing was almost adult-like. Although he was by no means a large boy, Derek took up a lot of room. He carried an aura of the rebel—even his hair, which was cut regulation length, seemed to flout such rules by flopping about with insouciance. Derek was like no one I had ever encountered before. He was light years ahead of us in terms of intellectual development—which isn't saying much—but I had much to learn from him, and learn I did. "Remember, chinas, it's us against them," said he, horking on his Bata Toughies.

If so, it wasn't much of a contest. After a breakfast that differed from dinner only insofar as it was served at a different time of day, we were subjected to a detailed and thoroughly particular flag raising. This was to ensure that Oom Piet (who was nowhere to be seen) would not be further scandalized by our fumbling ministrations at the evening's ceremony. Following that, we strapped all our possessions onto our backs and set out for what I hoped would be a short amble through the scenic Middleveld. If by short amble I meant twenty-mile death march, I was exactly right. We started out through town, which was but a few hundred yards from the *veldskool*. Waterval Boven's small houses are built on hilly terrain. Townsfolk sat on their *stoeps* staring at us as if we were the understudy cast members of Siegfried and Roy's white tiger Vegas act. The Bovenites, misshapen by inbreeding, their crumpled faces staring at us in a swirl of confusion, disgust, and loathing, were no less exotic to us than we were to them. Four limbs and a torso were a rarity in these parts, and we were subjected to a quick but definitive lesson on the ravages of genetic homogeneity.

Whether inbreeding has an inverse relationship to racial tolerance I cannot say, but it seemed that all the ingenuity in Waterval Boven and the surrounding villages was invested in segregating each and every aspect of everyday life, no matter how negligible. It wasn't enough for there to be a bench with a large sign stating "*Slegs wit mense*"—whites only—but there had to be a crappier bench nearby that said "*Slegs swart mense*"—blacks only. Examples of Petty Apartheid were everywhere. In Johannesburg such signifiers were less explicit, and the working parts of the Apartheid machine were far more obscure. Not so in the Eastern Transvaal. Shabby stores prominently displayed large "*Slegs wit mense*" signs. One of the more absurd instances of Apartheid I had ever encountered was to be found in the pedestrian tunnels under the railway bridge. With very little room to work with, the engineers were forced to create two tunnels: a nice one for whites, and a shittier one for blacks. This struck me, even at the age of twelve, as astonishingly pedantic, a fanatical adherence to the fundamentals of legislated segregation. The two-tunnel caper rendered the bridge structurally unsound and perfectly articulated everything about the system—even to a child. Two tunnels, side by side, painstakingly divided, an utter liability.

Through the dripping *"Slegs wit mense"* tunnel we marched and into the African veld. I'd love to say that the first five miles of goosesteppalooza were pleasant, but that would have meant ignoring the helpful information that the ooms were doling out to us. Speaking in their curiously formal English, spat out as if each word of the hated tongue would sear their lips if they didn't get it out of their mouths fast enough, they would say things like: "This here is *kooi-kerrie.* Very poisonous. If you are stuck in the veld with no food, you must boil them for at least twenty minutes. You will have a bad stomach ache, but you will not die." Besides recipe suggestions, they gave us helpful hints on where to stand if we found ourselves under enemy attack. As we moved through a valley gorge, an oom wheeled around and yelled, "Halt!" After completing the process of soiling our pants in terror, we looked at where his finger was pointing. "*Kyk daar, seuntjies*—Look there, boys," he said. "Enemy troops can fire at us from there, because we have not scouted for cover. Always scout for cover. Always!" As if to emphasize the martial nature of the proceedings, squadrons of Cheetah jet fighters flew overhead in low formation with a thunderous roar—either on training missions or on their way to strafe villages in Angola.[47]

At this point, I would have welcomed a refreshing barrage of Cheetah ground fire. That, or a real meal. There was still more to learn from these Martha Stewarts of the bush: which grasses burn best when setting an enemy encampment on fire; where best to set up a machine-gun nest; how to incapacitate rabid wildcats; what rodents go with what Stellenbosch cab sav; and other useful tidbits gleaned from the Boer Wars some eighty years earlier. A considerable part of the guerrilla insurgency that defined the two Boer Wars was fought in these very hills, and several of us found old bullet shells and larger casings from mortar rounds in the veld. The ooms would look over these findings and say, derisively, "*Ag,* they're English"; unless, of course, they were from the old Winchesters the Boers had used. Then their eyes would mist, and they'd finger the *objets de guerre* with the reverence of priests before the Shroud of Turin. "We triumphed," said an oom, "because we was always thinking."

By the time we returned to *veldskool,* I was no longer capable of thought—I would have gladly eaten a tonne of raw *kooi-kerries* and washed them down with a flagon of wildcat piss. Sadly, we still had the flag ceremony to deal with. Oom Piet

47. The Cheetah was a hodgepodge derivation of the Mirage III jet, cobbled together in South Africa because of sanctions. The planes were notoriously unreliable, and we were lucky that engines or bits of fuselage didn't land on us hikers below.

Angola was South Africa's Vietnam—a faraway war against a proxy Soviet client state. The South African Defense Force battled the Communist-backed government forces alongside the rebel group UNITA, with the CIA untidily in the mix somewhere. As far as dirty wars go, it was up there with the best of them.

stalked through the fog of my exhaustion and hunger like a demon god, offering more exhortations to the flag. "This is," said Oom Piet, his Hitler comb-over unmoving in the slight breeze, "a symbol of your country." His harsh Afrikaans accent made *country* sound like a dirty word. Behind me, Derek sniggered, "Cunt-tree." I sniggered, too. This outburst of mirth proved unwise. The ooms were on us like Boer guerrillas on a pith helmet. Oom Piet stalked through the ranks of boys and closed in on Derek. He knew this was a mind he had to crush. In slow and measured tones, as if speaking to an imbecile, he said, "We will fight for this flag. We will die for it. You think this is a joke? Our enemies wait for us, and will try to take this *cunt-tree* from us. And you make jokes. In Angola, right now, we fight to make sure that they do not come here for us. So what, *seuntjie,* is so very funny?" Oom Piet was one for rhetorical questions—he had the answers to everything he needed to know by the age of three—so he didn't wait for Derek's reply. He wrenched Derek by the scruff of his neck and dragged him to the flagpole. There, for twenty minutes, the ooms harangued him to get the flag off the pole in the proper manner. I felt bad for not having spoken up in allegiance to my friend, but not bad enough. I was especially thankful for my cowardice when Derek was dragged off in the direction of the outbuildings before we were dismissed to mess.

That night in the dorm, Derek showed off the three raised, purple welts just below his butt cheeks. We were impressed. No paramedic was present during the caning, and Derek admitted that he had almost cried (his red-rimmed eyes suggesting that the "almost" was not quite accurate). Still, you had to give the guy credit, and we did. "Those were the fucking hardest jacks I've ever got in my life," he claimed. Having seen the results, I believed him.

Once in bed, we all sniggered some more over "cunt-tree." But my twelve-year-old brain, tired as it was, was mulling over a thought. This being South Africa, I had encountered as many psychos in my short life as an FBI profiler does in a thirty-five-year career. The ooms, however, were a new kinda crazy. In Johannesburg, you'd see plenty of cynical acquiescence with the terms of Apartheid, and certainly plenty of racism, but never the kind of ideological fanaticism on show here. I had never thought that anyone truly *believed.* I didn't think anyone would *die* for our way of life because they believed in it as thoroughly as those in my Oupa's synagogue believed in God or a Jewish way of life.

The cunt-tree, all of a sudden, seemed like a confounding place.

"Oom Piet has many interesting things to say on different topics on the veld."

"Communists," said Oom Piet, as we all stood in a field of swaying grassland, "have no fear. They can come from anywhere. We must always be prepared." With that, he simply disappeared, as if he were a wizard performing a morning sleight-of-hand workout. We looked around, stunned, listening to the rustling of the grass. Oom Piet reappeared just as suddenly behind us. "We must always use the land," said Oom Piet after we were done screaming, "as if it is our best friend."

Oh, the ways in which the land is our friend: Pebbles for flints and makeshift arrowheads. Grass and mud for camouflage. Wood for sharpening into spears. Caves for shelter. Rocks for hand-to-hand combat. Snakes, bugs, and birds for sustenance. Indeed, all you needed to fight Communism was a combination of know-how, derring-do, and a healthy appetite for anything that oozed when you poked it. We dropped and rolled, we leopard-crawled, we bird-called. "And when the *kaffirs* and Communists come for us, we will be ready," Oom Piet assured us.

Maybe so, but we Johannesburgers weren't holding up our end. Perhaps inspired by the message of the land as one big all-you-can-eat buffet, our chaperone, Mr. Billups, and the thirty or so boys under his care (I, thankfully, not among them) had drunk freely from the waterfall pool (a pool so stunning that "drinking it in" seemed entirely appropriate, if incredibly unwise). It took the ooms no time at all to assess why a stomach bug was spreading so rapidly through the dormitories. The ooms and the Johannesburg chaperones had a strange relationship. The interlopers were clearly regarded as idiots and enemies, yet still addressed in a polite, gentlemanly manner—a throwback to the World War I concept of respect and adherence to social conventions regardless of how deep the ideological divide between you and your adversaries. In this case, however, the ooms' derision was unmistakable. Pails were set up by the bedsides of the stricken, and that night was a symphony of retching, weeping, intestinal gurgling, diarrheal splooshing, and the distant sounds of the ooms laughing their asses off.

"I am quite happy I did not get sick."

Note the qualifier "quite" in this scrapbook entry. Acute dysentery would have come as something of a relief at that point. My body was ravaged—blisters the size of silver dollars plagued my feet, now so swollen they could barely fit into my (well-polished) shoes. I had lost about five pounds walking what seemed the equivalent of the length and breadth of the African continent. Twice. And my fingers were chapped and swollen from all that damned washing-up. I stared enviously at the group members lucky enough to be leaking poison from their orifices. (Gluten/Lactose, the bastard, had managed to come down with diarrhea, even though he went nowhere near the offending water. I smacked him on the head—Derek was too weak to protest.) Given the morning's itinerary, a severe case of the flying axe handles actually looked appealing.

It was Obstacle Course Day.

Now, I was no obstacle-course virgin. Then again, I had also hiked before. Considering that *veldskool* ratcheted up even the most menial activity to unbearable levels of pain (that washing-up water was *hot*!), I knew that this particular trial spelled trouble.

The obstacle course would have posed a challenge for battle-hardened Delta Force soldiers, but for twelve-year-old boys it was a killing ground. The sheer rope wall disappeared into the clouds above us; the ditches, filled with fetid water, were topped with barbed wire that glinted like muggers' shivs. Group rankings depended on a good performance here, so it promised to be a fiercely contested exercise. The ooms spaced themselves along the course, and as we completed lining up in front of the rope wall, one of them, stopwatch in hand, yelled, "Go, go! *Maak gou!*" And off we went.

Mayhem ensued, followed quickly by pain, with injury fast on its heels. I saw a boy from my school, Ryan, lose his hold on the rope wall and fall close to six feet into the dust with a sickening *whomph*! An oom towered over him, yelling "Again! Again! *Maak gou!*" Any kid with a body mass index of over twenty-six—those individuals who did so well in the classroom portion of school—now found themselves the lowest link in the food chain. Intelligence was not highly prized at Waterval Boven. "Run, fattie! Run, boy! Hurry!" The heavier kids did not have a good day of it. Dimitri, the chunky chap who had devoted his off time to riding Gluten/Lactose like a petting-zoo pony, was on the receiving end of the most egregious genital injury I have ever witnessed. While swinging from one landing to another with great, gathering velocity, he was yanked by gravity down the rope to the point where his groin and a pole were introduced to each other with a sickening squelch. He screeched his throat raw, and I have yet to see a nastier bruise than the one he showed us that evening—a vicious piebald stain that leaked all the way down to his thighs and halfway up his belly. He wept for two days.

On that obstacle course, gravity worked with unremitting insistence; I, too, gave in to its ministrations. On a particularly intricate jump-and-swing manoeuvre, I wrenched my shoulder from its socket on the same rope where Dimitri had become Demitra, and dangled dangerously until a group member courageously dived across to swing me to the landing (thus earning us extra points for his selfless assistance to a comrade in need—in true Dirkie Uys/Ragel De Beer fashion). I finished that round of the course in great agony and was curtly waved toward the infirmary by an oom who had seen worse.

The nurse was a local woman, most likely a faculty wife, who had a bedside manner best described as Baathist meets Tamil Tiger, by way of Robert Mugabe. She was about as well versed in medicine as I am in post–World War II Macedonian poetry, and was far more interested in smoking her way through a pack of Rothmans Blue than in administering to her patients. It was a busy day for Nurse Nevermind. After a cursory "Wherzzit hurt?" she splinted fingers, splashed disinfectant on cuts and abrasions, and, in my case, made a rudimentary sling for my arm. Clearly, her orders were to patch 'em up and get 'em back on the field. She gave me my lime-green lollipop with such scorn that I—a lollipop aficionado—seriously considered flinging it onto the dirt. Good sense overcame my principles, and I returned to the battle suitably fortified with acetaminophen and sugar, ready for round two.

"My arm hurts."

Assembly that evening in front of the flagpole resembled a Flanders triage tent circa 1917. Filthy bandages, emaciated soldiers, bloodied clothing, dysentery—you could almost hear distant, mournful bagpipes playing "Amazing Grace." Oom Piet, in his freshly pressed safari suit, didn't seem to notice the dismantled state of his troops, and if he did, he was probably secure in the knowledge that the road to manhood lies potholed with just such hardships. Besides, he had other things on his mind.

I remember this line distinctly: "One day, you will know the sound of an AK-47 like you know your own heartbeat." Poetry. The Kalashnikov semi-automatic rifle was, of course, the Soviet Union's number-one export and, therefore, the ANC's weapon of choice.[48] Thus, when the war began in earnest, the report of

48. The ANC was supplied with arms and training by various Communist regimes within Africa and beyond. Their philosophical leanings had links to Communist, or Marxist, theories—thus, they were tarred with the pinko brush by the Powers-That-Were. However, Umkhonto we Sizwe (meaning Spear of the Nation), the ANC's military wing, was (revisionist history notwithstanding) not set up as a proper fighting force or full-fledged rebel army, like UNITA was in Angola. Therefore, Oom Piet's view of it as an organized, heavily armed Communist fighting machine was somewhat overblown.

the AK-47 would become the lingua franca of the enemy, while we retorted with sharp blasts of our standard-issue R-5s. "You will know," said Oom Piet, belabouring his point, "very well the sound of your enemy."

These rhetorical blandishments were getting me worked up, and not a little fearful. Nonetheless, I was indulging in reflection that Oom Piet would probably not have cared to broker. Most important, I saw a gargantuan chasm in the logic of the *veld-skool* curriculum. I lived in Johannesburg, dammit! When were *they* coming for us, who exactly were *they*, and when were we gonna get some firearms training? I didn't have the luxury of being able to remove the poison pouch of a *boomslang* and drench the tip of a sharpened stick with its deadly liquid.[49] What was I supposed to disguise myself as? A Volkswagen? A three-bed, two-bath ranch house? If *they* were coming to Johannesburg, damn straight I would know the sound of an AK-47. Right before I knew the sound of bullets ripping through my body. Veld fighting was all well and good, but what about urban warfare? We were from Johannesburg—*Johannesburg*—not some remote outpost in the bush.

"The ANC," said Oom Piet, unaware of my internal rant and following the course of his own inner logic, "is our ultimate enemy. Its intention is the overthrow of this great *cunt-tree.*

---

49. *Boomslang* literally means tree snake. A *boomslang* is pretty much the reigning sociopath of the veld—it is one of the few members of the animal kingdom (humans are another) that kill with malignant glee rather than any biological imperative. The snake's MO is to drop from the trees like death from above and inject its prey with a powerful hemotoxic venom that doesn't even provide a decent high before curdling the victim's blood and shutting down the internal organs.

After, the blacks will run the place, and destroy our Christian way of life. We will all be turned into Communists. Well, we have faced such things before. We must be prepared." I remember being somewhat alarmed by the tenor and the ferocity of these harangues. This was not the kind of thing we were used to at school—we didn't talk about the ANC or Communism or anything outside the tightly controlled curriculum. No—this kind of talk was reserved for *veldskool,* and for committed believers like Oom Piet.

But when I thought about the ANC, I thought not of running battles in the Drakensberg but exploding garbage cans and township violence. I was twelve, but I clearly saw the ANC as an urban threat, or at least as a threat to me as an urbanite. I was not yet sophisticated enough to feel any empathy for the ANC's cause. The ANC was the bad guys—the same as the bad guys the *A-Team* battled every week. I saw its bloodthirsty antics as completely unrelated to the disenfranchisement of black South Africans (not that I could spell *disenfranchisement* at the time, let alone explain it). Indeed, colour had everything to do with my acceptance of the ANC as an enemy of the state. They were black—and they hated us because we were white. Simple.

But what was it with this Communism stuff? It was something I just couldn't get my head around. Given that the writings of Marx and any other Commie theorists were banned in the country (and had been for years), and given that our educators were forbidden to speak about these theories, I was completely in the dark as to the conceptual engine that drove the spectre of the Soviet Union. What precisely did the Communists want with us? What was their mission here at the end of the earth? As far as I was aware, they wanted to kill our God. Well, if that meant no more hymns on Wednesdays, they had my vote.

The USSR sounded like a drag, no doubt about it. There the government told you what to do and when to do it. The bulk of the population, I was told, lived a poverty-stricken existence, while a privileged few enjoyed lifestyles of great extravagance. The state killed its citizens in bulk; torture was little more than a good way to get a confession out of someone who had nothing to confess. It snowed *all* the time, and the toilet paper, if you could find any, was like rough-grain sandpaper. I guess I needed Oom Piet to explain to me—snow and ass wipe notwithstanding—how this differed from South Africa. Mr. Billups had intimated these things in math class. Indeed, Oom Piet and Mr. Billups were opposite magnetic forces pulling my burgeoning worldview to shreds.

Maybe because of the comments Mr. Billups had made over the past couple of years, I had always seen the USSR and the Republic of South Africa as roughly analogous. I'm not suggesting that I was a twelve-year-old political scientist—I couldn't even begin to fathom the working differences between a capitalist/Calvinist state like South Africa and Soviet Communism, even if I had known the first thing about Communism. To a child, they looked one of a piece. Thus, I had a visual in my head that linked the two regimes. I thought of Soviet Russia as grey. Featureless. And despite the orgy of colour that surrounded me here in the Eastern Transvaal—the verdant subtropical fauna butting up against the rich reds and browns of the Lowveld, the ostentatiously adorned birdlife, the shockingly blue sky broken with white cumulus—I could picture South Africa as nothing other than grey, too. It had everything to do with folks like the ooms and the dreariness of a place like Waterval Boven—people who reminded me exactly of the politicians I saw on TV and the authority figures I encountered at school or on excursions just like this one. This graphical comparison was a child's way of drawing an analogy between two regimes, even if I didn't exactly understand the vast differences between the two. Still, if I was having trouble differentiating between us and our sworn enemy, the Soviet Bloody Union, then there had to be something seriously awry. I wanted to ask Oom Piet, "P.W. Botha and Khrushchev. What's the diffs, *boet*?"

I don't think he had a cane in his arsenal big enough to punish that offence.

For one half of an afternoon, we boy soldiers were allowed a few hours of reprieve. We had been constantly occupied up until that point, and it was almost eerie to have time without someone yelling "*Maak gou!* Hurry!" I can see why some become addicted to military life—quiet time can seem like a huge comedown. With my friends either puking in buckets or being patched up by Nurse Nevermind, Derek and I sat on the bank of the Elands, me nursing my shoulder and he nursing his still touchy stomach. I threw a stone into the fast-moving waters. This hurt, as did movement in general.

"*Jassis,* Oom Piet is *mal,* hey?" said Derek. "He's the kind of Dutchman that makes this cunt-tree truly special."

"*Ja, boet.* He *skriks* me out," I agreed.

He gingerly felt the welts on his butt. "*Ja,* I wish the ANC would come in here right now and deal with those bloody ooms. That would be *lekker* by me."

Naturally, I did not record this conversation in my scrapbook. I remember the gist of it because I remember Derek's attitude clearly, so great an impression did it make on me—his apostasy, in this case, mirroring my own. There was a distinct smell of bullshit in the air, an olfactory constant that would not leave my nostrils until I left the country, some four years later. A new chemical constitution was bubbling in my bloodstream, causing my nose to twitch into a sneer and my brain to reject any information it was given. With hindsight, I know what it is that made Derek appear so grown-up to me, what makes me remember him as somehow adult: It was his cynicism—a cynicism born of living in a system he didn't believe in, and being bound to rules and regulations that he saw right through. He was a little Billups, but without the bitterness. Yet.

I cannot remember the precise genesis of my own brand of cynicism, but I remember when it firmly took hold and stuck. It was now an ineffable part of my bloodstream, alkaline making way for acid in ever-increasing increments. In many ways, however, I wish that cynicism was my most memorable *veldskool* souvenir.

It wasn't, not by half.

I noticed them that afternoon while in the bathroom doing my daily obsessive-compulsive inspection for pubes. We had just had our first shower in seven days—a brief moratorium on the group punishment instituted for our association with Gluten/Lactose. The shower felt like needles jabbing into skin, so cold was the water. As I hurried shivering into a bathroom stall, I happened to notice that, although there were *still* no pubic hairs, there were, horrifyingly, three shiny black critters attached to my cold-wrinkled scrotum. Where the shaft of my penis joined said appendage, I located a fourth. Dread settled over me like the enfolding, papery wings of an Angel of Doom. I frenetically searched the rest of my body while hyperventilating noisily. Nothing. Only my genitalia were afflicted, which added irony to cynicism in my growing lexicon of adult sensibilities. I calculated the length of time remaining until I would be home. Four days. Ninety-six hours. A lifetime. My balls were under attack from vicious blood-sucking creatures, and I had few, if any, options. The nurse was out of the question, unless second-hand smoke would kill these things, which I doubted. Mr. Billups, stout of heart though he was, would probably run screaming into the *bushveld.* That, or cane me for having a supercilious look on my dick. The ooms would shrug, sever my privates with a bowie knife, and turf them into the dinner *sosaties.* My friends and group members were simply not an option—the mocking and piss-taking would make the actual ticks seem like a non-issue. No, on this I was solidly alone.

I bent double and tried to pull at one of the ticks, but it was clamped on with impressive tenacity. Tears sprung to my eyes. Before I could think of what MacGyver might do in such a situation, an oom banged on the stall door, interrupting my self-assessment (our stays in the bathrooms were restricted to mere minutes, to save us from the self-abuse endemic during preadolescence). As I gingerly pulled my underpants over my afflicted bits, homesickness and self-pity crawled into my throat and lodged there in a stubborn lump. I rejoined my team and completed packing my camping kit. We were going camping. Unfortunately, it looked like rain.

"It was raining hard."

It was raining hard.

For two days straight (incidentally, the length of our camping trip), rain fell with unremitting constancy. For the march to the campsite, a good ten miles from the *veldskool,* we wore large plastic bags over our raincoats and knapsacks. Without the sun the day became cold, and my teeth clattered like skeletons wrestling on a ceramic floor. The objective of this particular exercise was to survive off the land for two days and two nights. We were equipped with matches, packages of raw meat, other assorted foodstuffs, and old army tents. Of course, I was packing a little more than most—the four ticks attached to my genitals might have weighed twenty pounds a pop, so heavy in my mind were they.

We were left, my group mates and I, in thick, almost subtropical *bushveld,* with the patter of rain drowning out the curious noises emanating from the trees. The area was riddled with wildlife, most of it opposed to our intrusion. Either that, or we were considered nature's equivalent of ordering in. I have never been mechanically minded, and the vaunted opposable thumbs that apparently raise *Homo sapiens* to the top spot on the evolutionary rankings must have skipped a generation in my family. Pitching the tent was a two-man job, but given my injury and my long-standing handicap, only one boy—Derek—could do it. Thus, the task was performed less efficiently than we might have liked and, with the inclemency we were experiencing, even the slightest of gaps became a significant liability.

Those days were two of the longest of my childhood. We boys settled quickly into our *Lord of the Flies* social framework, with me crawling up the leaderboard using my sling as leverage. ("*Ag,* how do you expect me to do that, *boet*? I should be in a fuckin' hospital.") Others scouted for food and firewood (useless, of course, given the weather), and we set up watches so we would not be raided by wild animals and/or enemy camps and/or Commies and/or *kaffirs.* We did not kill the pig, as such, but L'il Gluten/Lactose left that bush so mentally scarred that I'm sure he is still but a shell of a man, secretly ingesting bread soaked in milk and enduring the agony that comes with it. Still, he was lucky. Another day and he would've been lunch. A day after that, and we would've beaten each other to death with his bones.

My injured right arm forced me to scribble in my scrapbook with my left, and the water from the heavens mingled with my tears to leave blue blotches of ink where words should have been. Thus, my scrapbook deserts me here. Still, I have forgotten very little of those few days. I have never felt so afraid, before or since, and this kind of emotional nadir does tend to make an impression. Six days of *bushveld* instruction had simply not been enough for this measure of roughing it, and the daily bouts of propaganda had stoked my steady-burning South African paranoia into a full-blown conflagration. I knew, however, that there would be no one swooping in to save us. We were on our own.

Derek and I lay in the tent in advanced states of abject misery, inches of mud squelching beneath us, staring up at the crushing blackness of the wet night. I recall invoking the comforts of home in an attempt to quell our fear and discomfort. "*Ag,* imagine a Dreyer's milkshake right now, *boet,*" said Derek. "*Ja,* or a hamburger. Or fucking *wors* and *pap,*" I said. My salivary glands, dusty with disuse, went through motions they had not bothered with in close to a week, just for practice.

That night, unable to start a fire (and if we had, I'm unsure what we would've done with it), we supped on raw meat, consumed caveman-style—all hands and incisors. The increase in my red-blood-cell count inflamed the hunger of my hangers-on—I imagined them sucking blood from my scrotum like pups on a teat. While Derek drifted off to sleep before his watch, I lay awake, rain and tears mingling in a muddy soup at the base of my head. "Is this what being a man is about?" I wondered. "Is adulthood about extreme discomfort, hard slog, abject unhappiness, and parasites attached to your genitalia?" This was remarkable prescience born of great duress. At least when *I* grew up, I wasn't surprised.

Night watch was an interminable, terrifying three hours. Staying awake wasn't the issue; it was staying sane that commanded most of my efforts. I imagined eight-legged wildcats scuttling across the veld like monstrous arachnids, fangs caked with the dried gore of their victims. I pictured *boomslange* slowly surrounding the campsite, converging in ever-tightening circles. This, combined with the terrifying array of real bugs and creatures of the Middleveld made for an unforgettable 180 minutes, two nights in a row.

The ooms, who were probably (hopefully?) never far away, pulled us out mid-morning of the second day. I almost wept when I saw their rain-soaked moustaches and mud-splattered knees. I left a part of my soul behind at that campsite deep in the African *bushveld,* and a chunk of my childhood besides. I looked stonily ahead as we marched through the rain back toward those blessed dormitories.

I was never before or since so happy to see a forty-gallon tub of margarine.

"The camping trip taught me much about life in the veld. You must always be alert for danger."

Ah, the resiliency of youth. That afternoon, the rain—and the rigorous fidelity to team loyalty—abated. "It was nice to see my friends again," said my rejuvenated scrapbook. Reunited with Jeremy, Leigh, and other school friends, we regaled each other with tales of our heroism. Night watch inspired the most fanciful recounts, along the lines of: "*Boet,* there was something out there. I sharpened a twig like Oom Fritz taught us, and I yelled at it. I swear it was a Communist." My dirty sling got plenty of admiring glances, and no doubt I played up the pain; if my stoic scrapbook is to be trusted, "it doesn't hurt very badly anymore." My balls, on the other hand, could have used serious medical attention.

Despite that, I remember the pleasure of napping in the *veld-skool* beds after the two nights of lying in mud. This pleasure—like most in life—did not last long. Shortly after heads met pillows, the ooms, in a seriously foul temper, awakened us with their barks. "Up! *Maak gou!*" We were forced into the court-yard, where two hundred groggy boys blinked rapidly in the dying sunlight. I cannot remember what the offence was, and my scrapbook leaves no record of it, but several boys were in big trouble for a misdeed. The ooms, though, were unsure of the culprits. Thus, we were seated in the courtyard like a massive cast in the denouement of an Agatha Christie novel (*Death in the Middleveld,* maybe, or *Foul Play at Veldskool*?), with Oom Piet as a crazed, Afrikaans Hercule Poirot.

"Who?" he asked simply as he walked through our ranks. Instead of using a Sherlock-like intellect, Oom Piet employed fear to smoke out the guilty. This is quicker and far more effec-tive—as his socks and *velskoene* passed by my face, *I* almost raised my hand in confession. Oom Piet was one of those rare people whose facial expression almost never changed. When Nelson Mandela was released from prison, Oom Piet probably had the exact same expression on his face as he did when he was firing off rounds at indigent villagers in Angola. He didn't look angry so much as have anger smouldering off him, in coiled tendrils of steam. The only visual clue to his rage was that a lifetime as a red-meat-and-potatoes eater had rendered his circulatory system so clogged with sclerotic plaque that he flushed a deep, worrying maroon. This obvious manifestation of his rage made the question, how, *how,* does this man maintain such outward calm when he is clearly so pissed off? even more urgent. My answer would be: because he's fucking crazy. You may have another theory.

One by one, the guilty slowly raised their hands. One by one, Oom Piet grabbed them by the ears, twisted, and lined them up before us. Although I was in a nap-befuddled haze—a state of being that lent the proceedings a suitably surreal aura—I have never forgotten Oom Piet's fulmination that afternoon. There was that face, a few degrees west of purple on a colour temperature chart; the flecks of spittle flying from his mouth like ash from a razed field; his pale blue eyes unblinking, mirroring the colour of the sky. He went through the list of his usual bugaboos, but I wasn't listening anymore—he and I were thinking differently by this point. My view was that the enemy was Oom Piet himself: inflexible, ideologically rigid, essentially unthinking, and a total fucking bore. A feeling of panicked frustration rose in me—the same feeling I now recognize when dealing with government bureaucrats, bank clerks, left-wing university students, right-wing MBAs, or the deeply religious—the sense that there is some vast, immutable edifice of righteousness propping up their convictions, a monolith that would remain unscathed under even the most consistent barrage of reason and good sense. So it was with Oom Piet and his khaki-clad minions.

Oom Piet *believed* in the system he espoused. My time in *veldskool* helped make me a devout non-believer in the system (insofar as I understood it) and those who perpetrated it. It would be years before I understood the full breadth of the system, but that didn't matter because, with the purple man in the safari suit screaming its virtues, I came to understand the impulses for it. I could never have articulated all this, but when I arrived at *veldskool* I feared Oom Piet because I figured that he had it all figured, that he'd covered the angles, thought it all through. Now I feared Oom Piet because of the smallness of his mind—his ignorance was a liability. In my mental statue garden, Oom Piet stands as a ten-foot-tall example of ideological inflexibility, a symbol of the dangers of living in a world of your own making. He was waiting for the Boer War to return to these hills, this time with a different enemy. Yet somehow, the Boers would still, of course, be the victims. For a mildly intelligent boy of twelve, this seemed a little rich. No matter how many bugs he ate or how well he hid in grass, Oom Piet, I remember thinking, was a complete dick.

"It was very sad saying goodbye to Derek, and many others also."

Our final breakfast was followed by an assembly, run by the man himself. He seemed in a fine mood—as if all his hard work would undoubtedly come to something as we headed out into the big, wide world. His speech was a fulsome article of praise of those boys who had distinguished themselves, and he handed out leadership certificates to about twenty or thirty of us. (I received one for continuing the obstacle course with an injured arm. Derek did not.) I felt like a fraud as I took the piece of paper from Oom Piet's leathery paws, his hand engulfing my own when we shook. There he was, right in front of me. I remember thinking that he wasn't even that tall. "You should've kicked him in the balls," whispered Derek when I sat down. The thought *had* crossed my mind. Oom Piet wished us the best of luck and, of course, reminded us who the bad guys were. "We must look for Communism everywhere," or something to that effect, were his final words to us.

The bus ride home was silent for reasons different from the ride in. Mostly, we were too battered, bruised, and exhausted to thigh slap or engage in preadolescent badinage. Also, I think all of us, to a boy, had one thing on our minds, one thing we had been missing for the past nine days. If we had been older, that one thing would have been pussy. Given that we were twelve, that one thing was television.

"It is nice to be home, but I miss the experience of Veldskool."

I've intimated that *veldskool* helped instill in me very adult sensibilities. That's different from saying it made a man out of me. A day after my homecoming, after a nice long lie-in, I awakened with a heaviness of heart I could not account for. Then, in a flash, those Angel of Doom wings engulfed me once more. The ticks! I had managed to forget about them in the excitement of eating a real meal, but now they once again loomed large in my consciousness. I had no choice. I had to tell my mother.

To her credit, she tried valiantly not to look horrified. She failed. Minutes later, this newly minted man and soldier was standing in the bathroom shaking as his mother examined his scrotum, her hands protected with rubber gloves. A call to the doctor, over my strident protestations, informed us that soaking the afflicted area in hot (not warm, friends, *hot*) water and disinfectant would do the trick. Bushy was enlisted to keep the finger bowls of liquid tick killer coming fast and furious, making this the single most humiliating experience of my life. "Be strong, boy," Bushy sniggered, handing my mother another testicular bath.

One by one, those ticks were soaked into the big sleep, lying belly up in the steaming liquid. I have spoken of the resiliency of youth—this is the only way to explain that my well-adjusted (or, more appropriately, typical) attachment to my genitals did not suffer any ill effects from this experience.

Freed from these last remnants of *veldskool,* I began to feel that Oom Piet and his minions were far, far away. It was a Saturday, and I dug out my action figures along with fellow *veldskool* vet Leigh. We set up our *A-Team* figures in the rec room and played war with much sounder tactical underpinnings than we would have prior to our nine-day excursion in the *bushveld.* As I took out Leigh's (newly restored) *A-Team* van with a flank manoeuvre, I thought, "*Ag,* being a man isn't such a bad thing after all." We drank orange juice, my mother made us lunch, and then we fried bugs under my magnifying glass. You know, business as usual.

There was, however, something new and shadowy lurking in my consciousness. The everyday no longer seemed quite so comfortable, or controllable. A low buzz of tension hummed in the air, a buzz I had not noticed before—both a constant sense of insecurity and the promise of … something. The quality of light had changed, the trees looked different, people moved differently. My world was newly washed with a fresh, shiny menace.

Oom Piet had become for me an icon—a *Day of the Dead* puppet whose mouth moved in jagged clacks, saying nothing. He was a dread symbol, and through his gaping puppet maw I heard the voice of all the authority figures I encountered. I understood that whoever was pulling the puppet strings, those pallid grey men in Pretoria were deadly serious about keeping things just as they were. At *veldskool*, through Oom Piet, I had been inside their minds, seen how they saw things. And it was, frankly, terrifying.

If, by extension, I had seen things through P.W. Botha's eyes, I had also seen things through the eyes of people like Derek. And things looked badly askew from that viewpoint. In a short time, the quotidian had become the absurd. I felt new kinship with the cynical, and a new enmity with hard and fast believers. I was becoming a doubter, with nothing else to replace the empty spots where what I once believed in used to be.

Is this what constitutes the making of a man? Maybe, or at least a certain type of man. For me and many of my peers, *veldskool* had failed in its central tenet—to make us working parts of the machine. In the machine we still were, but faulty cogs rather than well-burnished ball bearings. Some emerged from *veldskool* newly empowered; I emerged into a much darker place. When I handed in my scrapbook, with its dead leaves and even deader prose—a tract that bore absolutely no resemblance to the actual *veldskool* experience—I was only too happy to have it out of my possession.

It was the work of a little boy.

Muzak

My bobba, my father's mother, lived in a small flat in the Johannesburg suburb of Lower Houghton. Before she got so sick, and when I was very young, we'd play hide-and-seek among the trees in her apartment building's front garden—two towering jacarandas and a couple of gloomy camphors. We'd then sit outside on a bench, which, despite having each wooden slat painted a different colour in an exhausted approximation of a rainbow, did not bring any good cheer to the building, which was full of Polish bobbas, ancient before their time, with whiskers and shabby housecoats and warnings that swallowing even *one* dog or cat hair is fatal.

Dr. Poplak discovered the telltale white speckles of a tumour on the inside of Bobba's left cheek when he was cleaning her teeth at his surgery. Shortly thereafter, a sizeable piece of her face was removed, and her gums and molars could be seen through the gaping hole. This was frightening, and goes a good way to explaining my youthful *Fangoria* obsession. I resisted visiting, but when I did, she served me smoked chicken and Nestlé white chocolates, each with a different species of butterfly on the packaging. I hoarded them, a sort of confectionary lepidopteran collection that saved me running around a meadow with a net and one of those silly hats.

Anyway, there I was, in Bobba's flat, about ten years old, sitting with her on the couch watching *Pop Shop*, and on comes Michael Jackson's "Billie Jean." I loved that song. Stuffed to the gills with chicken and chocolate, I nonetheless went crazy, hopping off the couch and moonwalking across the carpet in the small living room. "Ah, Billie Jean, ah with my laaaa," I sang. Bobba had leaned forward and was peering at the TV intently. Maybe she liked the song too; she was, after all, a singer of some renown in her youth. So her interest in the King of Pop made good sense.

"He sinks so good!" she said. "But a *shvartze*?"

Then it hit me: Michael Jackson is black! That had never crossed my mind. He was so high above earthbound considerations such as skin colour that it hadn't occurred to me to classify him as either, erm, Black or White.

At that instant, while I was moonwalking to "Billie Jean" in front of my bobba, Michael Jackson was in the process of turning himself into a white teenaged boy, or Diana Ross, depending on whom you asked or what angle you looked at him from. If he had known that in faraway, much-maligned South Africa, a little white boy had seen him as completely outside, or above, the concept of race, would he have stopped the insanity?

Doubtful.

I had received the *Thriller* cassette for my ninth birthday, and I played it so often the tape warped, turning "Billie Jean" into a melancholy dirge—"Ahhh Biyliiiieeee Sheeean, ahhhhh with moiyyyyyy laaaahhhhh…" And I remember thinking that Michael Jackson was just a really *lekker* singer. Did it matter that he was black?

Well, to him it did; it mattered to my bobba, but only incidentally; it mattered to some of my classmates ("*kaffir* music," they called it); but it mattered not at all to me. If you were to analyze all four parties—Michael Jackson, my classmates, my bobba, and me—the person who had the largest issue with Michael Jackson's blackness was Michael Jackson (by a hair over some of my classmates). When it came to music—or, when it came to black American musicians—despite the notions of some of my pals, I was colour-blind. Whitney Houston, Lionel Richie, The Commodores, George Benson, the bassist from Culture Club—it didn't matter. So long as their music coalesced with the broad range of my discernment, they all made it into the scrapbook.

These scrapbooks depicted a journey—from the opening bars of delightful, meaningless chintzy pop in my early years to the closing guitar solos of dark, leaden 1970s rock of my mid-teens. From the innocuous (Olivia Newton-John) to the objectionable (Guns N' Roses), the journey is similar to that of so many music-obsessed kids, whether in Manitoba or in Mongolia. It just meant something different in South Africa—like the relationship my bobba had with Michael Jackson. A classroom wit once said to me at school, after I confessed to digging the new Whitney album: "If you like kraal music so much, *boetie,* come to my house and I'll get my maid to sing for you."

It started with ABBA. I have no recollection of this, but my mother and father insist that my musical interests were first piqued when I heard the Swedish quartet's "Mamma Mia" on the car radio. I was three, and I was hooked. Because the ABBA obsession amused them, they purchased the cassette, and when I got wind of Barry Manilow and Neil Diamond (this was uncool, even for a four-year-old), the car tape deck played these three artists on a rotating basis.

This nascent musical journey took flight on account of my friendship with David Eliakim, a sandy-haired tennis-playing youth who was a year ahead of me at school. I don't think David, who possessed a sharp, precise mind (he would go on to be class valedictorian at my high school), liked music so much as music provided a way for him to implement his meticulous organizational abilities. David's world revolved around the weekly syndicated broadcast of *Casey Kasem's Top-40 Countdown.* Every Sunday night, starting at 7 P.M. and running until well after my bedtime, Casey counted down the hits, much as he did all over the free English-speaking world.[50] The seven-year-old David taped each show, kept the cassettes in a library, listing each track, in order, in notebooks that resembled the work of anorak-wearing plane-spotters on the Heathrow Airport observation deck. In introducing me to Casey Kasem, David might as well have introduced me to God, and in introducing me to musical obsession, he could have found no better protege.

Kasem's authoritative voice, travelling over oceans and mountains and deserts, over glittering cities and shabby towns, arrived in my bedroom as the highlight of my week (even if it did coincide with the termination of the blessed weekend). The countdown—so American with its digressions, comeback stories, statistics, list-making, and hype—was serious business for me. I was allowed to listen until 9 P.M., which was my bedtime. Like generations of youths since the advent of the radio receiver, I took my white

---

50. I wonder how many youths Kasem influenced in the not-so-free world. There were certainly other South African fans, but what about the USSR, or Chile, or Cuba? His was a shiny, beautiful version of the United States, with his long-distance dedications from Omaha, Nebraska; Santa Fe; North Dakota. Casey Kasem broadcast the America that America was supposed to be.

Casio with me under the covers and listened until 11 P.M., when the number-one song was played (even though, with my David-inspired annotations, I pretty much knew whether it would be Madonna or The Eurythmics at the top of the heap long before Casey got around to playing the song). Regardless of the outcome, the countdown was an exercise in agonizing suspense. It was a four-hour serialized narrative that had an entirely novelistic approach. There were asides, bit players, new characters introduced along the way—it was high drama, and I was gripped. Strangely, whenever I hear Casey's gravely American accent, I think immediately of South Africa; he was as local to me as *biltong*. To Casey I owe my unadulterated love of music, my insistence on saving the best for last, and my intense distaste for Shadoe Stevens, who replaced him in 1988, thus shunting me further from pop and into the orbit of 1970s rock.

Radio 702—the station that broadcast *American Top 40*—was a combination talk–music format. The station's founder, the canny Issie Kirsh, observed that one of the Apartheid regime's more ignominious practices—the establishment of homelands—allowed a loophole for an outfit looking to start a mildly controversial talk radio station. Radio 702 was set up in the banana-fiefdom of Bophuthatswana, thus outside the government's official jurisdiction,[51] but within easy transmission

51. Here was the Catch-22 the government had rigged for itself: If it was suitably provoked, it could have pushed the Bophuthatswana authorities for the station's closure. But this would mean exposing the lie that Bop was independent of the South African government, and illuminating its quisling status. Also, the government knew that the Bop authorities needed every miserable penny to prop up its rickety regime. Thus the southern African capital of iniquity—the gambling/showgirl mecca of Sun City. And also, Radio 702.

distance of Transvaal, even on an AM frequency. Radio 702 became a rare voice, if not of outright dissent, at least of occasional reason. The station's news broadcasts were never as circumspect as the censored newspaper articles we read and certainly nowhere near as fictional as those on the SABC.

As the 1980s wore on, the signs of censorship became more and more prevalent. It was as though Oom Piet was vetting everything we watched or read or listened to. In mid-1985, when black sectarian violence threatened to get out of hand (meaning that the government's tacit plans of inciting a war between the itinerant Inkatha Freedom Party township hostel dwellers and the nominally more established ANC and Pan-Africanist Congress supporters was working to a T), the Powers-That-Were shook their grey, dusty heads, wrung their liver-spotted hands, and declared a state of emergency.

This meant that the government was now unhindered by even a cursory standing on democratic ceremony; it had finally arrogated its way into every facet of daily life. The state of emergency meant many things that affected me personally not at all—curfews after dark in the black areas, detention without trial—and one thing in particular that did.

Our house received two newspapers a day—the *Business Day* in the morning and *The Star* in the evening. On the surface, these publications appeared to be just like the broadsheets one would find anywhere in the free world. The front page blared bad news in headlinese; you could read about your favourite team getting their ass handed to them; and in the Tonight supplement of *The Star,* you could follow Madonna's exploits or read a review for "action-packed, thrill-a-minute" *Top Gun.* If you made a closer inspection of the front page, however, you'd find one ominous detail that changed the tenor of your newspaper-reading experience.

Somewhere, usually in or around the lower right-hand corner, you'd see a little grey box.

This little grey box was a courtesy to us, the reader, from the disgruntled editorial board. The editorial board was disgruntled for the usual reasons (wife/husband just split, cigarette prices went up again, cafeteria ham and cheese tastes like shit), and also on account of the fact that it was by no means the final word on its publication's editorial policies. Newspaper editors tend to be sincerely offended when anyone else grabs the still-warm scissors from their nicotine-stained fingers and starts snipping.

And thus, a compromise: "The material you find in this paper may have been altered by the authorities ..."

All in all—and despite some heinously far-rightist publications—the press in South Africa had a healthy history of coming down squarely against the regime. Many an editor found himself or herself on a one-way flight into exile (Donald Woods, played by Kevin Kline in the biopic *Cry Freedom,* was one such person), and there was a healthy alternative press that faced daunting odds. Any publication that printed more than eleven times a year was obligated to register with the government, and consequences were severe if the official line was not toed. Spokespersons for banned organizations such as the ANC could not be quoted; prison conditions could not be documented. Many courageous men and women toed no such line, and several liberal publications, including the now defunct *Rand Daily Mail,* were hounded mercilessly.

That little grey box was a perfect summary of our rulers: little, grey, boxy, short on prose, long on freighted subtext, ugly, upsetting. Still, it speaks of our addiction to news that we'll even consume *wrong* news, news that has been altered and is, by the time it has rolled off the production line, far closer to fiction than anything else. We swallow fantasy in broadsheet form because we are fundamentally dependent on a daily (or twice daily) dose of information. And so, in the evening, my father disappeared behind the pages; Oupa spread the paper over his card table; Gaga sat straight-backed, her glasses perched on her forehead, and neatly folded the paper in quarters. And they would read that strange mixture of capriciously censored fact and sloppily written fiction.

Me, I stuck to the Tonight section, where I'd do my own cutting. With a pair of large scissors, I'd carefully clip the pictures of music stars and paste them in my scrapbooks. It strikes me now that I must have looked, on the living-room floor in front of the anthracite heater, like a cadre of the DOP. *Snip, snip, snip.* When I was done with the Tonight section (and only after my father had read it), the paper must have looked much like the original version did when the little grey men gave it back to the editors earlier that morning.

At the outset of my musical journey, I did not think about such things as censorship. I thought about Madonna and Simon Le Bon. My mother took a surprisingly laissez-faire attitude to my obsession with pop music. In the car on the way to an errand or art class or school, she'd test me on the opening bars of a song. "Who is it?" she'd ask. "Kylie Minogue—'I Should Be So Lucky,'" I'd answer, without hesitation. In the five or so years we played this game, I was almost never wrong. She seemed bemused, if entertained, by this gift of mine—I suppose any small sign of intelligent life was encouraging. Indeed, at times she actively supported this obsession. As I waited for her to finish her shopping at the Norwood Pick 'n Pay, I'd pore over the music magazines at the newsagent, and she'd offer, unbidden, to purchase me a copy or two—"*Ag*, go on. I'll buy you a couple." At home, after studying the pages—*snip, snip, snip*—Rick Astley sidled up against Whitney Houston, who grinned at Bros, who scowled at Robert Plant in the pages of my chunky tomes.

Like any fundamentalist, I loathed as violently as I loved. As with videos, local music was an absolute no-no. "That's utter *kuck*," was my knee-jerk response to indigenously produced music. Anything sung in a language other than English (if the Swedes could do it, so could the Afrikaners) I dismissed outright. Even David Kramer, a local Afrikaans songwriter who wore trademark red *velskoene* and wrote witty tracks about the South African prosaic, failed to make the grade. Because he was banned by the SABC (his material, like that of Afrikaans short-story writer Herman Charles Bosman, was deeply subversive and satirical, even if it seemed innocuous at first listen; because it was in Afrikaans, the DOP got it only too well), it is now cool to have dug Kramer. Not me, no how. Compilations peppered with homegrown ditties—like the ubiquitous locally packaged *Springbok Hits*—were derided as rubbish. Likewise the vaguely hippyish (I didn't come round to the likes of Crosby, Stills, Nash & Young and Dylan until later). Anything golden oldie-ish was dismissed outright—with the exception of an old Motown record of the Supremes' greatest hits.

As for local black music, I tuned it out completely. It existed at the edge of my experience, wafting from tinny speakers in sculleries and laundry rooms and servants' quarters and other places I'd find black people. It found legitimacy with me—and only for a short time—through Paul Simon's *Graceland*. It was a question of packaging—only through the idiom of glossy industrial pop could the music claim any cachet. Africa could be appreciated only through a filter, one that had to come from the likes of Columbia Records, if it was to prove effective.

This tiny musical lexicon expanded slightly after my older cousin Lewis went to high school, and came by The Doors, Led Zeppelin, and Pink Floyd. "These *okes* are crazy!" Lewis assured me. "You should *hear* how crazy some of these *okes* are." He lent me his prized copy of *No One Gets Out of Here Alive,* a Jim Morrison hagiography that showed unequivocally that these *okes* were indeed crazy. After I heard that Led Zeppelin once fucked a groupie with a fish, teenaged prurience and lifelong musical fanaticism met in a glorious psychedelic confluence, and henceforth it was rock 'n' roll for me.

"Check this," Lewis would insist after a Sunday *braai.*

He'd sit on the edge of his bed and slaughter, painstaking chord after painstaking chord, "The End" or "Wish You Were Here," or, God forbid, one of his own compositions.

"*Boet,* please!" I'd beg.

"China—one more song," he'd say. "Kay—awright, I think it goes like this ..."

There was only one way to combat this, and that was to get a guitar of my own. Again, my mother was surprisingly accommodating. I was soon in possession of my own cheap acoustic six-string, and under the tutelage of Lewis's instructor, a loquacious Southeast Indian in his mid-thirties named Pravesh.

"Ogay—look vad I learn yesterday," Pravesh would say as he ran through an intricate Yngwie Malmsten medley. He was no rigorous pedagogue, Pravesh, and a lesson was as likely to involve a long breakdown on the status of his marriage as it was Supertramp's "Give a Little Bit." He showed little interest in how my own strumming was progressing.

"Vun sec," he'd say if I asked a question. "Vatch this: solo from 'Stairvay to Heaven.' Backvards."

When Lewis and I regaled each other with our limited prowess, birds fell from the sky.

"Check this," I'd say as Lewis shoved wads of cotton wool into his ears. "Clapton: 'Cocaine.' Kay—it goes like so—'If you wah-na hang out, you've got to—erm—ta-*aake* her out—cow-cayyne …' "

At some point in my musical journey, things got more complicated, and my free time more cluttered. In the drawer beneath my bed, alongside my DIY music compendiums, were my movie scrapbooks. Accompanied by a tall, dark Israeli-born kid named Tamir, I'd cram in as many movies as I could in a weekend—a secret, second life away from my tough-guy high school buddies. Tamir and I would table all the movies we had seen in separate mathematics notebooks, meticulously adding new entries directly after we had seen them. We had yet to develop any mechanism for qualitative judgment—any old shit, so long as it was projected onto a white screen, sufficed. Eighteen hours of Andy Warhol's *Empire,* or *Hamburger Hill*—what's the diff, *boet*? *Scritch, scritch, scritch*—both were inscribed in the notebook, as incongruous alongside each other as mismatched partners in 1980s buddy-cop movies.

The films we watched were, by an overwhelming margin, Hollywood productions. We did occasionally stumble onto screenings of the avant-garde, the *outré,* and the French. These we consumed with the same gusto as the latest Tom Berenger flick. Of course, we *preferred* action, but this was not necessarily a preference we could indulge when we saw three films on any given Saturday. We devoured the product; we didn't read the ingredients.

If we did, we would never have found anything that resembled our surroundings or referenced our own lives. Tamir and I would hop onto one of the increasingly rare double-decker whites-only buses that still hurtled along Louis Botha Avenue toward town and go to a Ster-Kinekor multiplex in the Carlton Centre. Granite Hillbrow gargoyles stared down at us from once regal blocks of flats as we sped toward the noon showing of *American Ninja* or *Three Men and a Little Lady*—somehow aware in their ancient stone sagacity that we were the last—the very last—white children who would pass through this once proud area in this proud way. The neighbourhood was already surrendering to a mutated underclass; the government had placed a moratorium on the Group Areas Act in Hillbrow—anyone could now live there. Africa was slowly moving in. No—not Africa, exactly. Africa is, after all, a big place, and varied besides. This was the version of Africa that Apartheid had made—a community of half people, chewed up by rage and drugs and violence and diseases we did not yet have names for. As I looked down Hillbrow's alleyways—with an estuary-like view of the world from the front of the clean, empty top deck—I can be forgiven for not knowing what I was looking at.

I was looking at our legacy.

We had no pop-cultural lens through which to try to decipher the world we lived in. What's more, the 1980s was film's suckiest decade to date—even Cinema with a capital C offered slim pickings (art films mostly about food or about how long films could be), and besides, culture of any description had to be aggressively tracked down and consumed before it scooted into the thick undergrowth of hegemony or became ensnared in censorship's baited traps. So, we chewed the gristle of *Who Framed Roger Rabbit* and *Jagged Edge* and *Major League* and *Rain Man.* Because release dates in South Africa followed those in the United States by at least six months, I had read the *MAD* magazine spoofs of these films long before seeing them. So, to add a twist to my relationship with popular culture, I viewed American movies through the filter of American satire. But I had never seen an Athol Fugard play performed, and I'm not sure what I would have made of it. After all, it hadn't been predigested by Mort Drucker and the usual gang of idiots at *MAD.*

I lived on popcorn during those film-going marathons, eating several bags a day. My lips shrivelled and cracked from the salt, my blood pressure rose to that of a ninety-year-old liverwurst addict. But this film obsession allowed me one thing, which was to view my surroundings with something approaching a measure of objectivity. Because of my interest in the medium, I would walk through town picturing a crane shot rising over Eloff Street, capturing both the colonial buildings and the slow but sure encroachment of Africa. As my crane shot stretched higher, I gained a perspective similar to that of my perch at the front of those double-decker buses. I saw everything as if through a film camera—and digested it in the same way. And I saw the potential for drama—the same sort of exotic setting and sizzling tension that gave the films I dug their dramatic impetus. "*Jassis,*" I'd say to Tamir, "someone should make a movie of this bloody place."

Film and music never overlapped in my obsessive scrapbook library, and I did not like it when they overlapped in actuality. *Yentl* or *Grease* and their ilk were—to quote the younger me—

"kuck." But the musical genre did grab my attention on one or two occasions. North American audiences of a certain age may recall *Breakin'* and *Breakin' 2: Electric Boogaloo.* These films were derivations of *Footloose,* except with breakdancing instead of whatever type of dancing was in *Footloose.* And they nudged a deep curiosity, a curiosity that started when I heard, for the first time, sitting at Gaga's kitchen table for lunch, a type of music the radio announcer called rap.

I think this must have been the summer of 1985. As Carolyn and I munched our way through a chunk of Gaga's famed pink layer cake, washed down with a flagon of Coca-Cola, we heard something on the kitchen transistor radio that made us look at each other and then spew a viscous cake-Coke compound through our noses. "What a *lag,*" I howled. This was one of those shows that, with a pseudo-academic anthropological disinterest, solemnly introduced various world music genres to middle-brow South African lefties. Once our laughter died down, Carolyn and I were entranced—we bopped our heads and spat out what was probably the first and only hip-hop rhyme ever composed in Johannesburg's northern suburbs during the Apartheid era. Of course, we'd heard stuff like this before, buried in mainstream pop, but this was the first time it had made such an impression (perhaps helped by the sugar rush of the cake-Coke elixir). The announcer informed us, in typical elevated SABC twaddle, that this music emerged from the economically ravaged American cities, where violence and depredation predominated.

All the other black musicians I'd heard before that, because of the music they played—and how much I loved that music—were colourless. I could sing the lyrics of "Ebony and Ivory" by Paul McCartney and Stevie Wonder, but it was really just a slightly more socially conscious version of "The Girl Is Mine" by Paul McCartney and Michael Jackson. It never made much of an impression, because fluffy pop music generally doesn't. All the black entertainers pasted in my scrapbooks were colourless—mostly because they brought no attention to their colour, certainly not in the pages of *Teen Beat* or on Casey Kasem's countdown. And if Zeppelin and Co. had ripped off their riffs from black bluesmen—well, that was news to me. How the heck was I supposed to know where rock 'n' roll came from? It had always been around, hadn't it?

Rap, however, was different.

This was genuine black music—it sounded spare and dangerous and alien. For the first time, I realized that black America (those inner cities the announcer spoke of) might be an entirely different place from white America. I had always viewed North American culture as homogeneous, just as I'd viewed South Africa's black and white cultures as utterly distinct. Now I realized that this was not the case. I had always hung on to this notion—that Casey Kasem's America was a halcyon place where ebony and ivory sat side by side everywhere, not just on piano keyboards. It's not that I harboured any particular desire to sit next to black people, but I suppose one part of me wanted to believe that we were an anomaly, South Africans—that our racial and cultural divide was a one-off. But a couple of MCs and a drum machine gave the lie to that assumption.

It's these little things that make an impression. They add up, item by item, eventually amounting to a worldview. Like the first time, moonwalking in front of my bobba, I realized that Michael Jackson was black. Or when Carolyn and I first heard rap over layer cake and Coke. If something as outlandishly foreign as rap could exist inside what I understood to be

America, then maybe I didn't understand America. And if Michael Jackson was willing to stain himself white, even though a white South African boy worshipped him regardless of his flat nose and afro, then maybe this race thing was more complicated than just, as the King of Pop would put it some years later, "Black or White."

How the hell was I supposed to make sense of all this? I never did pursue my cursory interest in rap with any of my characteristic zeal. I returned to the familiar. My musical journey—which in South Africa travelled over too many pitted roads—started to be fuelled by my hormones. The louder the guitar, the longer the solos, the more overt the references to Aleister Crowley, the better the song. As I got older, my musical tastes moved further back in time. I traded my moonwalk for an air guitar, and I rocked out.

Thing is, as a kid, I wanted everybody to love the music I loved. I was delighted that Bobba enjoyed "Billie Jean"; I loved watching *Pop Shop* with Dr. Poplak. I did *not* want everyone to love Led Zeppelin. Only the *right* people could dig Deep Purple. So, in the ruthlessly segmented, shrinking world I inhabited, my exclusionary musical snobbery was absolutely appropriate. My scrapbooks became depictions of the fenced-in area where I lived, and the further fences I erected inside those pens. From "Dancing Queen" to "Sweet Child of Mine." In so many ways, the typical teen journey.

Unless, of course, you read my scrapbooks' small print. The subtext, after all, tells an entirely South African story.

The Barracks

King David High School has no sign proclaiming its presence, sprawled as it is over a swath of the Linksfield Ridge, like a large creature sunning itself on the rocks. The property is surrounded by a high wall garnished with fresh, glinting barbed wire; a guard stands sentinel at the school's entrance, noting down the licence plates of cars as they come and go. The veld on the rugged high sections of the ridge—harsh clumps of fynbos and white-thorned acacia—threatens to pour over the southern fence and invade the campus, which moves steadily, sometimes vertiginously, downhill as a series of open-balconied brick-and-tile blocks, broken now and again by patches of fierce, subtropical green.

The school is quiet as we move north toward the low, terraced plains of the sport fields and tennis courts. Here, the shadows lengthen, the blocks are closer together, the vegetation thicker, more impenetrable. It is noticeably chillier; crepuscular, moss-slicked corners shiver with unseen life. Down here, where the assembly hall meets a two-storey block of classrooms in a part of the school that sunlight never touches, is a door, almost hidden by a steep overhang, on rusted hinges. Strips of ancient blue paint peel from it like curls of charred skin, but you can still make out the faded gold-leaf sign: "Boys."

This place has an air of fetid menace about it. Even if you are desperate for the bathroom, something—some undefined fear—keeps you from entering. However, if you do allow your bladder or bowels to override your better judgment, you immediately think yourself silly for your initial childish apprehension. You note, after your eyes have adjusted to the murk, that the bathroom is disused to the point of ruin—the stall doors hang from their frames, the wooden benches crawl with creatures as yet unclassified by entomologists, the urinal has not seen a mint in over a decade. Sure, the place would benefit from a makeover. But what is there to be afraid of?

Yet as the urine drains from your body and your senses return to the fore, fear creeps up your spine like one of the large spiders dodging the stream of your piss in the dusty urinal. You have the unmistakable sensation that you are being watched. You hear breathing. Absurdly, you smell fresh cigarette smoke.

"Hullo?" you call into the shadows. "Is anyone there?"

Right about then, when the terror shimmying up your back reaches your brain stem, as the scream inside your head threatens to reach your mouth—at that very instant, someone, or something, comes at you from the dark.

We called this place The Barracks.

Despite Dr. Poplak's strenuous and oft-vocalized protestations, my attending a Jewish high school was inevitable. Oupa was resolute: He wanted my Hebrew to be at least as good as my Italian. The crisis became painfully evident after I squeaked—literally and figuratively—through my bar mitzvah. The rabbi's solution to my inability to read Hebrew was for me to memorize the entire portion, section by section, and recite it by rote on the big day.[52] This made for a suspenseful ten minutes, and it was only by luck that I made it through without garbling the words into an Aramaic order for smoked meat on manna, with extra pickle. As it was, I sounded like a bad Israeli dub of the Chipmunks, sped up and pitched high. When the ladies threw candies from the high balcony, they threw hard.

Furthermore, I was at this point going through something of a religious period.

"We must make this kitchen kosher," I'd say to my parents.

Dr. Poplak would wave his arms around, shaman-like, and say, "*Alem hachem aza kabooh, lechem min ha-aretz.* There. It's kosher."

Holding a sandwich, I'd separate the pieces of bread and peer inside like a myopic triage surgeon examining an infected shrapnel wound. "Is this meat kosher?"

"It's Italian salami, and you've been eating it for years," my mother would say. "Why don't you go to the Europa Deli and ask Maria when last the Beth Din came by?"

My parents took great amusement from this bout of religiosity, placing it alongside my brief fervencies for, among other things, space travel, dinosaurs, medieval battle weaponry, and ABBA. They called me Little Rabbi.

I didn't know how they could be so cavalier about the whole God thing. This was not, after all, a guy renowned for His sense of humour. The God I knew from synagogue was harsh, unforgiving, and uncompromising. He did not debate. He smote. On Yom Kippur, as I watched the men in rumpled suits

52. I don't know where my parents found this man. I think he was chosen for convenience: His home formed the central point in the geographical triangle between judo, art class, and school.

with sneakers, stubble prominent on faces pale from a day's fasting, *doven* to the holiest prayers of the year, I understood that this was not a God to be trifled with. Those musty *siddurs,* with their reams of Hebrew text, spoke of an entity who proffered mercy only to the desperately faithful, and then only occasionally. That my parents came to be inscribed in the Book of Life year after year seemed to me a clerical oversight—a case of celestial bookkeeping gone awry.

I feared for them. Indeed, I prayed for them. When I told my father this, he'd say, "Thanks, Rabbi. Listen, can you put a few words in for my lower back?" Their amusement, however, turned to dismay when Oupa put the screws in, and they realized there was no way out of sending me to King David.

"Jesus Christ," said Dr. Poplak, getting his religions mixed up, "look at these bloody school fees!" What price a soul? thought I, also scrambling theologies. We had long discussions—my parents insisting I take solid advantage of the extra-curricular opportunities the school offered in addition to both secular education and religious edification. This way, they figured, maybe they'd get their money's worth. "I'll join the debating club," I promised. "I've always wanted to try chess, so I'll join the team. Young Zionists against Seal Clubbing sounds good. And I'll swim, too."

"*Ja,* right," said Dr. Poplak, rolling his eyes. He may not have been able to turn our kitchen kosher, but he could see the future with crystalline foresight. "We'll have this conversation again in a year." King David's unparalleled scholastic record somewhat mitigated my parents' (or my mother's, anyway) opposition: The institution had a storied history for furnishing the international capitals of the world with well-schooled Jewish professionals. Maybe I'd end up a neurologist in New York, a lawyer in London. "*Ja?* More like a layabout in Lagos," said Dr. Poplak. In fairness to him, those school fees *were* significant.

King David High School Linksfield had a reputation for providing what can be best described as a liberal Jewish education clumsily welded to an illiberal South African one. Although the school was legally bound to prepare students for government-prescribed standardized matriculation testing (with a track record second to none for doing so), the curriculum was certainly looser in its adherence to Apartheid-era pedagogical principles than, say, an Afrikaans boarding school in Eugene Terreblanche's hometown of Ventersdorp. Even Alan Paton's *Cry, the Beloved Country* made it onto our reading list.

For the most part, and for reasons already discussed, the Powers-That-Were allowed these transgressions to pass. That's not to say that the Special Branch, the South African secret service, hadn't paid the school's administrators the odd visit over the years. Famously, several King David teachers were indicted in the notorious Rivonia trials of the 1960s—trials that saw Mandela, Thambo, Mbeki, and so many icons of the struggle imprisoned or sent into exile. Furthermore, the moustached, beer-bellied, corduroy-clad Special Branch flunkies had on one occasion visited the principal who reigned during my three years at the school and warned him that several students were acting in a manner "contrary to the interests of the country." They likely informed Mr. Wolf—a gentle, slope-shouldered man of inordinate height—that if those students *didn't* want electrodes attached to their genitalia during the administration of a strenuous bout of water torture, they should perhaps cease and desist from engaging in their extra-curricular activities.

"Read what you want, say what you want (without getting too carried away), but *do* what we *say*." That was the prevailing mantra in the late 1980s. After all, this was a democracy. Indians and coloureds could now vote in their own tricameral parliaments and write their own legislation (in turn used as toilet paper—but only in emergencies—by the ruling party). And couldn't blacks vote for local representatives in their homelands? Sure they could. Mind you, if those local representatives weren't the right local representatives, they were removed and sent far, far away. But a vote's a vote, right?

Besides, in January 1987, with the world but a couple of years away from the End of History, the government had other issues with which to concern itself: facilitating Communism's death rattle in nearby Angola; opposing the independence of South West Africa (soon to be Namibia); implementing the blanket laws of a state of emergency; and keeping a watchful eye on townships riven by a de facto civil war that the National Party was fuelling and facilitating. When the wind blew northeast, we King Davidians would unwittingly inhale air wafting across from Soweto—molecules of burning petrol, rubber, skin, and flesh—detritus from a war we knew little of, and cared about even less. So, on the government's to-do list, "Make *Jood* school toe line" was priority #1712, right between "Review summer menu in black detention centres" and "Organize Good Monday halal *braai* and square dance for Qaddafi visit, April 1988."

Compared with Mr. MacMillan's Ridgeview Primary down the road—with its 180 students and two double-storey blocks of classrooms—King David was immense. The campus teemed with 1200 kids, all of Semitic ancestry, all vastly similar in appearance (well, the girls differed somewhat from the boys—in a good way, I thought). It was perhaps unfortunate to name the school for King David—the quintessentially brash, cocky, and ridiculously self-assured kid who would be king—a boy with both the balls and the bravado to go head to head with a massive Philistine, armed with only a sling and his self-regard. Self-assurance, self-regard, balls, and bravado were endemic at King David Linksfield. I had those in spades when I left Ridgeview. And now? Who were these kids who came from larger primary schools with ready-made cliques, who based their self-assurance on better grades, their self-regard on better sporting records, their bravado on larger (or *any*) muscles, and their balls on—well, their balls? Thankfully, Jeremy was also a new King David pupil, but he was in another class, and I barely saw him. I was a nobody. And it hurt. At home, I listened endlessly to a vinyl copy of A-Ha's *The Sun Always Shines on TV* on Dr. Poplak's record player. When you resort to mopey Scandinavian pop for solace, you know you're in a bad way.

I ruminated on my change of status with a brooding that rendered me almost invisible to my new classmates. Few remembered my name, fewer cared. No doubt this was tumbling around in my tormented brain as I entered the upper boys' washroom between classes one day, several weeks into my time at King David. I immediately sensed danger.[53] At the urinal stood a massive matric student who was so hard-core, he reportedly wore a feather earring outside school grounds. Word in the halls: He was *seriously* considering getting a tattoo. His

53. Boys' bathrooms were no man's land when it came to teacher supervision, and were policed by prefects (who, understandably, spent as little time in them as possible) or not at all. These authority-free circumstances allowed for students of a certain class to hang around and cause havoc as they saw fit; some of the worst cases of student-on-student violence I witnessed (or experienced, or perpetrated) occurred in boys' bathrooms.

chunky biceps, pocked with angry boils, were on display because he rolled his shirt sleeves to the shoulder in the manner of all high school toughs. A succession of chins coiled over his open shirt collar and met his gut in concentric circles of thick, slick flesh. "Ah, Jesus," I thought (still mangling faiths, but it had only been a couple of weeks), "here we go." I stared over at him nervously. That gave him his in.

"You staring at my cock, china?" he asked mildly.

"No, sir," I said.

This angered him. "Don't call me sir, you little *poes.*" He stared over to a couple of his henchmen, who were washing their paws at the basin.

"'Check this *oke,* chinas. The little *moffie* was staring at me pissing." He sheathed his much-discussed penis and zipped his fly.

"Izzit, broe?" asked a henchman, mock horrified.

"*Ja, boet.* Fuck, hey—you're not safe anywhere these days."

"No, china. Nowhere."

"Okay, *boet,*" said Reportedly-Wears-Feather-in-Ear, this time to me. "Now, we watch *you* piss. So *you* can see what it feels like." His two henchmen joined us on the deck of the urinal, crowding around me, hunching to stare at my crotch.

"Piss, *boet.* C'mon," he urged.

"No, I'm fine, really," I said, making to zip up and fly out.

"No one goes anywhere until you take a nice long piss, china."

So that was that. The four of us stood there, me suffering from extreme, urethra-paralyzing stage fright, the older boys snickering at my discomfort. I was mortified, and my dick, as if in complicity with my tormenters, shrivelled into negligibility. Finally, mercifully, the bell rang. With a slap on the back and a final "fucking *moffie,*" they were gone.

I was somewhat shaken by this episode.

Back in class, I opened my satchel and stared at the tallis and tefillin bags Oupa had given me for my bar mitzvah a few months before, and I was hit with sharp pangs of homesickness. I felt the velvet between my thumb and forefinger, and even though Oupa's house was close enough to walk to, it felt impossibly far away. A week or so later, when several prefects forced me and three other boys to hang from the straight bar connecting the rugby posts, my shoulder joints screaming and my spine clacking like a pair of ill-fitting dentures, I realized definitively that I no longer wished to hang from rugby posts. But I'd gladly hang *others* from rugby posts. How could I engineer this change?

Pray my ass off. That's how.

At the compulsory morning prayer services, I wrapped the leather straps of the phylactery around my arm in that centuries-old ritual, relieved to be among my co-religionists undergoing such solemn and devout proceedings, and especially glad to be keeping the Lord's wrath at bay by repeated and fervent prayer.

Other boys may have conversed quietly among themselves during morning services, but not I. Draping a tallis over myself like a holy security blanket and then attaching tefillin to both my head and my left arm were, in combination, startlingly effective rituals—medieval in nature and origin, weighty with centuries of practice and history. The man of faith is literally immersed in the word of God—the boxes of the tefillin contain scrolls inscribed with passages from the Torah, while the *siddur,* cradled in your hands, holds those same prayers, among hundreds of others. It's the theological equivalent of that old cop-movie cliché: "Freeze! You're surrounded!" The Word of the Almighty was heavy in its authority—it descended from the dome of the synagogue, it came up from the floor, it was intoned from the bimah, it throbbed at my left arm and my forehead, beat up at me from the book in my hands, and settled in the pit of my stomach like an unlaid egg—ready to crack and send forth an ecstatic religiosity as soon as I could decipher but one word of the Hebrew I was reading. Just imagine, I thought, if I'm this holy now, what I'll be like when I actually *understand* this stuff.

Watch out, *boet*! Little Rabbi's comin' for ya!

"Who, Poplak, is Lumpy?"

Mr. Astler, my Form One math teacher had affected a peculiar intonation and a series of strange mannerisms that had transformed him into a character from Dickens, as played by Van Damme, in an adaptation by Lynch. He was swarthy and well built, with disconcertingly large forearms and a furious unibrow that met on the bridge of his nose like a head-on collision between two airliners—causing him to look simultaneously captious, confused, constipated, concerned, and, ultimately, Cro-Magnon. Astler stood alongside my Hebrew teacher, Mrs. Lebanon (yup, Lebanon; you just can't make up shit like that), as the resident unhinged tyrants. Lebanon mangled English with a serial killer's psychotic proficiency, asphyxiating aphorisms ("She who is laughing be laughing first in de END!"), shivving syllogisms ("All childrens is idiot; all idiots is here: therefore you is IDIOT!"), and trepanating clichés ("Aha! So the grass is BETTAH on de other side of DE FENCE!").

"Answer me, boy," said Mr. Astler. "Who is Lumpy?"

There was a long answer and a short one. As I stared down at the margins of my algebra book with mounting horror, I realized that the short answer was: "Lumpy is a doodled caricature of you, sir." I opted for the long answer.

When my classmates saw how brazen a rendering of Mr. Astler Lumpy was, they had no choice but to be impressed. I should point out that this was an unintentional act of cruelty, interpreted by my comrades as an intentional act of sedition. I was (and still am) an inveterate doodler—and this doodle was mindless, if subconsciously revealing, as only doodles can be: I was as shocked to see Lumpy's resemblance to Mr. Astler as anyone else. I was saved by the fact that we are naturally inclined to see caricatures of ourselves as the work of Fools, and that's only when we happen to recognize ourselves in the caricature. Blessedly, Mr. Astler, like most of us, lacked self-awareness. And thank God for that.

Post Lumpygate, my classmates conferred on me the sobriquet "Mr. Mock," and I was slowly lifted from my position of miserable loner to the decidedly higher one of class Fool, a ceremonial position in South African high schools as important (and as dangerous) as it was in Versailles. Luckily this was a temporary, rotating position, and I wasn't bidden to say something witty (or, at least, what passes as wit to fourteen-year-olds) every class, every day, for the length of my scholastic career. Certainly, though, in my eighth year in the South African school system, I had come to a conclusion—authority was my enemy, an assertion backed up and endorsed by Pink Floyd and The Doors. The only way to combat this, to flail against the MacMillans, Billups, Oom Piets, and Mr. Astlers, was with a well-placed barb made under your breath for the benefit of the classmates who counted, while those who didn't stage-whispered "Shh, man" and dispensed dirty looks.

This notion strained the shaky religious period I was going through. Now that the cool kids had accepted me, I was having difficulty seeing the point of prayer, and whether it was prayer that had got me to my newly enhanced social position in the first place was not a metaphysical question I found worthwhile asking.

I don't know how he came to hear about it, but it was Kevin Bloom who told me about a place where we could practise smoking the Chesterfields we'd recently purchased in the safety of what was one of the school administration's few blind spots. A place of legend. And of hope.

Kevin was a rotating member of the growing cast of Fools; swarthy, dark-lidded, with a darker intelligence and a self-destructive streak that was well honed for a fourteen-year-old. There was also Martin, an angst-free kid of excessive cheerfulness who was motivated to misbehave for the sport of it, rather than for any ideological or hormonal imperative. And then there was Ari—short, thin, and rangy, with the swagger of a much bigger man, and unhindered by cumbersome baggage such as scruples, morals, or common human decency. Ari was a menace. We were an inseparable foursome and, therefore, we had to be separated. "Poplak and gang—disperse," Astler would order.

It was really, really tough to fall in with the wrong crowd at King David (the wrong crowd end up practising human rights law, while the right crowd end up as well-behaved corporate lawyers), so you had to assemble your own wrong crowd, à la Reportedly-Wears-Feather-in-Ear. Collectively, our little gang could not have outweighed one of his biceps, so violence and intimidation were, sadly, never our métier, at least not at first. As troublemakers, we were left with two activities: cutting class and smoking. Both were hanging offences. Thus the enormous premium placed on abandoned or remote sections of the school.

"Boet," said Kevin, "there's a jazz somewhere down by the assembly hall where *okes* can do what they *smaak,* and I hear from reliable sources that it's fucking *lekker* down there." To translate this schoolboy jargon: There was a toilet where the likes of us self-appointed rebels could do what we pleased, and it was most pleasant down there.

Now this *was* news. It sounded like an Atlantis, an Eldorado, a Canaan—a Pete Seegeresque land swathed in downy cloud where we could stare from a high place into valleys running with cheap whisky, fields awash in the green of tobacco plantations, and hills echoing with the bawdy chit-chat from similarly minded fellows. Females with sullied reputations would, of course, be welcome, but as Kevin pointed out, this *was* the boys' bathroom.

"But you don't just waltz in there, *boet.*"

How we found it, I don't know. Ari had older brothers—perhaps they had led him to it. Thus, some weeks after Kevin's tale, Ari and I stood outside the darkened, slightly ajar doorway, peering into the darkness. A sloped rock garden abutted the far wall of the bathroom, and many of the plants were of a genus I had never before encountered. The air was moist and cold. My memory insists that a stream of screeching bats poured from the crack in the doorway and partially decomposed corpses threw hunks of their rotting flesh at us.

But maybe I'm wrong about that.

"Some other time," I said in a small voice.

"*Ja,* man," said Ari. "We're young. What's your hurry?"

Nothing cures a bout of preadolescent religious devotion like repeated exposure to religion, and nothing cures preadolescence like the onset of puberty. When these two phenomena occur simultaneously, you have something of a perfect storm. My "isthiskosher?" period lasted six months, tops. The dark God of synagogue, that same God who wanted me to go hungry on Yom Kippur, who asked me to atone for my sins without giving any indication that I was forgiven—well, he had become just another authority figure among far too many. I didn't lose my religion so much as come to detest the God that crowded me at morning prayers. His rules were onerous, his lack of good humour an offence. God had become Oom Piet.

This should not be mistaken for atheism. It is anti-deism, a spiritually murky hinterland that subverts at least the first commandment, and probably a host of lesser ones. It's a mindset that sets you adrift from your co-religionists and sends you on an existential journey away not from a God who has ceased to exist, but from a God whom you now actively rebel against. The defining factor is not an absence of God—after all, you're not disputing his existence. The defining factor is fear. Because, ultimately, he's still God, and you're still you—puny and human and weak. And the time of reckoning will come.

This minor religious crisis simmered away on my mental burners—which were then turned to high by the music of The Eagles, Roger Waters, and other humourless dirge-meisters of the 1970s whom I listened to on the stereo I bought with my bar mitzvah money. I'd close my room door and exist inside the music, inhabiting it. What I did not do was go to Young Zionists against Seal Clubbing or join the chess team. Instead, I practised smoking.

"How's the debating club coming?" asked Dr. Poplak from behind his newspaper. "Chess not getting in the way too much, I hope."

Meanwhile, the Apartheid we learned about in class was the Apartheid of the 1960s and 1970s, a flat-toned canvas splashed with the occasional livid daub of 1950s American Southern-fried racism to bring out the grey. These were dusty, uncomplicated tales of good versus evil, with benches neatly demarking white and black, and edifices of righteousness and truth chiselled from the rich-veined marble of noble ideals. Who among us could remain unmoved by Harper Lee's characterization of an upstanding white Southern gentleman fearlessly defending a falsely accused black man against a jury not of his peers but of his enemies? "These hills," wrote Alan Paton, in diction far closer to Shakespeare than to *Miami Vice,* "are grass-covered and rolling, and lovely beyond the singing of it." Such books were redolent of the honourable nature of their authors and were borne to lofty heights by the scalding thermals of the indignities they exposed.

My burgeoning political identity was the least of my concerns at this point. I rolled my shirt sleeves up to the shoulder—the South African schoolboy equivalent of gang colours. I grew a rat's tail and gelled it into the body of my coif, I wore white socks with my shoes, I donned an undershirt with graphics under my regulation school button-up. In a Johannesburg Jewish day school, these were the signs and signifiers of teenage rebellion. Curse words and racist epithets peppered our slang-soaked discourse. As the country itself slid into all-out rebellion, I heard pronouncements, often from classmates, such as: "The *kaffirs* are going crazy. What kind of monkey rips his own home to pieces?" It did look like the blacks had taken leave of their senses. Watching mob violence on the eight o'clock news—scores of black men and women beating a scorched corpse with whatever township flotsam they could get their hands on, the *coup de grâce* a rusty panga jabbed into the side of what now looked like a rag doll salvaged from a house fire—well, what were we to make of all this? *This* was Apartheid *circa* 1987—black-on-black sectarian violence that seemed to be an indictment of the black man's ability to govern himself. Where were all the Reverend Stephen Kumalos? Where was all the dignity we read of in our textbooks? The rage kicked up on those dirt streets was animal nature, and it rendered what we read in class as wooden and ornate as antique furniture. *Cry, the Beloved Country* was about as contemporary and relevant to a fourteen-year-old living in the very system it depicts as *King Lear*. Especially to a fourteen-year-old rebel, who sat at the back of the class and drew comic-book characters with other fourteen-year-old rebels.

Our teachers could never make the link between the frayed, yellowed Apartheid of the 1960s with the fast-moving, mercurial Apartheid of the here and now, and that may have been because they couldn't see it themselves. The black men in overalls who moved through the King David campus, keeping the hibiscus clipped back from the pathways and the halls free of our Peppermint Crisp wrappers—their status was never discussed, and that's because they were invisible. And that's because, despite what we were reading in our schoolbooks, Apartheid had done its job. That menace I had felt after *veldskool* was very much there, but my mistrust of the authorities had coalesced as a hatred of authority because of what that authority forced on *me,* rather than what it forced on Apartheid's real victims. As my political understanding grew, my political consciousness narrowed. I was fourteen. I didn't give a fuck about the greater context, and in a perfect world, fourteen-year-olds shouldn't have to give a fuck about the greater context.

But this was not a perfect world. It was South Africa, 1987. The seams were starting to show.

Bunking was an art form. It required the duplicity of an Eastern European passport forger, the survivalist skills of a Delta Force soldier, the inner stillness of a Trappist monk, the subterfuge of a CIA operative on a Middle Eastern beat, and the doddering sweetness of a bake-sale granny ("What am I doing out of class now? Oh my, is it class time? Look at me—I'm turned all inside out!"). Our lack of expertise in these varied disciplines limited us in the early days to bunking morning prayers, as cutting actual class was still beyond our operational capabilities. That Atlantis we'd heard talk of was still off limits, so we had only two real options as hiding places. One was a runoff ditch behind disused playing fields. The other was in our homeroom, under our desks.

Why would we do this? The discomfort was extreme and, in retrospect, pretending to lay tefillin in a warm synagogue sure beat shivering in silence under a steady drizzle in a damp playing field or cowering under a desk, hidden by a ring of tog bags assembled around you as camouflage. Nonetheless, this was an expression of our escalating rebelliousness, and we bore it with grim determination. If we'd had a bumper to put a sticker on, it would have read "Bunk or die."

More often than not, we found ourselves in the mornings under the desks in our classroom, scrunched with our chins on our knees in the attitude we'd been taught to affect in preparation for the upcoming nuclear holocaust. We were well primed for such an event: After watching educational sixteen-millimetre films on the devastating results of an atomic strafing (I remember my awe at seeing the model houses blown to motes by the red, fiery wind of a nuclear onslaught), we put our evasive measures into practice. This included closing all the windows and doors of the classroom and assuming the crash position beneath our desks—surefire protective measures against thermonuclear holocaust. The mournful *wooooooooooooooo* of the air-raid siren bounced off the Linksfield ridge in performance of a harmonic requiem, and I'd stare at my kneecaps thinking of my mother and father and sister and Oupa and Gaga and how we'd find each other if the Soviet Union did finally lose patience and start sending neat legions of warheads, ordered in the same manner as the sardine soldiers my aunt Valda put on toast for us. If you believed the authorities—that we were the final bulwark between civilization and the metastasizing scourge of global Communism—well, then, the citizens of Johannesburg were a far more legitimate target than those soft-stepping pussies in Washington, D.C. Mushroom clouds in Linksfield were not so much a possibility as an eventuality.

King David was beset with both bomb drills (bombs were a classic Transvaal Education Department paranoia—ANC terrorists were not beyond slaughtering children) and actual bomb threats. Those less than well disposed to the existence of a Jewish day school called in hoarse telephonic warnings, cueing the bomb-threat alarm. The students and teachers would file rapidly to the bottom sports fields and stare up at the school, waiting for it to explode in a shower of brick, steel, wood, paper, corrugated iron, and tallis bags—1200 Jewish children momentary bedfellows with crazed anti-Semitic phone pranksters. "Blow," I'd think. "Blow sky-high, you motherfucker!"

Anyway, bunking:

There we huddled, under our desks, safe from nuclear attack and the prying eyes of teachers and prefects. It was impossible to roll call every student in the school during prayers—a security breach teachers remedied by keeping a close eye out for the presence (or, more important, the absence) of certain individuals. We, in turn, countered those measures by meticulously forging notes from our mothers. This process had several immutable rules of thumb:

1. Never forge your own mother's note. Always get another member of the bunk squad to do this for you.

2. A specific parent's signature is always forged by the same member of the bunk squad (I wrote in Mrs. Bloom's loping hand, while Kevin was Mrs. Poplak's chicken-scratch proxy).

3. Keep a stock of flowery letter paper on hand. Teachers are suspicious of a note written on the ripped-out leaf of an exercise book.

4. Keep the prose terse. Mothers are busy people. Loquacity invites suspicion.

5. Develop an individual voice for each mother. Base this on what you know about her: level of education, hobbies, what she keeps in the fridge.

6. Lay off big-issue diseases like leukemia or malaria. This tends to incite a worried phone call and a fundraising assembly. Keep it dental or gastrointestinal.

With these simple rules, we wove our web of lies and subterfuge and thus found ourselves particularly well poised to solve a series of crimes bedevilling the school.

Let's call this The Case of the Taken *Takkies.*

Takkies, my dear Watson, are what South Africans call sneakers. For a couple of weeks before the incident, *takkies* had gone missing from tog bags.[54] A few pairs here and there—nothing to warrant a full-scale investigation, but worrying nonetheless. The teachers decided that this had the

54. South African schools had no lockers, so we left our sports clothing in the homeroom during prayers or break.

hallmarks of student delinquency. The truth, however, is that crime was as rare inside the halls of King David as readings of the Catholic catechism, and crime was still not ubiquitous in Johannesburg.[55] I believe that my bunkmates and I were, that fated day, among the first to witness the warning ripples of the massive extended crime wave that would swamp the city in blood and gunfire over the next fifteen years.

From my well-sequestered position under the desk that morning, I could hear the group "Amens" wafting from the synagogue and through the school, adding a further element of the illicit to our activities. We four bunkers were super-sensitive to noise, and when we heard whispering outside the classroom, we stopped whatever whispered discussion we were having and communicated with our now equine-wide eyes, glistening as they were with fear.

"What the fuck is that?" asked several pairs of eyes.

"????!" answered others.

We sucked in our breath and waited.

The door of the classroom moaned opened. Through the rows of desks I could make out two pairs of legs in blue coveralls. The legs, which appeared to be attached to black garden workmen, moved slowly into the classroom. But what were they doing in here? As far as I could tell, there were no hibiscus bushes to clip. Seconds later, it became clear what they were up to. Our staying quiet was no longer a game.

---

55. Domestic servants were, at this time, by far the largest group of suspected criminals. If something went missing, it was always: The maid took it. You have to wonder why white South Africans, given that the maid was an assumed thief before she started her first shift, didn't just avoid the problem by preparing dinner and cleaning the toilet themselves.

Quietly they crept, bending slowly to open the zipper of two tog bags, their own eyes glistening and wide, also communicating though sharp, adrenalin-fuelled looks—two black men confirming all the prejudices of four young white South Africans: untrustworthy, thieving, scum. We didn't move an inch—my lungs burned with the effort of holding my breath. If they found us, things would get nasty.

Despite the danger inherent in the situation—and there was indeed danger—something in their eyes stuck with me, and I don't think it was just because those huge orbs mirrored my own—limpid with adrenalin and fear. There was something else.

Need.

I'm not talking about need in the imperative sense—those running shoes weren't going to feed anyone's family. I'm talking about the same kind of need I felt when I said to my mother "*Ja,* but I don't *want* the cheaper *takkies,* ma. I *need* the blue-and-red Reeboks, man!" Those two workmen, who couldn't have been that much older than the four boys secretly watching, they needed what they wanted, but there was absolutely no way they could get it without resorting to theft. I could never have spelled it out, this strange notion of relativism that made perfect sense in context—neither those workers nor I actually earned our *takkies.* The difference was that I was born lucky, and they weren't. Plenty of people born into destitution make it through life without robbing gym bags. But watching those two guys in the classroom that day, I knew I would never be one of those capable of accepting my lot without giving in to my appetites. This was a brief flash of empathy from the other end of the moral divide, and I'll never forget it.

The two young men grabbed several pairs of *takkies,* bundled them into the bellies of their coveralls, zipped up the tog bags, and left.

My companions and I sucked in air with a great, simultaneous *whoosh.* "Holy fucking shit!" I said (I'm approximating here—those expletives could have come in any order).

"*Jassis!* What do we *do*?" A moral dilemma (which wasn't much of a dilemma) stood clumsily before us. We could stay quiet and avoid whatever opprobrium came with outing the criminals. Or we could rat, and accept what would surely be a lesser punishment given that there would no longer be any need for veiled references to moral decline vis-à-vis the theft of *takkies* during Friday assembly speeches. With a Machiavellian understanding of what official recognition of this event could do for our reputations, there was only one choice.

We caught up with Mr. Wolf as he walked down the pathway to the administration building. After we related our tale, he stared down at us with that mixture of disappointment and disgust I was becoming so accustomed to.

"Describe the two men, please." He sounded like Matlock, except exhausted.

"No, they're two young, we think black, men in blue overalls."

He rolled his eyes: We'd just summed up the entire black population of Johannesburg.

"We'll deal with your absence at prayers later. Note that I will have my eye on you boys."

Case closed.

Shortly after that meeting (and by "shortly" I mean seconds), we started telling the story, and we didn't stop. We were a badass version of the Hardy Boys. Girls batted their eyelashes, guys stared glumly at us with a compound of envy and admiration, complicated handshakes were proffered, heavy elucidations and re-edits were devised.

Finally, we were sure, we had acquired the capital to earn us a slat on the bench in a certain deserted bathroom.

We stood at the doorway, Ari, Kevin, Martin, and I, and pushed our way in. The hinges protested with a tortured wail. The slight smell of cigarette smoke was evident through the dust and the mouldy reek of disused plumbing. Slowly, as our eyes adjusted, the shadows took shape—first the white of the regulation school shirts, then skin, then blazers and slacks and hair. And, finally, the dark, glinting eyes of the Boys of The Barracks, hardened miscreants all. They looked like the guys facing off against Michael Jackson in the "Bad" music video. (They would've taken this as a compliment.)

"What the fuck?" asked one of the shadows.

"*Ja,* no, we just came for a smoke," one of our number answered, in an attempt at nonchalance. We were on the cusp here. A beating was well within possibility. But, so, gloriously, was acceptance. After all, Ari had cachet through his brothers, and we had acquired enough of a reputation that some consideration would have to be accorded.

"Fuck off, man. Go *rook* somewhere else, chinas," we were told in a harsh whisper.

"Nah, *boet.* We're smoking here, chinas." With thumping hearts, we held our ground, unwrapped the Cellophane and foil that held our illicit goods, and fired up with the ceremony of a South American dictator sparking a Montecristo in front of the U.S. envoy at a trade mission. Tension buzzed in the reeking Barracks—veterans facing off against uninvited debutants. Ari, with his preternatural understanding of the human condition, held out his cigarettes.

"Jassis, boet," said the head shadow, grabbing the entire box. "Get inside here, man. And don't say a fuckin' word. If we're busted here, china, I'll come looking for you, and I'll kill your family, including your fuckin' pets, *boet.* I'm not *chooning kuck*—I'll lynch your fuckin' *zeida.* You *smaak*?"

We *smaaked.* With the quiet severity of bandidos hiding out in the jungle, we sucked on our Chesterfields and enjoyed the ambience of rot around us—satisfied in the manner of those who had found a long-sought spiritual home.

We were finally in The Barracks.

We'll call them Darryl and Brian. On the surface, there was little similar about them. Darryl was tall and effeminate, with a hunch at his shoulders that gave him the unfortunate appearance of the *Amazing Spider-Man* villain Vulture. Although he had no male friends, Darryl had a gathering of female friends who were outcasts themselves—brainy or borderline mentally retarded, too heavy or far too thin, with limps, or eyes that crossed, or acne that seemed viral rather than hormonal—their bodies constructed from bit parts left over from other botched creations, the luckless underclass for whom high school must be a type of hell that even Italian medievalists cannot fully articulate. This was Darryl's strange, ungainly harem. They had to be strenuously, vigorously ignored. Or destroyed. Darryl, however, was impossible to ignore, partly because he had a voice so deep and sonorous that every time he opened his mouth it sounded as though a roomful of tenors were warming up for an "Ave Maria" sing-off. This was accompanied by a habit he had of becoming extremely excited every time a teacher asked a question he knew the answer to. His hand would jet into the air and he'd say, "Mmmmmgghhhh, mnnmffffgrrr," in a horrendous growl. Darryl could not be muted.

Furthermore, Darryl was gay. We understood this even though we had no real comprehension of what homosexuality was. We King Davidians were astonishingly sexually immature for kids in our mid-teens in the late 1980s. One of my claims to fame was the ability to draw reasonable likenesses of naked women, and I was highly praised for this skill. I had never seen a naked woman: The closest my boys and I had come to sexual encounters was a trick we had devised. By throwing a pencil down in the vicinity of a comely female classmate, getting the angle right, and asking her to pick up the writing implement, you were almost guaranteed a quick flash of panty. This counted for sex. So when I say that we intuited that Darryl was a homosexual, I mean that we understood that he was somehow different.

And—hoo boy!—we did not like different. In a country of tribes hysterically segmented from one another—and in a school of people exclusively from my own tribe—the walls of our tiny world closed in around us like a booby trap in an Indiana Jones movie. Difference was a pejorative, no matter how much our reading lists stressed tolerance. Tolerance was a fine literary theme, but we weren't expected to put it into practice, were we?

Brian's case was a variant of the same theme. Although there was nothing amiss about his sexuality, he was from a troubled home, and he carried that trouble around with him as though it were a satchel filled with granite. And one of the rules of the jungle is that the wounded are the first to go. But, with his thick, sensuous lips and long lashes, Brian also had a femininity about him, a sense of the unknowable that mirrored the air of mystery hovering about our female classmates. Brian has stood for me as a splendid personal marker for how the male members of sexually repressive societies will, almost directly after their balls drop, turn to violence as an outlet. Don't believe me? Go summer in Tehran.

I quiver with shame at my treatment of these two kids, though I like to think that I was little more than a mere geometrical point on the circumference of the South African schoolboy circle of violence, which was nothing more than a speck on the greater South African circle of violence. When I think back to that time, I remember rage coming from everywhere—from within me, from the boys around me, and from outside the barbed-wire fences of the school. This energy had to manifest itself somewhere, and the schoolyard was as good a place as any.

Darryl would open his gym bag, only to find a ribbed condom, dripping with spermicidal jelly, inflated within. He'd screech, pull out the offending item, and try to stuff it into the garbage bin, a zeppelin trying to dock in a single-car garage. Mrs. Giangragoria would walk slowly toward the class as Darryl wrestled with the prophylactic; the cheeks of my ass twitched in anticipation of the caning they would shortly receive. "Don't respond!" the headmaster implored Darryl in a froth of rage. "Every time you respond to the tomfoolery of these animals, you will find yourself here, alongside them, in the dock. Is that what you want?" Darryl blubbered into his shirt sleeves while we looked at our shoes.

Brian's main tormentor was a thick-set swimmer with Popeye-like forearms and dark eyes sheltered by a thick plate of forehead, a kid we'll call Clifford. I went along with Clifford mostly because I was scared of him: He was a chilling mixture of cheerful good nature, racist vitriol, and random violence.

During a bullying session—his big lips shredded by a complicated construction of orthodontic work—Brian would stare at us as if he were in some way separate from this corporeal reality. Some coping mechanism allowed him to disassociate himself from the fact that we had him up against the wall, a chalk circle drawn on his crotch, and were whipping projectiles at our improvised bull's-eye with peals of harsh laughter. He lived in the airy province of so many bullied kids—well outside his body.

I remember, with remarkable clarity, him saying the following to us in his dead voice:

"Your time will come."

What did that mean? It incensed our ringleader, Clifford. His retort was pretty good, too:

"Who are you, *boet*? Nostradamus?"

"Your time will come," repeated Brian. Clifford liked that statement even less the second time.

Meanwhile, I occasionally went through the motions in the brightly lit synagogue that held pride of place on the northern frontier of the school property. I learned from our dusty textbooks that it was wrong to hate, I watched on TV the country burn itself with petrol-doused tires, I jerked off to ripped-out pages of ten-year-old *Penthouse* magazines, and I heard whispers of the coming revolution—"one Boer, one bullet"—and of special days put aside when the township hordes would allow themselves the indulgence of killing a white—a Kwanza of tribal bloodshed and mayhem, with us, we pure white children, the ritual offerings.

When I recall this time in my life, I remember a feeling of swinging away from myself—becoming another version of Richard Poplak. The cynicism and the anger that I had picked up on my travels—they had not organized themselves into a coherent ideological position against something but, rather, into an incoherent anger against everything. This is not unusual for a teenager. But what was unusual was the context. No one I knew talked politics (Billups was a mild exception, and he had only talked in code). Political discourse amounted to Kevin's ritually intoned "Fuck the government cunts" and Clifford's "Fuck the stupid *kaffirs*." Sure, I knew Apartheid was wrong.

But what, exactly, was right?

In the icy, dank confines of The Barracks, Kevin, Ari, Martin, and I went about the practices of the King David bad-ass—in particular, smoking—with an intensity and concentration usually reserved for high-level athletic endeavours. We crouched back in the dark corners with the several other resident reprobates and went about the grim, silent work of misbehaving.

"*Boet,* fuckin' inhale," Ari would whisper. "Smoke it like you mean it, china."

And we went about the increasingly joyless task of rebellion, often leaning over the moral divide.

Mr. Mitzhak, our religion teacher, was a precisely built miniature of a man. The peaks of his cheekbones threatened to tear through the skin, which was stretched taut over the sharp edges of his skull. On his right arm, I was told, there was a series of tattooed numbers, and his quiet voice hinted at an underlying subtext of psychic agony.

Mr. Mitzhak—and I wasn't alone on this—was an affront. He was a living reminder, and like most people, I like my reminders safely entombed in memorials and history books. His fragility was a wound that he not only bore but inflicted.

"Ven de juice move troo de desert for fordy years, vat vas Moishe tinking looking down over de land of Canaan—and never to go inside?" Mitzhak asked in his quiet voice. I dunno—that God was a big arse? How could this man—who had stared into the eyeball of the abyss—still go on about Moishe and Canaan and the milk and the honey? How could he derive any comfort from these fairy tales? We didn't need Moishe. We needed fucking Rambo. As far as I was concerned, if we were to learn from the lessons of the past, I'd take a fully loaded M-60 over a Talmud any day of the week (including Shabbos and High Holidays). I had become a dissenter within the walls of a religious school. Unfortunately for my ass cheeks, the debating club did not extend to class time, and in a Jewish high school (I assume the same applies to other denominations), one is required to at least respect the *existence* of the religion one is supposed to be practising.

"Don't you know what this man has gone through?" asked the deputy principal, Mr. Altsheuler. He was more baffled than angry—his eyes almost flickering with what remained of his interest in trying to solve a conundrum he would never quite grasp. But how could he? How could he bridge a generation and crawl around inside my mind, and see that the absence of future he saw with "these children" was perfectly mirrored in my own deep nihilism. We were at the cliff edge of the End of History—we were, I felt it!—and as our enemies—the stinking Commies—crumbled around us along with the Berlin Wall, others rose, in perilous proximity, to take their place. On TV, we watched the black hordes gathering in thick ranks—looking for a way in.

"Answer me," said Mr. Altsheuler, half yelling, half imploring. "Do you not know what he's gone through?" Asking a teenager for empathy is like asking a lead pipe for a cup of camomile tea— Altsheuler was as out of touch with his inner fifteen-year-old as anyone I've ever met. "Why do you boys speak to him the way you speak to him?" (Ari was usually beside me in the cramped office for these exchanges; spitballs his offence, rather than religious/philosophical insurrection.) My answer was always similar:

"I do know what he's gone through, sir. And I can't understand what he's talking about. I'm sorry, sir. I'm sorry. There's no logic to his way of thinking."

Mr. Altsheuler would look from one to the other of us and back again, eyes bulging, a Looney Tunes character following a tennis match.

"You know I'm going to have to cane you?"

"Izzit?" Ari said to me in a low whisper. "What a fer-hukkin' surprise."

"Your time will come," Brian had said, his sad eyes sheltered by those long lashes.

How right he was.

In retrospect, it's obvious that the incident had been meticulously planned. Four of us, with Clifford at the helm, were chasing Brian in a fast sprint. The chase ended abruptly in the shadow of the Linksfield synagogue, among a bed of thick green elephant ears. Brian simply stopped running and turned to look at his pursuers.

Something was up.

They emerged from the very soil of the earth. There were five of them: a tangle of bulging biceps, hard grimaces, slit eyes, and, God help us, stubbled chins.

I'd watched enough action flicks to know a trap when I saw one.

"What the fuck is this?" asked Clifford. Brian stood panting, bent over, resting his hands on his knees, looking at us with dead eyes.

"I said what the fuck *is* this?" Clinton's voice had pitched up an octave or two. "You can't fight your own battles, *boet*?" he asked Brian, with something approaching epic levels of hypocrisy.

These new fellows answered definitively, in a universal language called fisticuffs.

My mental crane shot, honed by the hundreds of hours of movies I'd watched, rose in a slow spiral over the battlefield. There were six or seven of them to our four. We met them with yells, while they attacked in silence. Mickey, my judo teacher, faded in over the scene in a glowing, translucent superimposition. "Okay, now remember your moves, Poplak. Get in nice and close and … Oooow, Jesus! Drop and roll! Drop. And. Roll!"

The crane shot hurtled groundward, falling into the elephant ears and gritty soil in a crumpled heap beside me, heaving, as I was, in agony from a nicely placed shot to what I later found out was my solar plexus. Until that point, I was unaware I had one. It was a rude introduction—like finding out that a part of your body spontaneously bursts into flames. Someone stepped on my face, and then spit on me.

We were no match for our opposition's size, numbers, strength, and moral rectitude. Their leader—a ruddy, sandy-faced boy with sizeable ears—grabbed a healthy fistful of Clifford's hair, shoved his face in the soil, and said, "Do not fucking touch him again or I will fuck you up with no mercy." I was as grateful as I was surprised to hear that any mercy had been bestowed on us in the first place. Clifford opened his mouth to say something, but instead of words, soil came out.

There we lay, as restful as if we'd just decided to have a casual yet tiring roll in the flower bed, while Brian and his protectors strolled off. He did not look back, Brian. Not even to check if we were okay.

Back in class, breathing in short gasps so as not to agitate my solar plexus, I again looked in my satchel and fingered the soft blue velvet tallis and tefillin bags my grandfather had given me almost three years previously. I remember the roughly embroidered silver Hebrew lettering—the significance of which I still could not understand. With that same feeling of self-pity I had experienced after my urinal humiliation so long ago, I wanted to be elsewhere, at home, with my family. I resolved at that point to be a better person. To do good. To live in a way that would make Oupa proud.

But in The Barracks, where our tog bags now hid flasks of booze alongside packs of cigarettes, what good could possibly be done? I had wrenched myself from my moorings and left something behind, some essential goodness that I may or may not have possessed before my personal dinghy, *Miss Behave,* drifted into the sludgy waters of reprobation.

And so we hardened and darkened, our shoulders stooped, our eyes lost that dewy glisten of untroubled youth, our fists clenched, and we became ornery, argumentative, quick on the draw. With each lungful of Chesterfield smoke, we moved further and further from our childhood. We swung away from ourselves. I don't believe that any generation has been as tethered as tightly to home and hearth as white South Africans of that time—we were practically throttled by the apron strings. We crawled forward interminably, like coyotes whose hind legs are caught in traps. And we spent the following decade making sense of the confusion of hatred and rage and guilt and need that had made mad dogs of us in the first place.

I spent only three years of five at King David; my time there was cut short by my family's immigration to Canada. But by the time I left, I was a fixture in The Barracks, as much a part of the setting as the rotted wooden slats, the dusty urinal, the stall doors desperately hanging to the dignity of their door frames, and the other mini-rebels who fashioned themselves after Billy Idol or Axl Rose. I remember thinking that it was an achievement of sorts, being on the other side of that darkness of which I had once been so fearful. I felt a rush of pride when new grunts tried to buy their way in with cigarettes and hard-earned reputations for causing trouble in class or having their ears pierced or wearing the wrong-coloured socks to two assemblies in a row.

They'd show up with their sleeves rolled up high over tiny, fine-boned arms—the universal sign of the 1980s South African schoolboy tough.

"Fuck off, man. Go *rook* somewhere else, chinas," we'd tell them in a harsh whisper.

"Nah, *boet.* We're smoking here, *boet.*" They'd offer up their cigarettes, and we'd take the whole box, threatening to lynch their *zeidas* if they spoke out of turn.

And I'd stare at them—feeling both old and brand new, like a godfather but also like a child—suck on my Chesterfield, and sink into the low shadows of The Barracks, a rebel in a country descending into rebellion. After a few minutes, Ari would make like a mother hen and fussily usher them out.

"*Boet,* come on, man!" they'd protest.

"You're young," he'd say. "What's your fuckin' hurry?"

Depths and Depths

In which we Travel the Lengths of Louis Botha Avenue; See the Ghost of a General; and Forget the Ending.

The General's Last Stand

After dark, Louis Botha Avenue feels like the gateway to a nightmare. Stygian and empty, it's a broad pathway winding through a mausoleum, where crumbling three- or four-storey buildings stand in for concrete sepulchres. Traffic lights act as votives, reflecting dully off the asphalt. If this is some kind of cemetery, kinsfolk have left no wreaths, no flowers, not so much as a scrap of greenery. This place is an epitaph written in decaying brick and tarmac.

"China, we're the last *okes* on earth," says Kevin (though it comes out more as "Shina, weerzz lassokes nerth") as my merry band—three of us in all—stumble our way south along the benighted boulevard. He has a point. After ten o'clock on a Saturday night in 1989, you can walk down this street and see not a single car for minutes on end, which on a major road in a major city makes you think of stuff like *The Twilight Zone* or Judgment Day.

"Woooooooooo!" says Ari, doing his best horror-house ghost imitation, which he follows up with his trademark cackle.

"Nah, *boet*," says Kevin, waving his hand dismissively. This is the thing with Ari: Where we see boundless terror, he sees Casper the Friendly Ghost. It's a question of perspective. For all our bravado, most of us are afraid of this street, where it leads, and what it can lead to. But when you have a skipper like Ari at the helm, you're bound to sail ever onward into unmapped regions, perils notwithstanding. Oopla! Over the edge, into the abyss.

General Louis Botha's political career was a spaghetti-tangle of trouble; Botha was a man who could not so much as get out of bed without causing a major fracas. Born in 1862 in Natal, the scion of a proud Afrikaner *Voortrekker* clan of German ancestry, he earned a reputation as a formidable commando in both Boer Wars. Although he became the first prime minister of the Union of South Africa in 1910, his continued negotiations with the British earned him the enmity of many within his own tribe. When he brought the Union into the Allied orbit during World War I, his loyalty to his German forbears was called into question by compatriots who had far more in common with Kaiser Wilhelm II than King George. General Louis Botha died clinging to power, his tribe bitterly divided, his own soul rent in twain—the only point of convergence between him and his detractors a hardening attitude toward the black population.

Louis Botha was as unlikely to rest in peace as anyone who walked this earth.

His troubled history perhaps goes some way to explaining the ambience of the street that bears his name. Louis Botha Avenue is a dark tributary that flows through suburban Johannesburg. Like the River Nile's until Livingstone stumbled upon Lake Victoria, Louis Botha's source is a mystery. Unlike the Nile, it has no delta marking the termination of its passage. It just peters away into nothingness at either end: to the north, the crumbling environs of Alexandra; to the south, the decaying streets of Hillbrow.

Putco buses screamed along Louis Botha Avenue, loaded down with a freight of black workers shipped into the city from the smoking townships and then shipped out again at night.[56] Often, these rotting hunks of steel veered off the road at Death Bend (a sharp downhill turn near my neighbourhood) and flipped onto their backs, wheels spewing grit into the sky, a viscous cocktail of oil, fuel, and blood leaking onto the asphalt. These buses, unmaintained and poorly operated, were sources of death all along Louis Botha Avenue, like feluccas manned by clandestine assassins who arrived in a screeching whir, metal flashing, body parts flying. When I was quite young, I saw the aftermath of a Putco incident—a black man lay crushed under the wheels of a bus. He lay inert on the tarmac, like a straw doll, the contents of his head pooling under the dripping chassis of the Putco, which huffed and puffed and snorted as it hunched over its victim. I suppose he must have been hit as he crossed the road—Putcos moved down the avenue at the speed of sound, and he was surely not the only pedestrian casualty in Johannesburg that day.

It wasn't *all* bad, Louis Botha Avenue. This was, after all, the key thoroughfare between the suburbs that were the settings of my childhood—Norwood, Orange Grove, Houghton, Yeoville. I remember the Orange Grove Library, where as a kid I spent hours of bliss opening the spines of

56. Putco was (and still is) a government-subsidized, white-owned transportation company. The buses were de facto gasoline-powered slave ships, critical to Johannesburg's cheap labour-based economy, and a key peg in the Apartheid mechanism that moved blacks between home and work in accordance with the Group Areas Act. These buses were in shocking disrepair, and the number of casualties they wrought must be added to the regime's grim tally.

musty books, their covers protected by meticulously wrapped plastic, or discovering worlds while I sat on a beanbag (always the blue one), listening to a librarian read Dr. Seuss, Enid Blyton, and other brat-lit stalwarts. Across the road from the library was a Kentucky Fried Chicken,[57] where I enjoyed my only taste of genuine North American cuisine; there were the banks and the post office where Dr. Poplak and I walked, my hand in his, so that he could do his banking and posting. At one of these banks I received my first bank card, and learned the (still relevant) pleasure of running an empty bank account. Also on Louis Botha Avenue: the Lido Café, where I bought my comics and my candy. And across from the library, my first girlfriend, Vanessa Tortello.

Sex (well, not quite), death, candy, chicken, literature, money. All life happened here.

For a time. Until the street started to die. Its sickness was most obvious at night, when the sidewalks were crowded with the melancholy vespers of Putco casualties and other restless, homeless spirits. Store windows were shuttered; scraps of litter rode the breeze like Hadean water birds searching for carrion. To walk along Louis Botha long after dark, something I did almost every Saturday night over the winter months of 1989, was to preview Johannesburg's future, and to sense the weight of its past.

I have a theory: It had everything to do with the General. And my thinking was (and still is): This avenue was his tortured soul's last stand.

---

57. International sanctions saved us from Big Macs, Whoppers, and Chicken McNuggets. Kentucky Fried Chicken (now "KFC") was the only North American franchise with outlets in South Africa.

No one seems to know why Solly's is called Solly's. It has no sign stating its name, and seeing as it's the house bar in the Sunningdale Hotel, by all rights it should be called Sunningdale's. But it's not.

This is where Kevin, Ari, Martin, and I, along with a cast of rotating guest stars, would convene before making our way south along Louis Botha toward our intended destination: The Thunderdome Nite Club. Thunderdome, named for the final chapter in the *Mad Max* trilogy, was our Shangri-La, a blue-and-pink neon-lit cavern full of all measure of iniquity. It helped that we were obsessed with the film, which starred Mel Gibson in his third go-around as the titular Max and Tina Turner as Aunty Entity, the benevolent madam of a post-apocalyptic city called Bartertown, which runs on the alternative energy source of methane derived from mountains of pig effluent. I'm not sure if Johannesburg's Thunderdome ran on pig shit, but it smelled like it ran on something at least as malodorous. I have no recollection of what type of music the club played (and neither does anyone else I queried, for reasons that will become obvious), and the clientele were a motley assembly of Johannesburg's bright white young things, whose bulbs were dimming by the minute. The club's doormen were notoriously tetchy, and this, combined with the fact that we were nowhere near of legal drinking age, meant it was impossible to know if we'd actually make it inside. But we would make a valiant attempt. And that attempt started at Solly's.

The Sunningdale Hotel was not actually on Louis Botha Avenue, but it was close enough. Kevin lived around the corner, so he was usually there first, hunched over the bar like Charles Bukowski nine weeks into a ten-week drinking binge. His growled "*Huzzit,* chinas" served as the evening's kickoff, swathed as it was in a black cloak of teen angst.

"*Ja,* no, *huzzit, boet,*" I'd say.

"No, *lekker,*" said Kevin, already working on something large and multicoloured.

My parents were bamboozled into dropping me at a nearby burger joint, and considering I'd be sleeping at Kevin's (who was sleeping at Ari's, who was sleeping at Martin's, if you get my drift), parental scrutiny was not an issue. Barring an implanted tracking device, there was no way my mother could know where I was or what I was up to. She would not have been pleased to learn that I was in the Sunningdale Hotel.

The lobby boasted, besides a threadbare carpet and a stained loveseat, hard-core *Ahh*-frika chintz: framed gazillion-piece puzzles of lion, buffalo, leopard, and other stars of the *bushveld.* There was the requisite portrait of P.W. Botha over the reception desk, which was manned by the requisite shabby, bespectacled concierge.[58] Like most three-star Johannesburg hotels, it earned one of its stars for working toilets, the second for disposing of corpses discreetly, and the final star for the pleasant disposition of the resident rat population. It also earned steady revenue from serving alcohol to patrons who were still a good year or so away from their first shave.

We sat, my crew and I, under faux beer kegs and the blinking Castle Lager signs, earnestly discussing what mattered, which was, mostly, Guns N' Roses' *Appetite for Destruction.* Ari and I, in particular, took that album very, very seriously. It was the octane in our hormonal fuel—a genuinely nasty, vitriol-drenched rock album that could inspire one to do harm to others and, of more

58. F.W. de Klerk, our new president, had yet to get glossy prints of himself out there to the masses—but after a watered-down Scotch or two, you begin to think the two men resembled each other precisely, so perhaps he didn't need to.

pointed concern, to oneself. "Welcome to the Jungle"? That song was *written* for Johannesburg. "Paradise City"? Bit of a stretch (the grass is green? the girls are pretty?), but entire stanzas applied. We could recite the lyrics word for word, and often did so with with solemnity, as if reciting a liturgy, or Milton.

The black barmen at the Capri Hotel, our second stop (and the first official port of call on Louis Botha Avenue), were entirely interchangeable with their counterparts at the Sunningdale Hotel. They wore stained penguin suits handed down through generations of previous employees, their eyes were red-rimmed and exhausted, and they used what they served with a conviction that was hard to match. They moved with a lethargy I associate with large underwater plant life.

"Mmm, *baas*?" they'd say drowsily, as we gathered around the bar, our size-eight Reeboks dangling a good few inches above the ground.

"*Ja,* no, four shots of chocolate liqueur and four peach schnapps on the rocks, hey."

The Capri stood back from Louis Botha Avenue, behind a large parking lot that also served a steakhouse and a liquor store. The hotel's architecture was a poor attempt at Miami-style 1950s art deco: the sign a jaunty, pink-splashed wave; the interior dotted with enormous, vaguely subtropical plastic vegetation covered in thick layers of dust. The Capri's claim to fame was its large event hall, and in the time before Johannesburg bar and bat mitzvahs became wars of one-upmanship—"The Cohens are having a ninja-themed barmie? Well, let's see their faces when they see the entire cast of *Cats* at Wayne's big day"—I'd find myself there once or twice a year, eating overcooked fish and under-frozen ice cream.

The bar was long and lit operating-room bright; there was an intense, clinical incandescence to the room, spoiled only by a carpet that gave me hives just looking at it. Unlike Solly's, the washrooms were spotless and reeked of heavy industrial cleaning product, so we were safe to puke up those early sugary beverages without the risk of an E. coli infection. The other advantage to the Capri was its proximity to Mean Machines, a destination hip with Johannesburg youth for the usual three-month period. Mean Machines was a theme bar without a theme, unless you counted the blue neon and a mild *Wild One* biker vibe. It did not serve alcohol to underage boys (this was a family joint), so we popped in, smelling like a mash-up of a candy store and a Tennessee distillery, to pay a visit to pals who had yet to go off the rails.

"Are you *okes dronk*?" asked those we considered pussies. We, of course, played up our inebriation, stumbling histrionically and yelling louder than was polite even for drunks.

"Why, you're not?" we'd ask.

"*Jassis, boet,* back off. You smell like chocolate milk that's gone off."

We didn't stay long.

Across from Mean Machines stood what was perhaps the avenue's most significant landmark. The Doll's House sign flashed pink neon, an attempt at a 1950s American diner in a pocket of Johannesburg that, come to think of it, was a botched tribute to 1950s-era America. Besides rampant civil rights abuses, what was it about this epoch in the United States that appealed to local sensibilities so? Suffice to say, it was something of a thematic phenomenon in the city at the time, and nowhere more prevalent than along this stretch of Louis Botha.

The Doll's House was built when the idea of eating in your car seemed a good one. The concept was simple: You drove into the parking lot, flashed the car lights, and a server shakily roller skated over to the driver's window to take the order (as Louis Botha Avenue went to rot and many a food tray ended up on the windscreen or a lap, this floor show disappeared). Their specialties—toasted cheese and tomato, burgers, milkshakes—were infused with so much grease, and were so addictive, that they made OxyContin abuse look mild by comparison. I can still perfectly remember the taste of a Doll's House toasted cheese, and how the cook managed to heat the tomatoes to a state of molten intensity that peeled layers of skin off the tongue and palate. It took days for charred taste buds to recover.

We ordered at the counter, where the Doll's House black clientele, such as they were, picked up their food. Clutching wax packets containing the smouldering toasted sandwiches, we batted tomatoes around on our tongues as we walked our way south, trying to avoid both potholes and third-degree burns in our mouths.

"Fug dis is haaa," I'd say.

"Welgum do da jungle, mudda-fugga," said Ari.

"Fangks," I'd say, soothing the pain with a dose of milkshake that sloshed around uneasily with the assortment of sweet liqueurs in my gut—a formidable, latent pool of burbling poison. By this time we were approaching Charlie C's, which, given its proximity to my house, would have been my local, assuming I'd had a local at the tender age of sixteen. This place shared none of the aesthetics of those other establishments; it was designed, I assumed, by a leprechaun with a drinking problem. Tables were too small, the lighting was low and sickly green, everything sloped. This is where drunken Irishmen go when they go to hell.

Here, in the green-tinged gloom, we'd lay out our plan of attack for storming the Thunderdome's ramparts.

"The Thunderdome," I'd growl, quoting Mad Max. "How do I get in there?"

"That's easy," said Ari, quoting Aunty Entity. "Pick a fight."

"Okes," said Kevin, "fuck off with that *kuck.* Let's get serious here."

Serious meant making sure we had an array of coloured markers so that I could draw counterfeit stamps on our hands if need be. We also had to pool our meagre financial resources to ensure we would only *mildly* insult the bouncer with a bribe.

With Forbes Street in plain sight (if I stood on tiptoe, I could probably have made out the peaked roof of my house), I turned my back on home and hearth and turned toward the city, my posse in toe, quoting lines from our canon as we made our way south.

I'm not convinced, although I am here to tell the tale, that hitchhiking down the length of Louis Botha Avenue was an exceptionally good idea. Living in the bubble as I did, I'd lost all—if I'd ever had any—fear of fellow whites, so I'd happily get into a hearse that had bloody handprints on the windscreen so long as someone of my own race was piloting it. There were no blacks on the streets this late, and few whites besides, so the wildlife picking up inebriated boys wearing pastel T-shirts and breakdance pants were a strange bunch indeed. I remember none of them specifically, but the compound image of those men driving south toward town at ten-thirty on a Saturday night adds up to a collage of Ted

Bundy, the two rapists from *Deliverance,* and Dick Cheney—crazy-looking, viciously inbred, bucktoothed white folk with quiet, genocidal intelligence.

As we zoomed southward, I'd see the markers of my childhood disappear behind us—Europa Deli, where we bought our crusty buns and salami, and where my mother, just a few years before, used to let me finish the sugary foam of her cappuccino; the rundown theatre where I'd seen a few pantomimes around Christmas time; the Lido Café; the road leading to my bobba's flat. My boyhood was soon swallowed by the cloud of emissions spewed out by the rust-bucket Ford Cortinas or Citi Golfs that we huddled in as we raced toward town in the charge of these anonymous men, the smell of their booze vapours and ours settling heavily over us like a cloud of Chernobyl fallout.

We sped up the great climb into Yeoville, past Dr. Poplak's surgery, and into Johannesburg's great experiment: Hillbrow. The inhabitants, hastily assembled bricolages of bone and rag, moved with herky-jerk zombie-like dance moves, converging on the city in a slow but inexorable shuffle. This was Nightmare Land—an amusement park filled with the wondrous detritus of ruined humanity. Street lamps turned everything the colour of late-stage cirrhosis; gliding through these streets drunk, in those strange, stinking cars, I could absorb the surroundings only in small, jagged hits—a yellowed eye, a rotted mouth framing a blackened tongue, a fading tattoo on a yellowed arm, squatting buttocks spraying steaming piss into the street.

From this haze, my movie-camera eye would run film through the gate—film that underwent a slow chemical process in my brain, removing the immediacy of the degradation I was witnessing, framing it as something outside my universe. Why, this was Gotham City, rendered in fierce, living detail, to be stored and used again in one of the imagined blockbuster buddy-cop films I had kicking around in my head. This wasn't real. It couldn't be. It was in no way analogous to my life during the day, during the week, in the safety of my usual surroundings. How could both realities be real? I could not in any way reconcile the Johannesburg of Hillbrow with the Johannesburg of Fellside or Linksfield. So Hillbrow became a set, and I the cinematographer.

I'd blink, and my internal Steinbeck editing machine would jump-cut to a little boîte named Comix,[59] so called because it was decorated with a catholic array of comic-strip characters: Superman, Prince Valiant, Charlie Brown, Wonder Woman, Hägar the Horrible. Personally, I couldn't tell Comix's rendition of Aquaman from Beetle Bailey—and I'm not sure that this was just because of the booze. They looked like they were the work of a seven-year-old boy who had angrily dipped his feet in a can of paint and smeared the walls during a tantrum. This was vandalism, not decor.

Comix, especially at this point in the proceedings, was aggressively surreal. The washroom was a claustrophobic closet wallpapered with comic strips, and I remember standing in there on one particular night, staring at myself in the mirror. Trying to quell wave after wave of nausea, and for a reason understood only by my drunken self, I quieted my thundering

59. The highlight here was a troubadour named Mick the Muff Diver, who acted as Comix's resident one-man band and dinner-theatre entertainer. He wore a snorkel and goggles, and his signature line, recited in a faux Cockney accent, was "Hi, folks. I'm Mick the Muff Diver! And I'm a real conniver!"

heartbeat and roiling gut by saying, repeatedly, "I'm Batman. I'm Batman. I'm Batman."[60]

"I want you to promise me something," my mother had said to me some months before. "I never want you going to one of those dancing places in town. I've heard stories about boys going there, and I don't want you to be one of them. Now promise me."

"*Ja,* Ma. *Jassis,* man. I promise."

"Good boy."

Why the hell hadn't I listened to her? What the hell was I doing here?

The walls in the bathroom closed around me until the room was as tight as a discount pine coffin, my skin oozed beads of sweat, and I desperately wanted to be home. But there was no way to get there, certainly not by myself. And sixteen-year-old boys don't base decisions on what they want, but rather on what their peers demand.

"I'm *Ba*tman," I promised myself.

There was only one option and that was onward—deeper into this journey I had imposed on myself, one that, absurdly, I could stop next weekend by saying, "Nah, chinas, I'm gonna go to the movies." I could go with Tamir and spend the afternoon at the Ster-Kinekor in town and then do the same throughout the evening. Yet, I was compelled to keep on, weekend after weekend, unwrapping the silver foil on packages of cigarettes and sucking back vile, watered-down cocktails in

60. This was around the time of the release of Tim Burton's *Batman,* and Ari and I quoted the film liberally to each other. So this is not quite as outlandish as it seems.

bars that were barely worthy of the name, in parts of the city clogged with misery. I had a choice, and I chose not to have a choice. This was, somehow, compulsory—like homework, or rugby.

Onward. Forward. Into the blank spots on the map.

The Thunderdome, according to Tina Turner's Aunt Entity, did not like Screamers. The first man to scream was a dead man. This was not exactly true of Johannesburg's Thunderdome, but herpes would certainly take the first man to sit on the toilet seats. The club, a large warehouse lit with that endemic garish neon, stood at the end of Claim Street like a heavily guarded fortress waiting to be stormed. As we approached, alighting from some strange car, my heart would start hammering with increased urgency. What if we didn't make it in? What if we got killed trying? What would Max do?

"We know the fuckin' plan, chinas," Kevin would say, "so let's fuckin' do this."

Town was not looking its best in 1989. It would get worse—much worse—but for those of us who knew it as a supremely ordered (if incredibly ugly) colonial city, with Victorian buildings standing alongside glass-and-concrete skyscrapers, the encroaching decay was suitably Aunty Entity's Bartertown. The area around the club was lit up like a military installation, and those in the lineup stamped their feet and blew into their hands and rubbed their shoulders to keep bare flesh warm from the stinging July cold. Along with the garbage-strewn streets and the odd scuffle, the whole set piece was perfectly apocalyptic. Remember Reportedly-Wears-Feather-in-Ear? The guy who accused me of staring at his penis in that high school bathroom? Let's put it this way: He was a regular, and he *did* wear a feather in his ear. A purple one. Welcome to the jungle indeed.

The air rippled with the *thunk* of bass emanating from the black, cavernous interior of the club; we straightened our shoulders and poufed our hair skyward to look bigger and taller, and took a few deep breaths.

"'Kay, chinas. Here goes. Remember, act eighteen," Kevin would say, walking in a locked-knee, stiff-backed gait suggesting that acting eighteen was similar to acting like you'd just had a colonoscopy.

Invariably, the large Indian bouncer at the door would crane his neck, look down, and tell us, very simply but with great meaning, to engage, along with several members of our immediate family, in a depraved sexual activity.

"Ah, c'mon *boet*!" one of us would say. And then in a whisper: "We got a little extra moolah, china."

Two things could happen here. One, he took the money and waved us in. Two, he took the money and didn't wave us in.

Or—a third option—he could get nasty.

Kevin and I once got on the wrong side of this gentleman's temper by employing Plan B—scrawling the club's admittance stamp on our hands with the coloured markers we had brought along for the occasion. There is no way I'd have been able to pull off this impromptu art project sober. Drunk, it was a disaster. We made our way up to the door with a couple of rudimentary Jackson Pollock's decorating our paws.

The bouncer grabbed my hand, looked close, and let out a low, pained sigh. He didn't even dignify Kevin and me with a punch to the face. He gave us two quick, open-handed slaps that rung my skull like the dinner bell at Gaga and Oupa's on Friday night.

"You *okes,*" he said, "are fuckin' *dooses.*"

We were duly shamed.

The times we did not make it into the club far outnumbered the times we did. And as bad as it was inside the Dome, it was worse outside. Pissed off and bitter, and drunk to boot, we'd wander around town, railing against the unfairness of it all.

I remember our wonky reasoning: "Fuck, what's wrong with that *oke*? If I was him, I'd let the younger *okes* come in, no questions asked. At least we don't cause any trouble." Hmm. Logic was of no particular interest to us, which goes a long way to explaining some of the places we made our way into. We'd drift, with Ari manning the rudder, to the nearby drinking holes, some of them catering to a drastically different demographic than our own. These establishments were often on the second or third floor of dying buildings, the stairs practically crumbling as we mounted them. They blend into one another, these pockets of nastiness, but I remember one in particular, in an old Victorian building with stately balustrades and walls that sweated a thick, stinking gunk from under William Morris–style wallpaper.

"What the fuck is this place?" Ari whispered to me.

"I dunno, *boet.* You fuckin' brought us here."

In this club, drinking was but a minor vice. From the look of things, the oldest profession in the world was doing a blistering trade. With wide eyes, we stared at the black whores who lined the room, their hips heavy, their hair teased into afros, their eyes darting across the room, looking for johns. Their clientele was, to my great astonishment, all white—scraggly men in tracksuits who looked over these women with unmitigated lust. This was the first time in my life I had seen blacks (I don't mean North American blacks—I mean local South Africans) in a sexual context. I had never even considered them sexual beings. This wasn't the Judy Blume "I'm feeling funny between my legs" variety of female sexuality, nor was it the *Penthouse* Forum "I fucked six chicks in a limo" version. Here, in this overlit place, I saw African women dripping with sex. They proffered it, in the way they stood, in the way they looked at their marks, in the way they leaned in and whispered something that made them giggle.

I watched in wonder as a white man and a black woman slow danced, grinding up against each other, and I understood for the first time what real sexual appetite was about. I fathomed the murk of desire, the peremptory nature of sexual need. In retrospect, I can see that this was something of a fetish club—a place for white men to pay for sex with black women in a country where both would face enormous reprobation for the offence. It was like bungee jumping from the top of Victoria Falls, another cheap African thrill. But to a son of Apartheid, even the genuinely appalling can be revelatory in a positive way. "Hey! They have sex!" I thought for the first time. "Who knew?"

We floated through the bar like players in a dream—the johns and the hookers so locked in their sordid jig that we were unnoticed until the lights flickered to indicate closing time. And then out into the night, with another mystery I didn't even know existed solved.

Depths and depths and depths—when did it all end? I had the dim understanding that it *didn't* end, that you could keep sinking interminably, and that unlike Dorothy in Oz or Joseph Conrad's Marlow on his dark cruise, there was no culminant *deus ex machina* to shed at least a little light on the enigma.

Nope, you kept going down and down. But occasionally, you came across a situation, or a person, that allowed you to understand just how deep bottomless actually is, and that no matter how far you were willing to descend, there was at least double that distance to go.

That was the night we stumbled into Club X-tacy.

That six-month period of debauching my way down Louis Botha Avenue smears into one composite night in my memory. Those nights were all more or less the same in tenor and pitch, and after each one I woke up with what felt like a large cinch tightly clamped to my brain, my tongue the flavour of boiled carpet, my bowels sizzling with a seltzer of booze and Doll's House menu items. Then the unease rolled in like fog off the ocean—the feeling that I was carrying the city's dark soul within me: the notion that I was not so much living in Johannesburg as Johannesburg was living within me.

I do remember waking up the night after that accidental visit to Club X-tacy. It was that feeling, to the power of ten.

X-tacy was in projectile-vomiting distance of Thunderdome; we never entered because the disastrous facade was about as inviting as a scissor kick to the genitals. Besides, the place had an unsavoury reputation. I have no recollection of who I stumbled in there with—Ari, more than likely. I learned later that it was the Mandrax capital of the city, which was, incidentally, the Mandrax capital of the world. Mandrax is the market name for a barbiturate-type drug, the active ingredient of which is methaqualone. Methaqualone is almost as addictive as a Doll's House toasted sarmie, and accompanied by alcohol, it was the street drug of choice in South Africa. Crushed Mandrax pills, or buttons as they were commonly known, were smoked from the cracked neck of a beer bottle. This process made people a little shaky on their feet and, in between highs, somewhat surly and unpleasant to be around. They developed chronic halitosis, and they were paranoid that someone was out to get them. In other words, much like members of the ruling National Party.

I knew none of this when I stumbled into Club X-tacy—and less when I crawled out. I did not smoke buttons, but I met a buttonhead, and he was one of the few spectres on our Tours de Louis Botha that I actually got to jaw with a little. I was a sixteen-year-old boy from a cloistered Johannesburg enclave—I met few people outside of my community, and I was, staggeringly, dangerously naive. So my buttonhead pal, like those hookers, represented something of an awakening.

"*Okes,*" he said, waving us over as we stumbled in. "Join a fellow for a drink."

This was new. I had seen *Barfly*, with Mickey Rourke, and this seemed like a *Barfly* kind of guy. That's the problem with drunks and junkies in movies—even the bad ones are usually the most interesting characters in the film. And this was a real drunk. I was enraptured.

"*Ja, lekker,* no problem," I said.

So, callow boys from Johannesburg's northern suburbs sidled up to this character and drinks were purchased.

Details: his teeth rotted to the gums, his hands charred at the palms (I later learned this is the telltale mark of a Mandrax smoker—the improvised pipes become scorching), his fingernails like blackened claws, his hair smudged back over his pate. And yet, there was a certain charm to the fellow, the essential magnetism of a junkie whose next high depends on benefaction and brotherhood, however fleeting.

It was a pleasant conversation. I don't remember the specifics, but we discussed the usual array of typical bar subjects—sports, music (I remember him saying that Rick Astley was a "fucking *moffie*" and that they don't make music like they used to), the finer points of female movie stars ("*Jassis,* Kim Basinger could make my brekkies any day, *boet*"). He was garrulous to a fault. I even got used to him placing one of those rotten hands on my shoulder as he spoke, waving a cigarette with his other hand. A real-life barfly. This was Life Experience. This was what being a man was all about.

The conversation, such as it was, at some point hit a snag. I'm not sure if it was something I said, but the tone changed. I was drunk, but I wasn't drunk enough to miss a certain alteration in the bar's atmospheric pressure. It was as though thunderclouds had rolled in. Mid-sentence, our barfly had metamorphosed into something else—a barspider, maybe. The cheerfulness vanished, and he went from garrulous to dangerous in a heartbeat.

"Let me tell you something, you little *poeses,*" said our new friend, his voice flat, his long fingers with their black talons spread on the bar.

He spoke of the end of the world. Or the end of our world, anyway. He railed, hunched over that bar, and spewed forth with a vitriol that I had never encountered before. About how the *kaffirs* will run us through and take us for everything and rape us and the white man is finished and this country is in ruins and his people will have to run for the hills and our women will be ripped to pieces and the black man will eat us alive and just look around you and see how they fuck everything up and make this beautiful city look like a fucking kraal in Natal and, say, *boet,* you *okes* don't happen to have a couple of rand you can spot a china, do you? Do you, china?

That wasn't a question.

"Chinas, you got any fuckin' money."

We emptied our pockets while this creature looked straight ahead, lost in ruminations of the coming blight, shortly to be numbed by the purchase he would make courtesy of our parents' money. I do remember his exit line more or less verbatim:

"Now fuck off, chinas, or I'll kill you."

He wasn't kidding, and we knew it. We started running, and we didn't stop until our burning lungs forced us to.

Stripped like a store-window mannequin, this rotting creature was the spirit of the country—a sepia snapshot of an era that was all but over. This must have been July or August 1989. In February of 1990, F.W. de Klerk would release Nelson Mandela, and turn the tide against centuries of abuse and minority rule. He was a soldier in a war that had been lost.

Which brings me, finally, back to General Louis Botha and his last theatre of battle: the winding avenue that was built in his name.

Getting home was always an adventure. The only vehicles on the streets were yellow police *bakkies* driven by rangy cops in their early twenties, not much older than we were, in ill-fitting hand-me-down uniforms. Their skin was aflame with acne and the thrill of authority, and they worked on desperate moustaches—starving caterpillars dying on their top lips. They'd give white teenagers a ride, as a public service, I suppose—a fact that would (and should) enrage every black person who lived under Apartheid. We'd sit in the pickup bed, huddling behind the cab to break the roar of the wind, and stare at one another in terror as the vehicle slowly nudged its way toward the sound barrier.

"*Wees versigtig*"—Be safe—they'd tell us as we clambered out of the trucks on weak legs.

Often, to calm what nerves we had left after those drives, we stopped in at Charlie C's for a completely unwarranted nightcap, chugging beverages called Depth Charges (a shot of mint liqueur dropped in a draft of beer—about as delicious as it sounds). These usually ended up in that bar's stinking toilet—among a spewed green-grey soup of junk food and booze and bile and fear.

And then it was back out onto the street—purged and wretched—to someone's home, to sleep.

I remember the feel of those nights, as I lay on an unfamiliar mattress wherever I had ended up—the feeling that things have somehow slipped horribly out of control, and the dreadful notion that I'd be impelled to do this forever, to travel that street in order to do ... What, exactly? Did we have fun? Intermittently, yes. But this felt more—much more—like a mission. If so, who was our commanding officer, and what was the mission's point? I can't speak for the others, of course, and this may not have applied to a guy like Ari, but for me, I think I needed to sidle up against that danger, to feel it slither against my skin, to get a notion of its menace. Indeed, these evenings became increasingly joyless; after I left for Canada, Kevin slipped further and further into that abyss—and took many years to clamber his way out. And still he keeps one foot in the water, and every so often feels the tug.

It was a horror show, a ghost story—the city at that time. It was sliding toward something, and while I couldn't articulate it,

I sure as hell sensed it. You think we didn't smell the blood—the fear and the terror—raging in the nearby townships? We knew, deep down, in that animal part of us, that all hell was breaking loose.

And some of us are drawn to hell, and the breaking loose thereof. This is a ghost story, and I love ghost stories. It's the tale of a long-dead general who became the first prime minister of a country he could unite with nothing other than hatred. The wisp of his wraithlike hand twisted hard at the wheel of those Putcos as they swerved off Death Bend and terminated their journeys as fireballs of roasting flesh and twisted metal. He breathed death into fading family businesses; he placed cartons of milk stout into the hands of the poor and the black so that they pissed away their cash and their dignity in a thick stream of urine, in the middle of the day, in the middle of the road. In a continent that has a radically different notion of death—where the spirits of ancestors are as real as you and me—is this such a stretch? Was this dark thoroughfare not another incarnation of broken tribal settlements dotted all over the country—places where the living no longer run the show but are subject to the whims of the dead?

The whole country in 1989 was a ghost story, playing out in ghostly enmities that refused to dissipate into the ether. Louis Botha may have informed the tenor of the street; he was but one spectre among many. It was where he could play out that uniquely millenarian sensibility that grabs so many South Africans from time to time. All our ancestors played out the conclusions to their bitter games along this river of pitted asphalt, even those in my little tribe—shoemakers and travelling salesmen, the scions of long-dead economic migrants who peddled their wares and meagre skills across this country. We drifted through in a bewildered, confused, and intoxicant-numbed terror, loving and hating the smell of the troubles, somehow needing to get a whiff of their noxious vapours. To make our way to the source, and then to scarper back—marked but unwounded. To play among the unmarked graves on the battlefield of the general's heroic last stand.

There was another Johannesburg.

It's one I saw on a bright Sunday morning as I made my way home after a night of carousing. On a Sunday, early, Johannesburg was peace. This Johannesburg did not recall, in any way, the set of a post-apocalyptic Hollywood B-movie. This city is full of trees, hundreds of thousands of them—a veritable forest. They absorb noise, making Johannesburg oddly quiet.

I could smell the dryness of the dead winter grass and the crisp freshness in the winter air. The sky in the Highveld is a thin, weak blue—a gossamer layer between us and the firmament. A few wisps of white clouds, a slight breeze. Or maybe a sky of cumulus—tumbling rollers of white on grey, stretching tens of thousands of feet into the stratosphere and catching the light of the sun in brilliant patches of luminescence. As the day wears on, these monuments to the ephemeral change in colour and tone—becoming melancholy orange and then a final, sulking blue-grey. In the afternoon, domestic servants will lazily pad back from church, enjoying their afternoon off. The smoke of a zillion *braais* makes the city smell of grilled meat, and there is a pervasive melancholy motivated largely by the fact that this day must soon end.

That other stuff—all the ghost story mumbo-jumbo—you could easily convince yourself was all a bad dream. If you wanted—and if you didn't feel the pull—the other Johannesburg, that of the general and his legions, did not need to exist.

Voetsak!

Memory has its own rules. For instance: I remember the early days of my childhood with remarkable clarity, yet I have almost no recollection of my final months in South Africa. September to December of 1989 have gone missing, as if I had a line on some covert, nefarious government plot (as opposed to the far more overt, nefarious government plot) and my memory has been wiped clean by a special branch of the Special Branch. As unlikely—although not completely impossible—as that may be, there is a scrubbed-clean quality to this gap in my recollection. I have the terrifying feeling that something important has been erased, that a fundamental key to my understanding—a cornerstone in the shaky edifice of my private posterity—is irretrievably AWOL. One moment I'm stumbling down Louis Botha Avenue and the next, the sliding doors of Toronto's Terminal 2 open onto an alien world.

I suspect many of us are confronted with this problem—we're like film directors with large chunks of important footage missing from the rough cut of our lives. The film is not quite ruined, but it is incomplete. We are left with two things: a straight-to-DVD release and a question. In my case, the question is not so much, What's missing from the gap? Rather, I'd love for someone to tell me what this gap *means*. Why the hole? Why that bright blaze of absence where a rich range of incidence should be? And what is the point of a personal story—or any story, really—with no final act?

My aunt Maxine, my father's sister, was not quite the skeleton in our family closet, but she did exist on the margins, the long shadow of loss and shame and sorrow that flickers at the corners of our history. When Maxine was two, she contracted a virulent strain of encephalitic meningitis. The disease left her emphatically and irreversibly mentally retarded. Stoked with the supernatural strength of the mentally otherwise, and with no way to control a temper that flared and ebbed with the caprice and ferocity of a sunspot, she was a danger both to herself and to those around her.

My bobba insisted on living with Maxine in her apartment in Lower Houghton—a situation that was fraught with peril for the old woman. One typical Maxine outburst occurred on the night my family and I were on the way to see Richard Donner's *Superman.* My mother, sister, and I waited silently in the car while my father attended to the situation in the apartment. The minutes slipped by, the Man of Steel already taking to the skies at the nearby 7 Arts cinema. After an interminable wait, Dr. Poplak returned to the car in obvious agony, favouring his back. Only he knows what went on up there. We drove off in silence, arriving late for the movie, missing the opening credits, which my friend Leigh insisted were unmissable. For a seven-year-old purist, I never quite forgave Maxine for this—it became the axis on which my discomfort and embarrassment with her turned.

Mercifully, before anything too terrible could happen—and before I could, God forbid, miss the opening sequence of *Superman II*—my bobba consented to have Maxine placed in a home for God's special people (as I had heard them called on more than one occasion): the Selwyn Segal Hostel.

When I knew her, Maxine's hair was already salt and pepper, cut into one of the two styles the in-house Selwyn Segal stylists practised: girl short (the other was boy short, which Maxine occasionally received when the stylists weren't paying attention). She was snaggle-toothed; sharp hairs grew on her chin. She was barely five feet tall and moved with a shuffling walk that could shift into high-paced jumping, skipping, or running with the quivered manipulation of strings from some unseen puppet master's hand. She was no longer as volatile as she once was—Selwyn Segal specialists medicated with a heavy hand. Her fellow in-patients moved with that same shambling gait, their feet anchored to earth with the weight of those rudimentary precursors to the drugs we're all now on—ancient psychotropics that wiped her clean of any personality that might have remained behind all that fried cerebral wiring.

Sentimentalists and romantics can say what they like, but there was no hint in the actual Maxine of what the potential Maxine may have been like. Her personality was whittled down to a nubbin. She loved Dr. Poplak and Uncle Percy above all else and enjoyed a series of rigorous obsessions that can be seeded in importance as follows:

1. The Royal Family.

Not any royal family. The British Royal Family. You could put pictures of Queen Beatrix of the Netherlands in front of her, and she'd quite rightly toss them across the room. Only two Western nations had monarchies worthy of the word: England and France. And French republicans did the English the favour of decapitating the competition. When Maxine visited us every second Sunday afternoon, she read through stacks of albums and compendiums and magazines, sitting on the couch for hours with her tongue protruding in concentration, lost in that gilded, plummy universe.

2. Cats.

Maxine loved cats, but this feeling was not reciprocated. She'd pet them against the run of their fur—something they strenuously object to, apparently.

3. The Orange Grove Convent.

In Orange Grove, a convent clock tower stands as a landmark. "We'll see the convent, heyyyyyy, Phillip?" Maxine would ask shortly after arriving. She loved to drive by on her way back to the hostel and look up at that tower (by tower, I mean it was three storeys to the adjacent building's two). I'm not sure what it was about the convent that attracted her so, but maybe she felt some small kinship with those cloistered women who had sacrificed so much in an effort to make everyone around them better.

4. All food groups in mouth at once.

A Sunday *braai* with Maxine was an exercise in stomach churning. With three swift movements of her fork, she had the contents of a heaping plate in her mouth. Rather than inhibit her conversational abilities, it stimulated them. "Slow down, Maxine," Dr. Poplak would say. She'd nod, and do the same with her second helping.

5. A buried, ticking biological clock.

I suppose this is where the tragedy of Maxine's situation bubbled up with an acid clarity. "I'm going to have a baby soon, Herbie!" she'd say to Dr. Poplak, referring to my father by his childhood nickname. "That's nice, Maxine," he'd answer in that measured tone of exasperation he used with her. I'm not sure whether she understood the mechanics behind producing children, but somewhere within her, this need—this buried imperative—called out. When we visited her at the Selwyn Segal, which stank of powerful industrial cleaner and misery—we'd sit outside on the hard benches overlooking the gardens and she'd point to a fellow inmate. "Him. We're going to have a baby." The poor fellow would shuffle by, unaware that he'd been singled out to stud.

Those hours at the Selwyn Segal were mostly torture for me and my sister, but they did hold us in a weird rapture. We'd stare in wonder at Maxine's fellow in-patients, envious that they were allowed to pick their noses in public and wear their pyjamas outside—privileges we were denied. Our visits were otherwise lessons in how time, when it felt like it, could stand still. When we left the hostel for home, I'd immediately relegate Maxine and the place she lived to the back of my mind. She existed in one small part of my universe and did not travel into other quadrants. I cannot say what she meant to my parents, but I know that they dreaded telling her that after a Sunday *braai* in the not-so-distant future, it would be a long time before we saw her next. She was the one major hitch in our immigration plans.

How were we to tell her? There would be practically no one to visit her (Uncle Percy and his clan were set to immigrate six months before us). I remember that my parents had no idea how she would take this—whether she'd even be able to grasp it entirely. Regardless, it would not be easy. Maxine, you see, had a keen understanding of the passing of time. She looked forward to things; halfway through a visit, she talked about the next. If she had a signature line, it was "We'll see, heyyyyyy, Herbie?" Maxine was only vaguely aware of the moment. She lived ten days in the future.

If I were to sum up how things felt in those months before our departure, I'd say that everything existed in Maxine time.

My whole world was like a pot of water in the moments before it comes to a boil, with those telltale bubbles rushing to the surface, sizzling away to nothing. Harbingers. In such a state, it feels as though the world has been tipped on edge. It's thrilling but also dangerous. When things happen, they take on a mystical significance. Everything feels like a prediction, or an omen. Everything exists in the realm of providence.

In class, our teachers earnestly discussed the changes in Europe. The TV showed roiling masses of drab, poorly dressed white people (white people demonstrating?—that was a change) waving placards with Cyrillic slogans that looked like the writing in the alien mini-series *V.* My classmates and I were divided into groups, given photocopied clippings of newspaper stories,[61] and asked to comprehend the complexities swirling around us. Would the Berlin Wall—that unfeeling symbol of Communism's might—crumble? Would Gorbachev and his principles of glasnost sway those featureless lands into submitting to justice, truth, and freedom for all? Would Soviet Russia soon enjoy the glories that we did here in South Africa, under our bright winter skies? Oom Piet, my old *veldskool* nemesis, was right. Those Commie fuckers didn't stand a chance against the righteousness of the Kingdoms of God.

The twentieth century was a busy one, but there had never quite been a twelve-month stretch like February 1989 to February 1990. Every day there was a new reality to grasp. A multi-party system of government in Hungary, whatever that meant. Solidarity taking over in Poland, wherever that was. East Germans taking to the streets, whatever that signified. And an

61. You can no doubt imagine how accurate these were.

unmentioned history happening right in our own backyard. International events were the muzak in the elevator that was dropping South Africans vertiginously downward to some unknown floor, where the doors would open to—well, what exactly?

"Okay, who can tell me why the people in Poland are so upset and want to change their government?" asked Mrs. Lieberman, my high school history teacher, who had the unenviable task of teaching history when it so beautifully coincided with current affairs. No idea, Mrs. L. Why are the people in Soweto so upset? Why are they setting one another on fire with such abandon? These questions we did not ask. Whatever was happening outside our very gates was beyond discussion. There was no point in trying to understand it. We had that old fallback, and we were using it. The blacks had gone crazy.

Frankly, I could not wait to be whisked off to the land of bubble gum and unlimited television channels, where there were no hard questions and where I could practise my brand of hedonistic esprit unburdened by the weight of either history or the present. In Canada, I imagined, I would be free of all this. There was no point to all this endless questioning. I was sixteen years old, and I was hatching a plan.

I was planning never to think again.

The night before Maxine died, Carolyn dreamt of her passing. I can't relate the specifics of the dream, nor can I suggest that it was a prediction so much as it was a twelve-year-old's way of processing the inevitable (Maxine was critically ill for a week or so before she died). Regardless, the dream, and my sister's intense, wide-eyed "I see dead people" vibe spooked the hell out of the rest of us—extra tinder on the conflagration of weirdness that was burning around me, further proof that the laws of the universe were being not so subtly redrawn.

Maxine's death occurs on the border of my memory, right before it falls off into nothingness. I remember that her life ended in a quick fizzle, like a seltzer past its best-by date dropped into a glass of water. The doctors had botched a simple stomach procedure and within ten days she had gone from a tummy ache to a better place. There are, undeniably, added difficulties administering health care to those who cannot communicate, but it seemed an egregious fuck-up—a terrible negligence so arbitrary that it was in many ways akin to a violent, random murder. In America, there would have been lawsuits aplenty. In South Africa, malpractice, like shit, happened. To assuage conflicted feelings (and how can there not be conflicted feelings when a severely handicapped member of the family—a burden and enormous responsibility—dies?), Dr. Poplak and Uncle Percy concentrated on recourse. They focused their anger on the doctors who had squandered a life, no matter how compromised that life may have been. This was easier than facing the mourning process. After all, how do you mourn for someone you've been mourning for all your life?

I recall nothing of Maxine's funeral except for my duties as pallbearer. Traditional Jewish burials insist on nothing more than an unadorned pine coffin. Maxine, or what was left of her, weighed nothing. I had a creeping suspicion that they'd simply forgotten to put her in there. But after a few moments, the weight, or lack of it, seemed entirely appropriate. There was nothing left. She had simply disappeared.

Maxine had tethered us to South Africa, and that hold had been tenuous. Once she was gone, so were we. Gaga and Oupa, as integral as they were to our lives, were as financially secure as it was possible to be, and they wanted us gone as badly as my mother wanted us to go. My parents had lived their entire lives in South Africa—their friendships were deep, but the deeper their roots sank into the earth, the less nourishment those roots found. There was no future, or at least none that my mother could see. Her friends were leaving one by one, as were many of mine (even Leigh's family had left Fellside for Sydney, Australia). She did not want me to do the mandatory military service; she thought that jobs and prospects would soon dry up. There was nothing ahead except darkness, and I don't mean that in the Joseph Conrad sense of the term: the incomprehensible plus the inconceivable plus black people. I mean darkness as in the absence of future. There was no hint in 1989 of the changes that were to come in the year ahead. The country was a roadside diner that hadn't altered its menu in forty years, and it seemed unlikely that a celebrity chef was going to come in and shake things up any time soon.

I had no love for the country. The very idea of patriotism was preposterous. Who was I supposed to get behind? Those dusty wax mannequins that ran the show, modelled as they were into poses of rage, anger, and indomitability? The chunky pugilist Nelson Mandela, alleged bloodthirsty Communist and killer of white men? Those raging black men on television, tearing one another to shreds? We were cut off from the international community (unless you count Libya, Israel, and a few clandestine CIA departments), our sportspeople and sports teams were not allowed to compete abroad, and there were constant demonstrations outside our overseas consulates. We were a *cause célèbre* without a whiff of moral authority. We could not say a word in our own defence, and that's because we were indefensible.

It is a strange thing to be severed from the community of man—to be an island—as we were in South Africa. Isolation, both cultural and geographic, causes a certain kind of backwardness. The pastiche you create of the world, assembled from snippets of popular culture, hearsay, half-true news, and folkloric assumptions, is a patchwork quilt. Adrift, you create a world that only nominally hints at civilization. We were a quasi-democratic quasi-dictatorship, with a culture as anemic and as weirdly translucent as those deep-sea species of fish seen on the Discovery Channel. The flag Oom Piet raised with such reverence, the national anthems we sang with such forced gusto at assemblies—these were dead symbols for a dead country.

Like my parents, my roots could sink only so deep. There was just no sustenance down there, and when it came time for me to be yanked from the earth, I gave with ease.

There are many who would tear their (or, more appropriately, my) hair out at this cavalier notion of rootlessness, many whose ancestors' blood and gore lie splattered all over that land, and who would never, *ever* leave—regardless of how dark their future looked. They would walk into that black hole, their history as their hope and their salve. This land was as their flesh, and to be peeled from it meant death, or worse. And, of course, there were the legions who couldn't leave, the hordes crowded into the hellholes of Khayelitsha, Alexandra, Soweto, or the poor whites in *dorps* like Pofadder and Upington and Pietermaritzburg. For them, there was no choice. The future meant twenty minutes from now, not a liberal arts education at an international university and the attendant job possibilities that came with it.

So, my family had a choice, and we made it. Or, rather, my parents did. I can only know how I felt, and for a sixteen-year-old, it was the adventure of a lifetime. I *was* North American, or at least a strange version of it. I was steeped in a cynical, satirical *MAD* magazine smarminess, not realizing that besides a few thirty-six-year-old fat dudes who lived in their parents' basement, knew the lyrics to every Monty Python song, and recorded every episode of *Moonlighting* on their VCR, I was the only person who read *MAD* magazine. It's not just that I wasn't plugged in. I didn't even have any prongs.

And so, Maxine could not have scripted her sacrifice any better. We would have left whether or not she had recovered from her stomach illness, but this was one less box of guilt to pack with our possessions. Meticulously, everything we owned was placed in cardboard by four black men. First they wrapped our belongings in the pages of *The Star, The Citizen,* and, absurdly, *The Sowetan,* then carefully assembled a box, filled the box with more paper, and placed the packages inside the box, finally taping it closed. And so on, until all was packed. (They wrote their names, carefully, in marker on the side of each box—Twana, Kweli, Moses, Shona—presumably so that if we arrived in Toronto with little more than crushed glass and bone china dust, we'd know who to curse.) The boxes were loaded onto a tractor-trailer, the detachable trailer was locked, the truck was driven away to the harbour, and the trailer unloaded onto a ship and sent to Canada. Forty-one Forbes Street was emptied, but I don't remember it empty. I barely remember those four men packing our possessions. I do, however, remember the sound of dirt being shovelled onto Maxine's simple pine coffin. Jewish burial rites ask that the males present drop three shovelfuls of earth onto the coffin, using the back of the shovel to indicate reluctance for the task. Each *thunk* of dirt sounded like a footfall. As the dirt piled up, the *thunks* faded in tenor, until there was no sound at all.

Snippets of memories here and there: My mates calling me from the airport, before hopping on an El Al flight for a school trip to Israel. But of that snippet, I remember only one brief conversation.

"See you later, *boet,*" I said to Kevin Bloom.

"Nah, china," said Kevin. "You won't." Which put things, definitively, into perspective.

As with everything that happens when you're sixteen, the Big Gap has a soundtrack. The other detail I remember is Ari coming by with a gift, a cassette of Phil Collins's *But Seriously,* which had a cover photo of Phil looking incredibly ponderous, perhaps mulling over the issues of the day, which, as we've already established, were legion. I don't have the heart to go into a Bret Easton Ellis–esque postmodern critique of Phil and his oeuvre, or to take myself to task for such dubious musical taste (I subscribed early to the apophthegm "Bad taste is a form of bad morals"), but I will say this: Phil's music, because of its simplicity, gets into your head with deadly virulence and never lets go. "Another Day in Paradise," conveniently the first track on side two of the cassette, was rewound so often in my big white knock-off Walkman that it warped. Phil's unsubtle conjuring of the great yawning gulf between Us (the wealthy) and Them (the poor) clearly hit a nerve. Despite that my excitement at leaving South Africa was paramount, I had the first niggling of that guilt specific to the white person from a (relatively) liberal upbringing. Look at me! I thought. I get to cut and run, but what about those others? What about the people I leave behind, and what about those untold millions living in hell? What will happen, I thought, when whatever was bubbling under the surface boils over? What happens when the unwashed masses decide that they wanted to spend some quality time in Paradise? I had to stop thinking, and soon.

My anger at God (or circumstance, or fate) for his unfairness was based on one principle: the burden of responsibility that came with having been given so much. I *had* to fulfill my promise—I *had* to make it big—simply out of fairness to my position. I had no right just to live and let live. I had to live and prosper. I had to cash in the mountain of chips I'd been given, and then turn over at least as much again at the high-stakes craps table of life. I couldn't just sit at a beach somewhere and drink mai tais. That's where Phil Collins and I met in some brief confluence, for a month or so of my life. If you pay attention to the lyrics of "Another Day in Paradise" (and I'm not suggesting that you do), you'll probably figure, like I have, that Phil encountered a female bum(ette?) on the street and wrote this little confection around her. That the track went to number one in every known country in the universe, outgrossing the mean GNP of most African nations combined, is the precise problem with hit pop singles about serious subjects. Phil, the record company execs, and I (by virtue of the fact that I was schlepping this tape along with me to my new home in North America) were all further established in Paradise. And once you're in, it's tough to leave.

So, in one of the biggest boxes that Twana or Kweli or Moses or Shona packed into that tractor-trailer sat the smouldering ball of lava that was my white man's burden. It was the first thing they packed, and the last thing I removed.

Which brings me, in a roundabout way, back to my last coherent South African memory. Like my sister, who for those late tumultuous months foretold of deaths (if only by a few hours, and outside of the realm of utility), I saw dream life as a stage thronged with players who crowded my boyhood—Mr. MacMillan, Oom Piet, kids from primary school whom I had not seen in three years, Bushy, Manson, Gaga, Oupa,

Mevrou Du Toit—the whole cast and crew, waving their bouquets, taking their final bows.

I think I had fallen asleep in the afternoon. The dream was impossibly vivid, as only afternoon dreams can be.

I am back in Fellside, and I'm on my favourite toy, a green and yellow British Petroleum scooter. My feet push against the warm asphalt of the sidewalk, which is dotted here and there with clumps of itchy-balls that had fallen from the sparse oak. I can feel by the sun that it's winter. The hard plastic of the wheels of my BP scooter make a satisfying, rumbling cacophony, while my mother stands a few paces ahead of me, beckoning. Suddenly, vertiginously, I am ripped from my body and torn heavenward. Up and up I go, looking down on tiny, blond-locked Richard on his green machine as he gets smaller and smaller. So, too, does Forbes Street, and Fellside, and Louis Botha—from river to vein to capillary in a manner of seconds. Johannesburg is laid out before me, like the opened, filigreed mass of a still-live organ. But as I rise, I notice that the edges fall away into darkness. And the higher I rise, the more my perspective allows that Johannesburg is ringed by a smoking, roiling clot of gore—a vast moat of tenebrous murk that is, despite all appearances, alive with something …

I suppose I jerked awake. I suppose I was sweating. But that's it. That's the last thing I remember. It doesn't speak terribly well of me, and the dream harbours some uncomfortable, disquieting symbolism. Sixteen years and three months in South Africa, and it amounted to this.

Oh, the mind of the white African.

I wonder what my grandparents said when we left. All that time spent with Gaga and Oupa—an entire childhood's worth of devotion—ended here. I would see my grandfather again only a handful of times, and as for Gaga—well, she now spends her days singing show tunes in a North Toronto flat.

Manson? I wonder what he had to say. Those friends that remained? Teachers like Billups?

More than anything, I wonder what Bushy said to me when we said goodbye. I know she probably used that quiet voice she used when saying goodbye before we left for vacation, or the even quieter one she saved for giving me advice. In these instances, she was almost shy. I hope she said, "Ree*shat*! *Uswaba, wena.*" That would've been appropriate. But I simply don't remember. If I have one small scrap of sentiment left, I'd love it to be spent on some sort of appropriate closure there.

That's the thing about the Big Gap. It comes down to closure, or the lack thereof. We need narrative to make sense of our lives, we need to develop some sense of story—and key to any narrative, of course, is the final act. The neat tying up of loose ends. Closure.

I suppose I could meticulously reconstruct those final few months, but if this account is indeed an act of memory, then the point here is that *I do not remember*. So I'll resist the temptation to fill in the blanks, and I'll try to make sense of that gap in my memory.

What it amounts to is this: That bright flare of absence is my mind's way of telling me in no uncertain terms that there *is* no closure. There is no way to say goodbye. My boyhood will never, ever, be over. What's the point of a narrative with no final act? The point is that the story can never be shelved, accessioned, forgotten. It lies open on your bedside table, forever.

Oh, I almost forgot.

One final snippet of a memory. I'm not entirely sure, but this may have been from the very week we left—and only a couple of weeks before I'd be wrestling a mannequin in a Canadian art class.

I think I had just returned from a jog, about to go into Gaga's house for dinner. I was stretching out my legs on her large front patio when I heard something. At first, the absurdity, the incongruity, of the sound allowed me to ignore it. That did not last long. I shook my head, and hoped desperately that I was losing my mind. Nope.

Grieg's *Peer Gynt.*

"Mr. Poplak," said a voice. "If it isn't our very own Mr. Poplaaaaahhhhhhhk!"

It took everything I had to stifle a scream.

The Whistler was perched high on a ladder, tending to something under the eavestroughs. I recalled that MacMillan moonlit as a beekeeper, and he was dealing with a hive that had fastened itself perilously close to Gaga and Oupa's front door. He wore a beekeeper's net over his head, partially obscuring the pudding face and the huge grin. The conversation went something like this:

"And how is Mr. Poplak?"

"No, fine, sir. How are you?"

"Splendid, thank you. You've grown some."

"*Ja,* probably."

It was odd batting pleasantries around like a tired shuttlecock, but he seemed cheered by the business.

"Shipping out, eh, Mr. Poplak?"

"Sorry, sir?"

"Flying the coop, eh?"

"Oh, *ja.* That's correct, sir."

"Your mother tells me Canada."

I nodded. I sensed an incoming celestial piss-take and braced myself. I was not disappointed.

"Perhaps we shall be neighbours," said The Whistler.

"Huh?" said I.

"Neighbours, Poplak. We, too, make for the frozen north."

I was speechless.

"Western Canada, mind you. But Canada is Canada."

That's when I realized that you can run, but you can't hide. As much as I wanted to forget, I'd be carrying South Africa along with me wherever I went, for as long as I lived.

MacMillan was preparing to apply smoke to the nest.

"I'd clear out for this, Poplak. They might get a leeee-tle ornery."

I cleared out in a hurry.

Outroduction

It was my initial intention to end this account with a definitive, comprehensive state-of-the-nation think piece on the New South Africa—what has come to pass, what will happen in the years to come. Then I thought, Nah.

For one thing, I'm not qualified for either summation or prophesy—a four-month research trip between January and May of 2006 and a few holidays back over the years are not enough to earn expert status. Besides, what makes someone an expert on a country—and especially a country like South Africa? Would I be tested on topography, geology, ethnography, and current events by an independent expert-status-granting NGO? I'm not sure I'd pass such a test. Let me revise that. I'd fail such a test miserably.

Oh, I read the newspapers. I closely followed the major political stories—all stale now—intending to use them as case studies to help me interpret the past and foretell the future. I interviewed the inhabitants, I consumed the pop culture, I put my finger on the pulse. Three weeks in, I had it all figured out. Two weeks after that, I was hopelessly confused. Two weeks after *that,* I could no longer pretend to fathom how I had expected to bring all the strands together, to render the New South Africa in a few thousand words. The notion seemed blessedly naive, the what-I-did-this-summer essay project of a precocious fourth-grader.

So, I'm left with moments, impressions. Like, for instance, ManFest. This is the South African version of *Cosmopolitan* magazine's annual sexiest man competition, and no, I was not a contestant. The competitors are a range of rugby stars, TV personalities, musicians, actors—of the twelve men on stage, more than half were black. The event takes place in Sandton (Johannesburg's Beverly Hills), in the Civic Centre, in January 2006. This is where I learn that—at least on a superficial level—South Africa's middle-class elite are indeed a cosmopolitan mélange of black and white, standing cheek by jowl as glittering fashion plates, chattering on cell phones, networking, connecting. ManFest tells me that the post-Apartheid years have been a splendid success. Such an event would have been all but impossible in the old days.

ManFest doesn't quite tell the whole story. Yes, there is a rapidly emerging black middle class—a demographic that marketers refer to as the Black Diamond. Purchasing power is huge, influence grows by the day. But the rich get richer, and the poor get swallowed up. These middle-class blacks are like the emerging middle classes elsewhere in the developing world. They're in a rush; they must buy everything *now*. This alarms people from the ranks of the hoary (white) Western middle class, who do not have penury and abjectness nipping at the heels of collective memory. The rapacity of those so recently disenfranchised is, inarguably, astonishing—urban centres are awash with bling—luxury cars, new electronics, high-fashion clothing. People live on credit; they're leveraged to the hilt. This sense of rush is, in a way, a poignant part of Apartheid's legacy. South Africans barely look in the rearview mirror. They seem afraid that the party could end at any second. I get a sense of nihilism, of millenarianism. What happens when interest rates increase, when the borrowing stops, when the piper calls, they ask? They look up, waiting for the other shoe to drop.

Johannesburg is jacked, harried, manic—as if a bomb is about to explode. Money is everywhere; people are constantly pitching. Everyone is a consultant. This has always been a mining town, and right now it's slap bang in the middle of a gold rush. Anything, I'm told, is possible. Initially, I mistake this for optimism. But optimism is not optimism if it has a best-by date. Make money *now,* because this is the window. Prevailing wisdom insists that after the 2010 World Cup—to be held in South Africa—all this comes to an end. When I leave Johannesburg to do research elsewhere, I feel the tension seep from my bones. My old hometown needs a therapist.

Louis Botha Avenue—the general's last stand. As I walk south past Fellside, taking notes, I step into one of the time warps that lie hidden away all over the city. In a flash, I'm transported back twenty years, walking with Carolyn to the Lido Café. Everything looks the same, smells the same. Then I catch, pasted to a utility pole, a large ANC sign declaring a candidate for the upcoming municipal elections. Vote ANC, it says. A cartoon-like *doing!* sounds in my head. *Vote ANC?* The poster, placed inside this time warp, makes me dizzy. In so many ways, this country is a miracle. What could have—by all rights should have—descended into all-out chaos never did (but boy, it came so close—especially after the assassination of the influential political activist Chris Hani by a far-rightist gunman in 1993). Johannesburg did manage to become the murder capital of the world. But South Africa was never Iraq, Sierra Leone, the Democratic Republic of the Congo. It stood on the edge of the precipice but never tipped over. It never did fulfill its darkest destiny.

Mpumalanga, driving south toward White River from the Kruger National Park, and then onward to Waterval Boven.

Shantytowns as far as the eye can see. The poverty is astonishing, more so because of the contrasts (there are a slew of luxury game-park compounds nearby, to say nothing of suburban Johannesburg). I have travelled to many poor countries but only one where I was on the winning end of the regime that rendered it so desperate in the first place. So it hits a little harder. It's not a question of guilt, because that's not what this is about. But I do feel connected to it, linked somehow.

I think about justice and fairness a lot while I'm in South Africa. I sit on a deck chair at my cousins' beautiful home perched on the Johannesburg ridge, watching legions of cumulus gather over the northern suburbs. The Truth and Reconciliation Commission comes to mind. To me, the TRC and its series of courtlike hearings—which gathered testimony from both the victims and the perpetrators of Apartheid-era atrocities, with the authority to grant amnesty in exchange for truth—are a bedtime story. At a certain point—after you've crossed so many lines in the sand, after offences to body and soul run groundwater deep, after millions upon millions have borne the brunt of humiliation, violence, and degradation—earthly justice can no longer be the prevailing concern. How many times can you sentence a man to hang for a thirty-year career of pistol-whipping domestic servants for neglecting to carry their passes? We don't possess the capability to even those scores. Justice becomes a secondary concern, because justice is impossible where Apartheid is concerned. Forgiveness is marginally less impossible. But that's exactly what the TRC asked of the country.

I'm realistic, and I know that there were (and still are) many who were bitterly disappointed by the outcome of the TRC. Amnesty was granted to monsters, and not everyone was forthcoming in clearing the air. Revisionists had a podium; liars had the floor. But so many hatchets were buried—in shallow graves, yes, but buried nonetheless. No one has the right to give up on humanity until they've fully investigated the TRC. They will see us first at our worst, and then at our best. To me, the TRC sums up all life. By that, I don't mean it's a metaphor—I mean that it literally encompasses every aspect of the human experience. There are those who disagree, but we choose our bedtime stories, and this is mine.

Editors, journalists, writers, commentators, artists, people on the street—all tell me how complicated the country has become. During Apartheid, it was simple. You knew who the bad guys were (who they were, of course, depended on your point of view). Now, as one prominent newspaper editor put it at a panel discussion I attended, "We haven't developed the ability to deal with the complexity." Everyone's playing catch-up. Events happen fast: No one seems able to forecast or to prognosticate or to sum anything up with any degree of insight. So South African stories—people complain—are not being told. AIDS and violence: That's the totality of the South African experience. So much more goes unremarked, undocumented. No one is explaining the complexity with any clarity.

Perhaps not, and even if they were, I'm not sure how I'd be able to judge. I dip my toe into the fast-running water of the South African narrative and instantly I'm swept into the roaring confusion. Others seem just as gun-shy. Most whites I encounter ignore the municipal elections that take place in March 2006, while I'm there. Their votes are meaningless, their voices lost in the din—a complete role reversal. Politicians make baffling pronouncements based on strange intellectual positions justified by "culture"—a deliberate swipe at a colonial past that bulldozed indigenous culture. "My culture" this and "my culture" that, as if culture is an immutable impetus, a catch-all excuse for acting outside the bounds of a universal morality that must be the ballast for reasonable governance anywhere. Governance is anyway always cultural, but this is not one of its finer points. In North America, I know why a politician makes a decision, even a bad one—I see the connections between ethos and constituency, policy-maker and lobbyist. It's logical, or a type of logical. In South Africa, I see no such connections. I don't know if anyone else does. I don't get the impression that they do.

In the Radium Beer Hall—a drinking hole on Louis Botha Avenue renowned for its decent jazz and soaked journalists—I look outside at the street I grew up on. I remember walking back from the Orange Grove Library with Leigh or my sister, books in my arms, and I think that I am *of* this place. I think this also when I look out at the twinkling lights of the city when I'm high up on the ridge, or when I walk down Green Street—past Gaga and Oupa's old house—and smell the green, or when I see the peaked roof of 41 Forbes Street, or when I eat *boerewors* at a Sunday *braai*. What does it mean to feel an almost painful pang of nostalgia for your childhood and boyhood when those years played out under one of the vilest regimes in history? I thought I would come up with an answer for this (part of the point, I'll confess, of writing this book). Yet, I have no answers.

The last months have been an exercise in looking back. It dawns on me that this project—which I hoped would state something universal about Apartheid, and therefore about racism and hatred and the human condition—is more personal than I ever expected it to be. I have what feels like a profound revelation: When I undertook to write this book, I thought I could communicate something elemental. I'm not sure if that's true, and I no longer care. Throughout this process, I have been staring the past dead in the face, coming to terms with it, trying to understand it, trying to decode my behaviour and the behaviour of those around me. After a time, I realized that I had regained an essential part of myself—the little me who used to ride the green and yellow BP scooter—and not the subsequent me contaminated by a rotten system. Perhaps the only thing I can reasonably share, besides my experiences, is the notion that confronting the past is a way to regain ourselves. We can be innocent again, if we are true. This is completely distinct from redemption, which is a religious impulse largely motivated by the need for absolution. Encoded in my realization is the idea that something like Apartheid leaves no one undamaged, and there can be no redemption until every last soul is healed. Absolution is not the goal. Can you allow me a cliché? The truth, I believe, will set you free.

This probably means little to those who suffered so terribly under Apartheid. But if you, like me, believe that the TRC had something to do with forging a Rainbow Nation (no matter how compromised) from a *bête noire,* then the idea of some sort of regeneration from a hard-nosed examination of the past is not so absurd.

The past is a foreign country, but so is the future. I have no idea what will happen to South Africa in the coming years. If you like happy endings, then I suppose this precise moment in the country's history counts as one. Many have been irrevocably failed, but there is still a wave of optimism, even if it may go off, like milk. There is a free press, there is discussion, there is an impulse to make things better. Millions and millions are lost to disease and poverty. But the millions more on the cusp have not yet been forsaken. There are saints in South Africa, albeit human ones. And there is a culture of forgiveness.

It is time to add my scrapbook to the great mosaic, to the balance of stories. It's time to say goodbye to the past. Indeed, many young South Africans waved me away when I tried to talk about Apartheid. They have no memory of it—it's history to them, and uninteresting history at that. You can't move forward, I tell them, without looking back.

If I was in the Radium Beer Hall right now, I'd stare out at Louis Botha Avenue and raise a glass to the future.

Glossary

Baas: Afrikaans. Boss.

Babotie: Afrikaans. A tasty stew with many variations; everyone who makes it has his or her own recipe, and claims to have perfected the dish.

Bakkie: Afrikaans. Pickup truck.

Bantu: Literally, people. Sweeping general term used to describe the black population of Africa. No longer in use.

Biltong: Afrikaans. Dried, salted meat, often game. Not unlike jerky. A South African staple.

Boerewors: Afrikaans. Farmer's sausage. Spicy, succulent, delicious, and essential on the *braai.*

Boet: Afrikaans. Literally, brother.

Braai: Afrikaans. Barbecue. Given the pleasant South African weather, a *braai* is a frequent ritual that takes on ceremonial importance, especially on Sunday afternoons.

Bunk: Cut classes.

China: Cockney rhyming slang. "China plate" is a mate. Widely used.

Doos: Afrikaans. Literally, box. We used it to mean "idiot," as in, "You drove the *bakkie* into the wall? What a *doos*!"

Dorp: Afrikaans. Small town.

Dronk: Afrikaans. Drunk.

Dutchman: Pejorative for Afrikaner, referring to his colonial roots. I was never quite sure why this was considered an insult.

Goggas: Creepy-crawlies.

Hadeda. The hadeda ibis (*Bostrychia hagedash*) is a large brown bird with iridescent patches on its shoulders. Common in Johannesburg.

Highveld: The eastern part of South Africa is sectioned into a series of plains, divided by the escarpments and riven by the Drakensberg mountain range. The plains are named according to their relative elevation, hence the high, middle, and low prefixes.

Hiy ko-nah: Zulu. Exclamation of alarm, as in, "*Hiy ko-nah,* it is too hot today!"

Homeland: Designated areas within South Africa in which the "native" black population lived, under the rule of quisling administrations or monarchies. Cramped, poor, and without resources, they were the result of one of Apartheid's most notorious policies, because they meant the displacement and relocation of millions of people.

Jack: Caning, as in "*Boet,* the headmaster jacked me so hard I almost fainted."

Jassis: Afrikaans. Derivation of Jesus, but meaning more along the lines of "gee whiz."

Jazz: Bathroom.

Kaffir: Derived from the Arabic *kefir:* non-believer. Extremely derogatory term for blacks.

Kiff: Durban surfer slang meaning "awesome." Interchangeable with *lekker.*

Lag: Afrikaans. Laugh.

Lank: Afrikaans. Literally, long, but we used it to mean "very," as in, "*Jassis,* that *boerewors* is *lank* juicy!"

Lekker: Afrikaans. Awesome! (Translated literally as "delicious.")

Loerie: Corythaixoides concolor, also known as the "go-away bird" because of its distinctive cry. Many varietals, but the most common in Johannesburg is the grey loerie, which resembles a large, lanky pigeon with a mohawk.

Lowveld: See Highveld.

Mal: Afrikaans. Crazy.

Mevrou: Afrikaans. Mrs.

Middleveld: See Highveld.

Moffie: Homosexual. South African Airways flight attendants were referred to as *koffie moffies.*

Muti: A general South African term for traditional medicine, or any item that is said to hold magical or curative properties. For instance, there are some who believe that rhinoceros testicle *muti* can help with impotence.

Oke: Guy, buddy, dude.

Oom: Afrikaans. Uncle. Attributed to an elder as a title of respect.

Pap: White maize dish, the perfect accompaniment to *boerewors.*

Poep: Afrikaans. "Crap" or "shit," as in, "*Jassis,* I'm *poep* scared of all those big *okes,*" or "That movie *skrikked* me so bad I almost *poeped* myself."

Poes: Afrikaans. Pussy.

Rook: Afrikaans. Smoke.

Skrik: Afrikaans. Frighten, or freak, as in, "He *skriks* me out."

Smaak: Afrikaans. Literally, taste. We used it in the sense of "like," as in, "I don't *smaak* that *oke.*"

Sosaties: Afrikaans. Wieners.

Stoep: Afrikaans. Porch. A great place to sit, shotgun at one side, brandy and Coke at the other, and stare sullenly at those walking past your property.

Takkies: Running shoes.

Uswaba, wena: Pidgin Zulu. "Beware you!"

Velskoene: Afrikaans. Also called *vellies.* A rough and rudimentary leather walking shoe with a tough, rubber sole. I was astonished to find, upon my immigration to Canada, that an Australian footwear company was marketing these shoes as fashion items. It baffled me that anyone would want to wear those things when not on a safari. Indeed, wearing *velskoene* in Johannesburg was a fashion crime so severe that only a medieval punishment such as hobbling could bring any real justice to bear on the perpetrator.

Voetsak: Afrikaans. "Be gone!" As in "*Voetsak,* man! I'm trying to vacuum the carpets!"

Wors: Afrikaans. See *Boerewors.*

Acknowledgments

If you'd told me, when I started my writing career, how many people it takes to write a book, I would have called you a crazy person. *Ja, No, Man* would simply not have been possible without the care, time, and dedication of several people whose names do *not* appear on the book's jacket.

Shared genes and motherly devotion do not explain the amount of work my mother, Lorna Poplak, put into this book to ensure that it is an accurate and comprehensible account of my years in South Africa. She fact-checked meticulously, read draft after draft after draft, and allowed nothing to slide. I cannot thank her enough for her assistance—it would be a much lesser book without her. While I cannot blame her for any inconsistencies, I can thank her profusely for culling their number.

Others also gave generously of their time, reading and re-reading cringe-worthy early drafts of the manuscript. South African journalist par excellence and ex–high school carousing buddy Kevin Bloom combed these pages on numerous occasions, correcting facts and, perhaps more important, improving the depth and tone of the final work. (His pointed criticisms led to the odd sleepless night in Johannesburg, and also to a much better book.) His obvious enthusiasm for my early drafts, his constant words of encouragement, and his close reading of the text were more helpful than he can know. I am eternally grateful. I hope the finished work does him proud.

In South Africa, I was forced to readjust my notions of hospitality. My cousins Ernie and Elinor Brenner opened their home to me for nearly four months, putting up with my idiosyncrasies (half bananas for breakfast, de-koshering the kosher kitchen) for much longer than they should have. I would not have been able to spend as much time in South Africa if it wasn't for their generosity, and the book would have suffered for it. Elinor also helped immeasurably with my research, giving me endless phone numbers, leads, literature, and family lore. I can't thank both of them enough. Also, I would like to thank ex-Fellsiders Ester, John, and Claire Richards in Cape Town for putting me up for two weeks and allowing me the use of one of their rotating supply of hatchbacks. I would like to thank John for his help and insight on Chapter 9. Thanks also to Dr. Irv Lissoos in Johannesburg for helping me with research, and to Jeffrey Brenner for the Colnago. I'd like to thank all those who took the time to speak with me and share their stories and experiences—in particular Pauline Carr, Elliot Wolf, Errol Judelman, and Maureen Chalom. There were dozens of others whom I can't list here, but I am grateful for their time. While I read far too many texts to cite, I must acknowledge Rian Malan's *My Traitor's Heart,* the short stories of Herman Charles Bosman, and *The White Africans* by Gerald L'Ange for expanding my perspective as a white South African.

At Penguin Group (Canada), I must thank my editor, Helen Reeves, for her belief in this project. She knew—even when I wasn't so sure—that we'd get a book out of this. Her wit and insight have done much to shape *Ja, No, Man,* and it's been a pleasure working with her. I'd also like to thank Abby Gainforth, who is, to all intents and purposes, this book's sparkplug.

I'd like to acknowledge the generosity of my lawyers (how often do you hear *that*?), Heenan & Blaikie—in particular Ken Dhaliwal and Bob Tarantino—for their excellent work and for so generously discounting their services. I must also acknowledge the benefaction of the Toronto Arts Council for awarding me a grant early on in this process.

Finally, I give my immense thanks to my family for their continued support and devotion, and for being such good sports in allowing me to portray them, warts and all. Cheers to my sister, Carolyn, and my cousins Lewis and Janine for a childhood of memories. Thanks to my uncles Alan and Neill Judelman for helping to keep me in beer and *biltong* in SA, and to my grandmother, Shenella Judelman, for information and show tunes. And cheers to Tamir Moscovici, long-time partner in crime, for all those years of toil in the basement (and other dodgy locales). This is one of the fruits of our labours.